Michelle Roberts

KETO DIET

FOR WOMEN OVER 50

The Amazing and Ultimate 2 in 1 Healthy Diet Guide with a Tasty and Delicious 28 Days Meal Plan to Regain Confidence and Boost Metabolism by Intermittent Fasting

THIS BOOK INCLUDES

BOOK 1:

KETO DIET FOR WOMEN OVER 50
The Ultimate and Complete Guide to Lose Weight Quickly and Regain Confidence, Cut Cholesterol, Balance Hormones and Reverse D at The Same Time!

BOOK 2:

KETO DIET COOKBOOK FOR WOMEN OVER 50
Discover How to Enter The Keto Lifestyle by Cooking Tasty and Delicious Low Carb and High-Fat Recipes to Stay Healthy and Boost Your Fat Also Over 50!

Table of Contents

KETO DIET

FOR WOMEN OVER 50

The Ultimate and Complete Guide to Lose Weight Quickly and Regain Confidence, Cut Cholesterol, Balance Hormones and Reverse D at The Same Time!

Introduction

The woman's body, at any age, is an amazing thing. We begin as tiny babies and grow up to have babies ourselves. We can hold down a job, carry a pregnancy, nurture tiny humans, and take care of our mates—all at the same time! Any woman who has reached the glorious age of fifty, or even beyond, should celebrate. You have experienced more changes, especially in your body, than men ever will. Unfortunately, all of the things that make the woman a glorious creature can also work against her when trying to be healthy and active long into her senior years.

The first major experience a woman of fifty and over will experience is menopause. That monthly inconvenience will be gone forever, and you will be able to experience life without it.

But the joy of freedom from that monthly event can also mean an increase in developing belly fat and possibly other health consequences. That's because the onset of menopause means the cessation of your body's production of estrogen.

The estrogens in your body are the hormones that your body produces related to your sexual orientation. They are what make you a woman. The estrogens start and maintain the things that make you a woman—the breasts, the reproduction, and your monthly cycle.

All of the forms of estrogen have a particular responsibility in your body. One of the types that decrease dramatically in production after menopause is the one that helps you regulate your metabolism and keep your body weight under control.

This is why many women tend to accumulate fat around their midsections. This fat collects around their internal organs and is not only unattractive, but it is also dangerous. This visceral fat can lead to stroke, heart disease, diabetes, and some forms of cancer. And older women often tend to move less than they did when they were younger.

Since they no longer have children to chase, and many no longer work, they find themselves with less reason to move and more excuses to sit. Unfortunately, this not only leads to weight gain but also the stiffening of their joints.

Young women often have poor dietary habits but do not gain weight because the estrogens help them to keep their metabolism running high. This also helps to keep the level of cholesterol in the blood at a normal level. When you pass fifty, cholesterol levels begin to rise, and if they rise too high, you might be at an increased risk of heart attacks and strokes. Cholesterol is made naturally by the body. The body will make the amount that it needs for its normal functions. When processed foods, sugary foods, and unhealthy fats are consumed regularly, they will cause a buildup of excess cholesterol, which will lead to the formation of plaque in your arteries.

Part of the problem with the older woman's joints is the excess weight that she is carrying around. Being overweight puts enormous strain on the lower body joints, causing them to wear faster than they normally would.

Weight gain comes from consuming a diet that is high in processed foods and excess sugar, which will lead to obesity, which will lead to joint pain and deterioration. On the more serious side, all of this indulgence can lead to the development of osteoporosis, which can begin with the loss of estrogen and be made worse by excess weight and lack of exercise.

A degenerative condition where your bones become more porous and stop regenerating happens when you get older and known as osteoporosis. It is the main reason why older people, especially women who tend to have smaller bones than men, often suffer hip fractures from falls. In osteoporosis, the bone can't grow quickly enough to replace what is deteriorating.

It is normal for your muscles to lose some of their natural elasticity and strength as you age, simply because the muscles are getting older, and you are not moving as much. But maintaining good muscle tone is the key to keeping you moving throughout the remainder of your life and living it since the loss of muscle strength is the biggest reason many older adults find themselves unable to take care of themselves.

Strong muscles will help to keep you from falling. You need them to help reduce pain in your joints, keep your weight at a healthy level, and help to keep your bones strong and functional.

While it is not possible to stop the effects of aging, you can minimize them and keep yourself healthy and active far into the future by mixing a combination of exercise with the right kind of diet to give you the nutrients you need. And that diet is the keto diet.

I also experienced those parts of my life feeling unhealthy. I tried almost everything, even drugs, and nothing worked for me, except for the last four weeks, I discovered a natural method that is quick, simple, and straightforward that immediately developed my body with 100 percent natural. Since I discovered the keto diet, it is very rewarding and fun to eat and enjoy such wonderful healthy food. I started a keto diet on December 26 last year and lost 37 pounds by this time. It is great, and I feel great. I want to lose 50 pounds more to remain healthy and live a lot of time with my husband. I love to travel with him, and we travel to many places around the world. Suppose you are interested in losing weight, healthy eating, and living a healthy and long life. In that case, I recommend you to try the keto diet to overcome your obesity problem.

Why Is the Ketogenic Diet So Effective?

Some people think that the biggest reason keto is so effective is that you're cutting carbs out of your regimen and you're focusing on leaner meats and healthy fats with high-quality protein to make up the difference. I have to say; it certainly doesn't hurt your efforts.

The thing that makes keto so effective, though, really is the process of ketosis. Once your body makes that switch, it becomes so much easier for your body to access the stores of fat that have become stubborn and stuck in over the years.

However, it is vitally important that you ensure the quality of the food you're taking on is higher. You want foods that contain Omega fatty acids, you want foods that contain a lot of vitamins and minerals, and you want foods that are generally very healthy. That isn't to say that you can't have bacon and cream, but make sure you're taking on lots of greens, vegetables, fiber, and all the good stuff!

One of the most important things that you'll learn is that you need to balance your macronutrients. Macronutrients are quite simply a type of food that is required in large amounts in a diet. Typically with keto, the macros you will most commonly hear talked about are carbohydrates, protein, and fat. You want to make sure that your macronutrients are consumed not in specific amounts, but in a ratio with one another.

- **Protein** – 15%–30%
- **Fat** – 60%–75%
- **Carbohydrate** – 5%–10% (with a cap of about 15g per day)

On keto, it's not necessary to track all your calories and macros to the percent. It is helpful to know a ballpark for each of these and try to keep them in that balance. Once you get used to eating in this way, you'll be able to eyeball it, more or less.

CHAPTER 1:

What Exactly Is the Keto Diet?

A ketogenic diet is very low on carbs, but high in fats and is average on protein. Over the years, Ketogenic diets have been used to remedy several illnesses that human beings have come to face. The Ketogenic diet forces the human body to use its fats rather than burn its carbohydrates. Usually, the body's carbohydrates, which are found in the foods you consume, are converted into glucose. The glucose results from the body burning down its carbohydrates and is usually circulated around the body. Glucose is a very important element in that it ensures the day-to-day functioning of your brain. However, the liver is forced to convert fats into fatty acids and ketone bodies if only very few carbohydrates are left in the food substances that you consume. These ketone bodies assume the place of the glucose in ensuring the day-today functioning of your brain. Elevated levels of ketone bodies in the human blood (a metabolic state known as ketosis) lead to a reduction of epileptic seizures. Ketosis is actually normal. It is a consequence of a low-carb diet or as a result of fasting. Ketosis provides an extra source of energy for your brain in the form of ketones.

The Keto Macros for Weight Loss

Your body needs to go through a calorie deficit to lose weight, which means that your body has to consume more calories every day than you eat.

Indeed, your body has a continuous energy demand and utilizes the calories from food to keep functioning. The excess is stored within your body as fat. In contrast, when you are in Ketosis, your body utilizes the fat stored corresponding to your calorie deficit.

For example, a calorie deficit of 3500 calories will result in one pound of body weight loss. So, if you plan to lose one pound per week, you must have a deficit of 3,500-calories per week, which results in 500 calories per day (3,500 divided by seven days).

So, it takes a 3,500-calorie deficit to lose a pound of fat then, if you burn an extra 500 calories per day with physical exercise, you will expect an extra pound of fat loss in a week.

Depending on your physical activity, your body has a particular need. Let us assume that your body needs 2100 calories to keep your current weight. Eating only 1600 calories per day will result in a 500 calories deficit and induces one pound of weight loss per week.

What Are the Macros on the Ketogenic Diet?

An effective ketogenic diet consists of low carbohydrates, high fat, and moderate protein intakes.

This implies that you must keep carbohydrates down to the minimum value (generally 5%) while eating healthy fats (typically 75%) and proteins (typically 20%) for most of your diet.

However, though respecting the following ranges, the ratios can be changed as needed as standard ketogenic diet macronutrient:

- **Carbohydrates** – 5 to 10% of daily calories.
- **Fats** – 65 to 75% of daily calories.
- **Protein** – 25 to 35% of daily calories.

With these ratios in mind, you may now be able to calculate your macros depending on your calorie deficit goal.

By following this scientific approach, your body will enter in Ketosis, and you will lose weight following your expectations.

Fasting Over Fifty

Lower metabolism, achy knees, diminished muscle mass, and even sleep disorders are a few factors that make it difficult to lose weight after age 50. At the same time, losing weight, especially hazardous belly fat, can significantly decrease the risk of serious health problems such as diabetes, heart attacks, and cancer.

Of course, the risk of contracting many diseases increases as you age. In some cases, when it comes to shedding weight and decreasing the risk of usually contracting age-related diseases, intermittent fasting for women over 50 might serve as a virtual fountain of youth.

How Does Fasting Work?

You would not be forced to starve yourself by intermittent fasting, also referred to as IF. It also doesn't give you a license when you don't eat tons of unhealthy food. You eat within a fixed window of time, instead of eating meals and snacks all day.

Most individuals make an IF schedule for 12 to 16 hours a day that allows them fast. They eat regular meals and snacks for the majority of the time. It's not as complicated as it sounds to stick to this eating window, since most persons sleep for about eight of their fasting hours. You're also encouraged to enjoy zero-calorie beverages, such as wine, tea, and coffee.

For the best intermittent fasting results, you should build an eating routine that works for you. For example:

- **12-hour fast:** You might actually miss breakfast with a 12–12 fast and wait until lunch to eat. You could eat an early dinner and skip evening snacks if you want to eat your morning lunch. Older women find it pretty easy to stick to a quick 12–12.
- **16-hour fast:** With a 16–8 IF schedule, you can enjoy a quicker performance. Within an 8-hour window, most individuals tend to eat two meals and a snack or two a day. For instance, between noon and 8 in the evening or between 8 in the morning and 4 in the afternoon, you could set your eating window.
- **5–2 schedule:** Limited times of eating cannot work every day for you. Another choice is to stick for five days to a 12-hour or 16-hour fast and then relax your timetable for two days. You might, for example, use IF during the week and usually eat on the weekend.
- **Every-other-day fasts:** On alternative days, another variation calls for very few calories. For instance, on one day, you might keep your calories under 500 and then eat normally the next day. Note that regular IF fasts never call for tiny calorie limits.

As with every diet, if you're consistent, you'll get the best results. Same way, on special occasions, you should allow yourself a break from this sort of eating routine. To find out which kind of intermittent fasting works best for you, you can experiment. With the 12–12 method, lots of individuals ease themselves into IF, and then they progress to 16–8. You should aim to stick to the schedule as much as possible after that.

What Makes Fasting Work?

Some people think IF has succeeded for them simply because the small eating window inherently helps them minimize the number of calories they consume. For example, they may find that they only have time for two meals and one snack rather than eating three meals and two snacks. They become more conscious of the types of food they eat and try to stay away from refined carbs, unhealthy fat, and calories that are zero.

Of course, the types of healthy food that you prefer can also be selected. Although some people want to minimize their total consumption of calories, some combine IF with a diet of keto, vegan, or other forms.

Fasting benefits for women can extend beyond the restriction of calories.

Although some nutrition experts argue that IF works only because it allows individuals to reduce food consumption naturally, others disagree. They assume that with the same amount of calories and other nutrients, intermittent fasting outcomes are higher than traditional meal schedules. Studies have also shown that abstaining from food for several hours a day does more than just minimize the number of calories you eat.

There are some metabolic changes caused by IF that may help account for synergistic advantages:

- Insulin: Lower insulin levels can help increase fat burning during the fasting phase.
- HGH: Although insulin levels decrease, HGH levels increase to promote muscle growth and fat burning.
- Noradrenaline: The nervous system will deliver this chemical to cells in reaction to an empty belly to make them know they need to release fat for food.

How to Know You Are in Ketosis

How do you know if you're in ketosis?

- **Dry mouth and heightened thirst.** You can have a dry mouth because you drink enough water and get enough electrolytes like sodium. Try one or two cups of bouillon a day, plus as much water as you like. In your mouth, you can experience a metallic taste as well.
- **Increased urination.** Acetoacetate, the ketone body, can end up in the urine. This makes it possible to use urine strips to screen for ketosis. It can also lead to having to go to the toilet more frequently, at least when starting out. This may be the primary cause of increased thirst (above).

- **Keto breathe.** This is due to the escape of a ketone body called acetone through our breath.
- It may make the breath of a person smell "fruity" or close to the nail polish remover. Often when working out this scent can even come from sweat. Sometimes it is temporary.

Alcohol

Consuming a glass of wine or whiskey occasionally won't do much harm, but make sure that you stay away from beer. Beer is extremely rich in carbs and you should keep that out of the way!

Did you know that hard liquor such as whiskey, vodka, etc., have no carbs as long as you don't add sweet mixers to the alcohol? This doesn't mean you should drink hard liquor excessively as they still have calories. A moderate drink here or there is fine. I love my single malt scotch!

CHAPTER 2:

Benefits of the Keto Diet

- **Strengthens bones:** When people get older, their bones weaken. At 50, your bones at likely not as strong as they used to be; however, you can keep them in really good conditions. Consuming milk to give calcium cannot do enough to strengthen your bones. What you can do is to make use of the Keto diet as it is low in toxins. Toxins negatively affect the absorption of nutrients, and so with this, your bones can take in all they need.
- **Eradicates inflammation:** Few things are worse than the pain from an inflamed joint or muscle. Arthritis, for instance, can be extremely hard to bear. When you use the ketosis diet, the production of cytokines would be reduced. Cytokines inflammation and so, their eradication would reduce it.
- **It eradicates nutrients deficiency:** Keto focuses on consuming exactly what you need. If you use a great Keto plan, your body will lack no nutrients and will not suffer any deficiency.
- **Reduced hunger:** The reason we find it hard to stick to diets is hunger. It doesn't matter your age; diets do not become easier to stick to. We may have a mental picture of the healthy body we want. We may even have clear visuals of the kind of life we want to leave once free from unhealthy living, but none of that matters when hunger enters the scene. However, the keto diet is a diet that combats this problem. The keto diet focuses on consuming plenty of proteins. Proteins are filling and do not let you feel hungry too easily. In addition, when your carb levels are reduced, your appetite takes a hit. It is a win-win situation.
- **Weight loss:** Keto not only burns fat, but it also reduces that crave for food. Combined, these are two great ways to lose weight. It is one of the diets that has proven to help the most when it comes to weight loss. The Keto diet has been proven to be one of the best ways to burn stubborn belly fat while keeping you revitalized and healthy.
- **Reduces blood sugar and insulin:** After 50, monitoring blood sugar can be a real struggle. Cutting down on cars drastically reduces both insulin levels and blood sugar levels. This means that the Keto diet will benefit millions as a lot of people struggle with insulin complications and high blood sugar levels. It has been proven to help when some people embark on Keto. They cut up to half of the carbs they consume. It's a treasure for those with diabetes and insulin resistance. A study was carried out on people with type 2 diabetes. After cutting back on carbs, within six months 95 percent of the people were able to reduce or totally stop using their glucose-lowering medication.
- **Lower levels of triglycerides:** A lot of people do not know what triglycerides are. Triglycerides are molecules of fat in your blood. They are known to circulate bloodstream and can be very dangerous. High levels of triglycerides can cause heart failures and heart diseases. However, Keto is known to reduce these levels.
- **Reduces acne:** Although acne is mostly suffered by young people, there are cases of people above 50 having it. Moreover, Keto is not only for persons over 50. Acne is not only caused by blocked pores. There are quite a several things proven to cause it. One of these things is your blood sugar. When you consume processed and refined carbs, it affects gut bacteria and results in the fluctuation of blood sugar levels. When the gut bacteria and sugar levels are affected, the skin suffers. However, when you embark on the Keto diet, you cut off on carbs intake, which means that in the very first place, your gut bacteria will not be affected, thereby cutting off that avenue to develop.
- **Increases high-density lipoprotein levels:** HDL refers to high-density lipoprotein. When your HDL levels are compared to your LDL levels and are not found low, your risk of developing heart disease is lowered. This is great for persons over 50 as heart diseases suddenly become more probable. Eating fats and reducing your intake of carbohydrates is one of the most assured ways to increase your high-density lipoprotein levels.
- **Reduces low-density lipoprotein levels:** High levels of LDL can be very problematic when you reach 50. This is because LDL refers to bad cholesterol. People with high levels of this cholesterol are more likely to get heart attacks. When you reduce the number of carbs you consume, you will increase the size of bad LDL particles. However, this will reduce the total LDL particles as they would have increased in size. Smaller LDL particles have been linked to heart diseases, while larger ones have been proven to have lower risks attached.

- **May help combat cancer:** I termed this under 'May' because research on this is not as extensive and conclusive as we would like it to be. However, there is proof supporting it. Firstly, it helps reduce the levels of blood sugar, which in turn reduces insulin complications, which in turn reduces the risk of developing cancers related to insulin levels. In addition, Keto places more oxidative stress on cancer cells than on normal cells, thereby making it great for chemotherapy. The risk of developing cancer after fifty still exists, so Keto is literally a lifesaver.

- **May lower blood pressure:** High blood pressure plagues adults much more than it does young ones. Once you reach 50, you must monitor your blood pressure rates. Reduction in the intake of carbohydrates is a proven way to lower your blood pressure. When you cut down on your carbs and lower your blood sugar levels, you greatly reduce your chances of getting some other diseases.

- **Combats metabolic syndrome:** As you grow older, you may find that you struggle to control your blood sugar level. Metabolic syndrome is another condition that has been proven to have an influence on diabetes and heart disease development. The symptoms associated with metabolic syndrome include, but are not limited to high triglycerides, obesity, high blood sugar level, and low levels of high-density lipoprotein cholesterol. However, you will find that reducing your level of carbohydrate intake greatly affects this. You will improve your health and majorly attack all the above-listed symptoms. The Keto diet helps to fight against metabolic syndrome, which is a big win.

- **Great for the heart:** People over the age of 50 have been proven to have more chances of developing heart diseases. The keto diet has been proven to be great for the heart. As it increases good cholesterol levels and reduces the levels of bad cholesterol, you will find that partaking in the Keto diet proves extremely beneficial for your health.

- **May reduce seizure risks:** When you change your intake levels, the combination of protein, fat, and carbs, as we explained before, your body will go into ketosis. Ketosis has been proven to reduce seizure levels in people who have epilepsy. When they do not respond to treatment, the ketosis treatment is used. This has been done for decades.

- **Mental focus:** Even the keto diet is based on protein, fats, and low carbohydrates. As we've mentioned, this forces body fat to become the key source of power. This is not the normal diet plan program conducive to nutrition acids that can be needed for appropriate brain functioning. Suppose folks suffer from cognitive diseases, like Alzheimer's. In that case, the mind isn't consuming enough sugar, thus becomes lacking at heart, and the brain has trouble functioning at a higher degree.

- **Increased energy:** It is not odd, also has become ordinary to feel drained and tired due to a poor food plan after the day. Fat is a much more reliable way to obtain energy, leaving you feeling a lot more vitalized than you would on the "sugar" rush.

- **Keto and anti-aging:** Several diseases are an all-organic effect of the aging process. Scientific tests on mice demonstrate brain cell improvement within the keto diet regime program, even though there have been studies done in humans. Studies have demonstrated that a favorable result of the keto diet program. We understand that a daily diet full of good antioxidants and nutrients, lower in sugar, high in carbs and nutritious carbohydrates, whereas saturated in carbohydrates, enhances our general well-being. It shields us from the toxic compounds of the diet plan. Research indicates that fatty acids such as fuel rather than sugar may slow the process down, possibly. Also, consuming some energy and ingesting is an issue of well-being since it prevents obesity and its particular negative effects. Scientific studies are constrained. However, considering the positive effects of the ketogenic diet on our health, it is plausible to assume that this daily diet helps us grow old. There are packed with sugars and foods. A typical diet plan is damaging to warding the indicators of aging.

- **Keto and eyesight:** People with diabetes understand that high blood glucose can cause a higher chance of developing cataracts because the keto diet program plan regime controls sugar levels, which can help protect against cataracts and maintain eyesight. This has been shown in several studies involving diabetic people.

- **Combats brain disorders:** Keto doesn't end there; it also combats Alzheimer's and Parkinson's disease. Some parts of your brain can only burn glucose and your body needs it. If you do not consume carbs, your lover will make use of protein to produce glucose. Your brain can also burn ketones. Ketones are formed when your carb level is very low. With this, the Ketogenic diet has been used for plenty of years to treat epilepsy in children who aren't responding to drugs. For adults, it can work the same magic as it is now being linked to treating Alzheimer's and Parkinson's disease.

- **Helps women suffering from polycystic ovarian syndrome:** This syndrome affects women of all ages. PCOS is short for the polycystic ovarian syndrome. The polycystic ovarian syndrome is an endocrine disorder that results in enlarged ovaries with cysts. These cysts are dangerous and cause other complications. It has been proven that a high intake of carbohydrates negatively affects women suffering from the polycystic ovarian syndrome. When a woman with PCOS reduces carbs and embarks on the Keto diet, the polycystic ovarian syndrome falls under attack.

It is beyond doubt that the Keto diet is beneficial in so many ways that it almost looks unreal. If you are to embark on the Keto diet, there are several things you must know.

Although the ketogenic diet is more called a speedy fat loss diet regime program, it is truly more to this than meets the eye. The truth is that high rates of energy and weight loss have been still only byproducts of this keto diet, a kind of reward. It has been clinically shown the keto diet program regime has many additional medical benefits.

Let us start by stating that a higher carbohydrate diet regime, together with its lots of ingredients and sugars, has no health advantages. All these are empty calories, and most processed meals fundamentally function to rob your body of that nourishment it needs to stay healthy.

Try not to be hard on yourself. A regulated Ketogenic diet is hard. If you have depended upon an eating routine for a couple of years, you're going to discover the change hard. Your body has turned used to the sustenance you have been eating. Your psyche is used to your routine. They are caught. So, it will take time for you to get in the swing. You'll be ideal. Keep the trust in yourself. Stick to the eating routine, and the results will come. It's a certainty. Keep it up.

CHAPTER 3:

Figure Out What to Eat

Now that we have gotten to the exciting part, it is time to learn what you can and cannot eat while following your new diet. Until this point, you have most likely followed the food pyramid stating the importance of fruits and vegetables. While they are still going to be important for vitamins and nutrients, you are going to have to be selective. Below, you will find a complete list of foods you get to enjoy on the ketogenic diet!

Keto-Friendly Vegetables

Vegetables can be tricky when you are first starting the ketogenic diet. Some vegetables hold more carbohydrates than others. The simple rule you need to remember is that above the ground is good and below the ground is bad—understand? Some popular above-ground vegetables you should consider for your diet (starting from the least carbs to the most carbs) include:

- Spinach
- Lettuce
- Avocado
- Asparagus
- Olives
- Cucumber
- Tomato
- Eggplant
- Cabbage
- Zucchini
- Cauliflower
- Kale
- Green Beans
- Broccoli
- Peppers
- Brussels sprouts

The below-ground vegetables you should avoid include:

- Carrots
- Onion
- Parsnip
- Beetroot
- Rutabaga
- Potato
- Sweet potato

Every food you put on your plate is comprised of three macronutrients: fat, protein, and carbohydrates. This will be an important lesson to learn before you begin your new diet, so be sure to take your time learning how to calculate them.

The golden rule is that meat and dairy are mostly made from protein and fat. Vegetables are mostly carbohydrates. Remember that while following the ketogenic diet, less than 5% of your calories need to come from carbohydrates. This is probably one of the trickiest tasks to get down when you are first getting started; there are hidden carbs everywhere! You will be amazed at how fast 20 grams of carbs will go in a single day, much less a single meal!

When you are first getting started, you may want to dip your toes into the carb-cutting. As a rule, vegetables that have less than 5 net carbs can be eaten fairly freely. To make them a bit more ketogenic, I suggest putting butter on your vegetables to get a source of fat into your meal.

If you still struggle at the store, figuring out which vegetables are ketogenic, look for vegetables with leaves. Vegetables that have left are typically spinach and lettuce, both that are keto-friendly. Another rule to follow is to look for green vegetables. Generally, green vegetables like green bell peppers and green cabbage are going to be lower in carbs!

Keto-Friendly Fruits

Much like with the vegetables, many berries and fruits contain hidden carbs. As a general rule, the larger the amount of fruit, the more sugar it contains; this is why fruit is seen as nature's candy! On the ketogenic diet, that is a no-go. While berries are going to be okay in moderation, you should leave the other fruits out for the best results. You may be thinking to yourself, I need to eat fruits for nutrients! The truth is, you can get the same nutrients from vegetables, costing you fewer carbohydrates on the ketogenic diet. While eating some berries every once in a while won't knock you out of ketosis, it is good to see how they affect you. But, if you feel like indulging in fruit as a treat, you can try some of the following:

- Raspberries
- Blackberries

- Strawberries
- Plum
- Kiwi
- Cherries

- Blueberries
- Clementine
- Cantaloupe
- Peach

Keto-Friendly Meat

On the ketogenic diet, meat is going to become a staple for you! When you are selecting your meats, try to stick with organic, grass-fed, and unprocessed. What I do want you to keep in mind is that the ketogenic diet is not meant to be high in protein; it is meant to be high in fat. People often link the ketogenic diet to a high meat diet, and that simply is not true. As you begin your diet, there is no need to have excess amounts of meat or protein. If you do have excess protein, it is going to be converted to glucose, knocking you right out of ketosis.

There are several different proteins that you will be able to enjoy while following the ketogenic diet. When it comes to beef, you will want to try your best to stick with the fattier cuts. Some of the better cuts would include ground beef, roast, veal, and steak. If poultry is more your style, look for the darker, fattier meats. Some good options for poultry selection would be wild game, turkey, duck, quail, and good old-fashioned chicken. Other options include:

- Pork loin
- Tenderloin
- Pork chops

- Ham
- Bacon

On your new diet, you will also be able to enjoy several different seafood dishes! At the store, you will want to look for wild-caught sources. Some of the better options include mahi-mahi, catfish, cod, halibut, trout, sardines, salmon, tuna, and mackerel. If shellfish is more your style, you get to enjoy lobster, muscles, crab, clams, and even oysters!

Keep in mind that when selecting your meats, try to avoid the cured and processed meats. These items, such as jerky, hot dogs, salami, and pepperoni, have many artificial ingredients, additives, and unnecessary sugars that will keep you from reaching ketosis. You know the better options now; stick with them!

Keto-Friendly Nuts

As you begin the ketogenic diet, there is a common misconception that you will now be able to eat as many nuts as you would like because they are high in fat. While you can enjoy a healthy serving of nuts, it is possible to go too nuts on nuts. Much like with the fruits and the vegetables, you would be surprised to learn that there are hidden carbohydrates here, too!

The lowest carb nuts you are going to find macadamia nuts, Brazil nuts, and pecans. These are fairly low in carbohydrates and can be enjoyed freely while following the ketogenic diet. These are all great options if you are looking for a healthy, ketogenic snack or something to toss in your salad.

When you are at the shop, you will want to avoid the nuts that have been treated with glazes and sugars. All of these extra add sugar and carbohydrates, which you are going to want to avoid. The higher carb nuts include cashews, pistachios, almonds, pine, and peanuts. These nuts can be enjoyed in moderation, but it would be better to avoid them.

The issue with eating nuts is that it is easy to overindulge in them. While they are technically keto-friendly, they still contain a high number of calories. With that in mind, you should only be eating when you are hungry and need energy. On the ketogenic diet, you will want to avoid snacking between meals. You don't need the nuts, but they taste good! If you want to lose weight, put the nuts down, and stick to a healthier snack instead.

Keto-Friendly Snacks

On the topic of snacks, let's take a look at keto-friendly ones to have instead of a handful of nuts! Before we begin, keep in mind that if you are looking to lose weight, you will want to avoid snacking when possible. In the beginning, it may be tougher, but as you adapt to the keto diet, your meals should keep your hunger at bay for much longer.

If you are looking for something small to take the edge off your hunger pangs, look for easy whole foods; some of these basics would include eggs, cheese, cold cuts, avocados, and even olives. As long as you have these basics in your fridge, it should stop you from reaching for the high-carb foods.

If you are looking for a snack with more crunch, vegetable sticks are always a great option! There are plenty of dipping sauces to add fat to your meal, as well. On top of that, pork rinds are a delicious, zero-carb treat. Beef jerky is also a good option, as long as you are aware of how many carbohydrates are in a commercial package.

With the good options in mind, it's always good to take a look at the bad. When you are snacking, avoid the high-carb fruits, the coffee with creamer, and the sugar-juices. Before you started the ketogenic diet, these were probably the easy option. You'll also want to avoid the obvious candy, chips, and donuts. Just remember, when you are selecting your foods, ask if it is fueling you or not.

Keto-Friendly Oils, Sauces, and Fats

On the ketogenic diet, the key to getting enough fat into your diet is going to depend on the sauces and oils you use with your cooking. When you put enough fat into your meals, this is what is going to keep you satisfied after every meal. The secret here is to be careful with the labels. You may be surprised to learn that some of your favorite condiments may have hidden sugars (looking at you, ketchup.)

While you are going to have to be a bit more careful about your condiments, you can never go wrong with butter! Up until this point, you have probably been encouraged to consume a low-fat diet. Now, I want you to embrace the fat! You can put butter in absolutely anything! Put butter on your vegetables, stick it in your coffee, and get creative!

On the other hand, oils can be a bit more complicated. You see, natural oils such as fish oil, sesame oil, almond oil, ghee, pure olive oil, and even peanut oil can be used on absolutely anything. What you want to avoid are the oils that have been created in the past sixty years or so. The oils you'll want to avoid include soy oil, corn oil, sunflower oil, and any vegetable oil. Unfortunately, these oils have been highly processed and may hinder your process.

Stick with these for your diet instead:

- Butter
- Vinaigrette
- Coconut oil
- Mayo
- Ranch dip
- Mustard
- Guacamole
- Heavy cream
- Thousand island dressing
- Salsa
- Blue cheese dressing
- Ranch dip
- Pesto

When it comes to dairy, high fat is going to be your best option. Cheese and butter are great options but keep the yogurts in moderation. When it comes to milk, you will want to avoid that as there is extra sugar in milk. If you enjoy heavy cream, this can be excellent for your cooking but should be used sparingly in your coffee.

Keto-Friendly Beverages

Remember that staying hydrated, especially when you are first starting your new diet, is going to be vital! Your safest bet is to always stick with water. Whether you like your water sparkling or flat, this is always going to be a zero-carb option. If you are struggling with a headache or the keto flu, remember that you can always throw a dash of salt in there.

CHAPTER 4:

Starting the Ketogenic Diet

You have already done much of the work to change over to a healthy lifestyle now that you know how Keto works. Of course, to make the most of the knowledge, you still have a lot to learn.

You'll also learn some of the common mistakes new Keto followers make and how to avoid them.

You'll learn how to be proactive in your approach by keeping a log of your daily eating habits. Your Keto journal will make sure you are making real progress.

Before we cover the common mistakes women make with Keto. First, we need to look a little deeper into Ketosis itself. As you know, practitioners of this diet are doing it as a way to trigger Ketosis.

Ketosis is the biological process in which your liver produces Ketones that cause your body to burn fat for energy. You get this to happen by depriving your body of its usual source of energy: carbs.

But it is actually a little more complicated than that, despite what other Keto books might have you believe. This is a way of explaining Ketosis that understandably simplifies it, but by doing so, it ignores some of the important components of Ketosis.

First of all, it isn't quite true that your body burns carbs for energy. Instead, your body uses those carbs to burn something else for energy: glucose. Glucose is the sugar that comes from the food that you eat.

It is different from the sugar you have in your pantry. Your digestive system breaks down everything you eat into its most basic parts so it can use the food for energy. Glucose is what comes out of this process of digestion. You could say it is the basic source of energy for your body.

When you put your body through Ketosis, this is a way of getting your system to use Ketones for the job that carbs would normally do. Meanwhile, the Ketones themselves get your body to burn more fat.

What makes Keto attractive to many women is the fact that it uses biological mechanisms already present in your body to burn fat. You aren't taking a pill to lose weight that won't actually work. Your body can already go through Ketosis without any medication; all you have to do is follow the Keto diet.

It isn't exactly true when people say you put your body through Ketosis to get these Ketones to burn fat. The job of Ketones is not to burn fat, but to aid in the process of burning through glucose.

When you don't eat a lot of carbs, carbs don't do the job of burning your glucose anymore. Instead, your liver produces ketones that burn fat.

There is a lot of misinformation that spreads because people learn about Keto from word-of-mouth or other unreliable sources instead of learning about it directly from a book.

Getting Started the Keto Diet

We've covered all the nitty-gritty details of the ketogenic diet for women over 50. Now it is time to get down to business—getting you started on keto. There are a few tips and tricks that I found that made my transition a stress-free one. This includes ditching all the non-keto food and restocking my kitchen with low-carb staples. I have some rules to share with you that will guarantee your success.

7 Rules to Success

1. **Pre-plan your diet:** If you're prepared, you'll eliminate the chance of you throwing your hands up in the air and giving up before you drive to the nearest fast-food restaurant. If you pre-plan what you're going to eat throughout the week, it will also make shopping a much more straightforward process. You'll have a shopping list to work from and won't aimlessly wander through the aisles.
2. **Prepare your meals:** If you're a busy woman and don't have time to spend hours a day in the kitchen, or maybe you just don't like cooking that much, a prepared meal may be the answer to your problems. When I first started eating keto, I found it convenient if I cooked a week's worth of meals every Sunday. It's an excellent way to make sure you don't use the excuse "I don't have time to cook" as a reason to eat processed and carb-heavy foods.

3. **Take it slow:** Getting into ketosis and staying there is not going to happen overnight. Persistence will win over extreme carb-cutting that will lead you to crash and burn a few days into the keto diet. Similarly, don't expect to see the positive health benefits immediately and then feel discouraged if you don't. You can't expect to undo a lifetime's worth of damage in only a few days.

4. **Try intermittent fasting:** If you want to speed the process up in a healthy manner, you can try intermittent fasting. This will get you into ketosis faster, meaning all the healing processes will start sooner than expected. The premise of intermittent fasting is you'll only have a window of X number of hours to eat in, and the rest of the time, nothing that contains any calories is allowed. There are different timeframes; for example, 16/8, which means you'll fast for 16 hours and eat for 8.

5. **Ignore the scale:** Women have this weird love affair with bathroom scales—they just can't leave them alone. Do you want to know a secret? They're actually pretty useless considering that your weight fluctuates throughout the month, depending on where in your cycle you are and how much water you're holding back. Various other factors also influence the number on the scale. Let's say you've decided to weight train. Well, the day after the training, when your muscles are sore, you'll weigh more!

6. **Keep a food journal:** This isn't even a recommendation but an instruction, especially in the beginning. There is no way you'll know how many carbs you're eating if you don't make a note of them. Now, when I say journal, I don't mean you have to write everything down on paper. There are carb and calorie-tracking apps you can use, which will do all the hard work for you. I mean, calculating net carbs, protein, and fat sounds like a complicated and tedious task. Another reason why I think food journals are terrific is that it gives you an idea of what time during the day you experience cravings, or when you're hungriest. If you have that information, you can be prepared for when it happens and have a healthy snack on hand.

7. **Clean out your kitchen:** Getting rid of all the carb-heavy and sugary foods is probably the best thing you can do for yourself. You'll be maximizing your chances for success since you won't have easy access to unhealthy foods. There's going to be a period when you won't have any of the foods you miss in your house. I recommend that you start stocking up on some healthy, nonperishable "fast food" choices before you start cutting out the junk. So get rid of the junk, stock up on some good foods, and be sure to have a well-stocked kitchen with healthy foods regularly. It's easy to eat unhealthily. If you open up your cabinets and pantry and look closely, there probably isn't much healthy.

Here's a list of foods that you should get rid of and ban from your house!

Fridge and Freezer

- Fruit juice
- Soda
- Margarine
- Store-bought salsas
- Any low-fat items
- Jam
- Cakes
- Store-bought waffles
- Buns
- Ice creams
- Ketchup
- Ready-made spice mixes

Pantry

- Chocolate
- Muffins
- Breakfast cereals
- Sugar of any kind
- Cookies
- Potato chips
- 'Healthy' processed snacks (granola bars, etc.)
- Dried fruit
- Crackers
- Beans
- Popcorn
- Candy
- Wheat flour
- Bagels
- Rice
- Bread
- Pasta
- Canned soup

This list isn't extensive—that would take pages and pages—but it includes some of the most popular high carb and sugary foods in American households. I suggest you read the labels on any remaining food you're not sure of. If it contains any sugar or carbs, ditch it.

Keto Staples

Okay, I'm not going to leave you with an empty kitchen. Here's a list of items you can restock your kitchen.

Quick Protein Sources

- Beef jerky
- Salami
- Pepperoni
- Canned fish (tuna, salmon, sardines)
- Smoked oysters
- Cheese
- Eggs
- Pork rinds
- Healthy keto fats
- Extra virgin olive oil
- Ghee
- Avocado oil
- Coconut oil
- Butter

Vegetables and Fruit

- Asparagus
- Brussels sprouts
- Cauliflower
- Celery
- Cucumber
- Green beans
- Broccoli
- Spinach
- Olives
- Cabbage
- Blueberries
- Kale
- Peppers (red and green)
- Swiss chard
- Zucchini
- Avocado (technically a fruit)
- Lettuce
- Tomatoes

Cooking Essentials

- Coconut flour
- Almond flour
- Sesame flour
- Shredded coconut
- Cacao butter
- Ground flaxseed
- Chia seeds
- Pink Himalayan sea salt
- Baking soda
- Baking powder
- Cream of tartar
- Gelatin
- Bone broth
- Xanthan gum
- Extracts (apple, vanilla, maple, lemon, caramel, etc.)
- Stevia
- Monk Fruit sweetener
- Sugar-free dark chocolate chips
- 85% dark chocolate
- Whey protein powder

Condiments

- Low-carb (and sugar-free) salad dressing
- Sugar-free ketchup
- Hollandaise sauce

Snacks

- Macadamia nuts
- Pecans
- Almonds
- Walnuts
- Unsweetened peanut butter
- Unsweetened almond butter
- Unsweetened coconut butter
- Seeds (pumpkin and sunflower)
- Olives

Prepare Your Kitchen

Before I move on to the recipes, I want to list some of my most-used gadgets to cook keto-friendly meals. I'm by no means suggesting that you have to have all of this in your kitchen to follow the ketogenic diet successfully, so please don't go out and buy anything you won't use.

You'll see I'm not listing cutlery and crockery and other items commonly found in a kitchen. I think in your 50 years on earth; you've spent enough time in a kitchen to know the basics required to cook food.

- **Kitchen scales:** Out of all the things on the list, this is one I would highly recommend buying. In the beginning, you won't be able to eyeball your macros as the more experienced keto dieters can. You will have to use a kitchen scale to weigh your food to know how much you are eating. You can then punch these numbers into a carbohydrate and calorie tracker app, and it will let you know if you're on track.
- **Storage and prepared food containers:** Essential for meal prepping and storing leftovers.
- **Slow cooker:** If you plan on prepping your meals in advance, I suggest investing in a slow cooker. You're able to cook a large amount of food at once and then divide it into portions for the week. If meal prepping is not your thing, you can still use the slow cooker to prepare a keto-friendly meal in a fraction of the time.
- **Spiralizers:** This is a nifty little gadget if you want to fool your eyes into thinking you're eating pasta. You can spiral different veggies into forms and sizes that resemble spaghetti, fettuccine, or other shapes.
- **Egg cooker:** Okay, you'll soon come to find that you'll be eating more eggs than usual. They're high in fat and protein and low in carbs, and that makes eggs a great snack. Boil a few eggs, pop them in the fridge and enjoy when you're a little hungry.
- **Immersion blender:** This is a baby food processor that you can hold in your hands to blitz up smoothies, make your own Hollandaise sauce, ground nuts, or whip some cream to add to your coffee. Just make sure you buy one with multiple attachments.
- **Frying pan/skillet:** You'll be eating a lot of steaks, so why not get a frying pan or skillet to cook it?
- **Roasting pan:** A whole chicken or beef roast surrounded by veggies, roasted in the oven, and then covered in a creamy cheese sauce. Doesn't sound like you're on a diet, does it? A roasting pan is a perfect container to make delicious meals in the oven.

CHAPTER 5:

How Ketogenic Metabolism Works

Ketosis is a standard metabolic procedure that offers various well-being favorable circumstances.
During ketosis, your body changes over fat into mixes known as ketones and begins to utilize them as its essential wellspring of vitality.
Studies have found that the consumption of calories that energize ketosis are very valuable for weight reduction owing to some degree to hunger suppressant impacts.

Rising examination shows that ketosis may likewise be valuable for, among different conditions, type 2 diabetes and neurological issue.

That said, accomplishing ketosis can set aside some effort to work and plan. It's not as simple as cutting carbs.

Here are some productive tips for getting into ketosis.

Reduce Your Carbohydrate Consumption

Expending a low carb diet is by a wide margin the most critical factor in achieving ketosis.

Typically, your cells use glucose or sugar as their essential fuel source. In any case, the majority of your cells can likewise utilize different wellsprings of vitality. This includes unsaturated fats, just as ketones, which are otherwise called ketones.

Your body stores glucose in the liver and muscles as glycogen.

At the point when the utilization of starches is extremely little, the glycogen stores decline and the hormone insulin focuses on the decline. This empowers unsaturated fats to be discharged from your muscle versus fat shops.

The proportion of carb obstruction required to cause ketosis is somewhat individualized. A couple of individuals need to bind net carbs (complete carbs short fiber) to 20 grams consistently, while others can accomplish ketosis by eating twice, so a great deal or more.

Subsequently, the Atkins diet confirms that carbs should be confined to 20 or fewer grams consistently for around fourteen days to ensure that ketosis is cultivated.

After this stage, modest quantities of carbs can be familiar with your eating routine a little bit at a time, as long as ketosis is ensured. In one-week research, people with type 2 diabetes who had limited carb utilization to 21 grams or less daily experienced day-by-day urinary ketone discharge rates that were multiple times more noteworthy than their standard fixations.

In another exploration, grown-ups with type 2 diabetes were allowed 20–50 grams of edible carbs every day, in light of the number of grams that allowed blood ketone focuses on being kept up inside the objective scope of 0.5–3.0 mmol/L.

These carb and ketone ranges are prescribed for people who need to get ketosis to energize weight reduction, control glucose fixations or lessening hazard factors for coronary illness.

Helpful ketogenic abstains from food utilized for epilepsy or exploratory disease treatment, then again, regularly limit carbs to under 5 percent of calories or under 15 grams for each day to additionally build ketone levels.

Nonetheless, any individual who utilizes an eating regimen for restorative reasons should just do as such under the direction of a clinical expert.

Restricting your starch utilization to 20–50 net grams for every day lessens glucose and insulin fixations, prompting the arrival of putting away unsaturated fats that your liver proselytes to ketones.

Incorporate Coconut Oil in Your Diet

As a general rule, it has been proposed that the utilization of coconut oil might be perhaps the most ideal approach to help ketone focuses on people with Alzheimer's ailment and different sensory system diseases.

Although coconut oil incorporates four sorts of MCTs, half of its fat is gotten from the sort known as lauric corrosive.

Use MCT Oil Regularly

Enhancing with MCT (medium-chain triglyceride) oil will help you get into ketosis regardless of whether your glycogen stockpiles aren't completely exhausted.

MCT's are promptly utilized into ketone bodies and utilized for vitality as opposed to experiencing your stomach for assimilation While numerous individuals think coconut oil is equivalent to MCT, they are molecularly unique.

MCT oil comprises 100% medium-chain triglycerides—caprylic and capric acids—while coconut oil contains 35% long-chain triglycerides and 50% lauric corrosive. Coconut oil is just comprised of 15% medium-chain triglycerides. So your body needs to experience its stomach-related tract to transform coconut oil into vitality. In contrast, MCT oil is changed over legitimately into vitality.

A few examinations propose that fat sources with a more noteworthy extent of lauric corrosive may produce a progressively consistent measure of ketosis. This is because it is more continuously used than different MCTs.

MCTs have been utilized to cause ketosis in epileptic children without restricting carbs as definitely as the exemplary ketogenic diet.

In actuality, a few preliminaries have found that a high-MCT diet including 20 percent of starch calories creates impacts tantamount to the great ketogenic diet, which offers under 5 percent of sugar calories.

While adding coconut oil to your eating routine, it's a smart thought to do, so gradually limit stomach-related reactions; for example, stomach squeezing or loose bowels.

Start with one teaspoon daily and work up to a few tablespoons every day for seven days. You can find coconut oil in your neighborhood supermarket or get it on the web.

Devouring coconut oil offers your body MCTs that are quickly retained and changed into ketone bodies by your liver.

Enhance Your Physical Activity

An expanding measure of examination has demonstrated that ketosis can be helpful for certain sorts of athletic execution, including continuance work out.

What's more, being progressively dynamic may help you get into ketosis.

At the point when you practice, your body will be drained from its glycogen shops. Typically, these are renewed when you expend carbs that are separated into glucose and afterward changed to glycogen.

In any case, if the utilization of sugar is limited, the glycogen shops remain little. In response, your liver improves the yield of ketones, which can be utilized as an elective wellspring of vitality for your body.

One examination found that activity improves the rate at which ketones are produced at low blood ketone levels. Be that as it may, when blood ketones are raised, they don't increment with practice and may viably diminish for a short timeframe.

Also, it has been demonstrated that turning out to be in a fasted state is driving up ketone focuses.

In a little examination, nine old females performed either preceding or after a supper. Their blood ketone focuses were 137–314 percent more prominent when utilized before a supper than when utilized after a dinner.

Remember that even though activity raises ketone yield, it might take one to about a month for your body to acclimate to the utilization of ketones and unsaturated fats as principle energizes. Physical execution might be diminished immediately during this second.

Taking part in physical activity may support ketone fixations during carb restriction. This effect can be improved by working in a quick-paced state.

Exercise yourself as well as possible.

An awesome way to spend your time while you're on keto is to take walks, go swimming, take hikes, and other outdoor activities. It's a great way to spend some of the extra energy you find yourself with so that you're not up at night!

Ramp up Your Healthy Fat Intake

A lot of good fat can expand your ketone focuses and assist you with accomplishing ketosis.

Indeed, an exceptionally low-carb ketogenic diet limits carbs as well as high in fat.

A ketogenic eats fewer carbs for weight reduction, metabolic well-being, and exercise proficiency by and large give between 60–80 percent of fat calories.

A three-week exploration of 11 sound individuals differentiated the effects of fasting with particular amounts of fat utilization on ketone centralizations of relaxing.

In general, ketone focuses are tantamount in people who expend 79% or 90% of fat calories.

Additionally, because makes up such a major extent of the ketogenic diet, it is fundamental to pick top-notch sources.

Extraordinary fats consolidate olive oil, avocado oil, coconut oil, spread, oil, and sulfur. Moreover, there are variously strong, high-fat sustenance's that are in like manner little in carbs.

Nevertheless, if your goal is weight decrease, it's fundamental to guarantee you don't exhaust such countless calories inside and out, as this can make your weight decrease delayed down.

Exhausting on any occasion, 60 percent of fat calories will help increase your ketone centers. Pick the extent of sound fats from both animal and plant sources.

Try a Fat Fast or Short Fast

The other method to get into ketosis is to abandon eating for a couple of hours.

Actually, numerous people have gentle ketosis between lunch and breakfast.

Youngsters with epilepsy now and then rush for 24–48 hours before they start a ketogenic diet. This is accomplished to get into ketosis quickly with the goal that seizures can be diminished all the more quickly.

Irregular fasting, a wholesome technique including intermittent momentary fasting, may likewise cause ketosis.

A 1965 exploration uncovered a significant loss of fat in overweight patients who followed a speedy fat. Be that as it may, different researchers have called attention to the fact that these discoveries seem to have been incredibly misrepresented.

Since fat is so little in protein and calories, a limit of three to five days ought to be followed to evade an inordinate loss of bulk. It might likewise be difficult to adhere to for more than a couple of days.

Fasting, irregular fasting, and "fat fasting" would all be able to help you get into ketosis relatively quickly.

Maintaining Adequate Protein Intake

Showing up at ketosis needs a protein use that is fitting anyway, not over the top.

The commendable ketogenic diet used in epilepsy patients is obliged to increasing ketone centers in both carbs and proteins.

A comparative eating routine may be important for infection patients, as it would restrain tumor improvement.

In any case, it's definitely not a not too bad practice for the vast majority to decrease proteins to enable ketone to yield.

In any case, it is basic to eat up enough protein to effortlessly the liver with amino acids that can be used for gluconeogenesis, which means' new glucose.' In this strategy, your liver offers glucose to the couple of cells and organs in your body that can't use ketones as fuel.

CHAPTER 6:

Challenges Women over Fifty Face during Keto Diet and How to Avoid Them

Insomnia

Your body may be adapting to your new keto lifestyle and to how your body absorbs the energy you now have if you have trouble sleeping. If this is a tough time for you, then there are a few things that you might consider trying to handle. Taking melatonin in the evenings before bed is one of the things you should do. It makes it simpler and more peaceful for you to slip away, and it will help you stay asleep through the night. If you notice that you're eating meals a little bit later in the evening, try to bump them up a little bit and quit between your last meal and the time you go to bed for around two to three hours. If you usually drink more than a cup of coffee each day, you might also want to cut back on your caffeine intake. Try changing your carb intake to earlier parts of the day so that at night you don't carbo-load. In the evening, keep your room cool, as being hot will prevent you from being able to sleep. You may also find that for thirty minutes to one hour before bedtime; you need to reduce the light you have on in your house or your room. This will inform the brain that it's time for you to cool down.

Keto Flu

You've read about this one, probably. This is the one that, when it comes to keto disadvantages, receives the most attention. You could find yourself feeling achy, sore, nauseous, sluggish, exhausted, hot, and just all-around crummy in the first month or so of keto. If you discover that this is the case, just get plenty of rest, stick to the scheme as best you can, and work through it by keeping the macros at the right level. The keto flu has enabled a reasonable number of keto dieters to discourage them and prevent them from hitting the most rewarding, best parts of keto. If you can struggle through the effects of keto flu, you'll find it's certainly worth it for you to do so. When you exit from the other end of it, you'll feel like a million bucks, and you'll find that you don't have to deal with those symptoms again. Staying rested and hydrated is one of the most important things to consider when you're moving through the keto flu. With electrolytes, drink plenty of water and get plenty of rest. You should be right as rain in just a few days, and you should start to experience a steep rise in your level of energy from then on!

Muscle Cramps and Dehydration

You're not alone if you've ever had unexpected, serious leg pain on a ketogenic diet.

While this high fat, low carb diet can help with weight loss and even help cure some medical conditions, several side effects, including leg cramps, have been associated with it.

Involuntary, localized muscle contractions that are frequently painful are cramps.

Usually, these contractions occur at night and can last from seconds to minutes. In less than a few minutes, most leg cramps have stopped.

Although their exact cause is not always clear, multiple factors can increase the risk, including pregnancy, medical treatments, inadequate blood flow, and the use of some medicines.

For several reasons, the keto diet can make you more prone to leg cramps.

Too Few Electrolytes

A deficiency of electrolytes is a possible cause of leg cramps.

Electrolytes are minerals that, like cell communication, are essential for critical functions in your body.

Your nerve cells could become more responsive if your levels become depleted. In addition, this contributes to pressure on nerve endings, which can trigger muscle spasms.

Your body may lose more electrolytes when adjusting to the keto diet by urinating in response to decreased blood sugar and insulin hormone levels.

This loss is normally highest during the first 1–4 days of the transition to keto, so during this time, muscle cramps due to electrolyte imbalance can be worse.

The Dehydration

Owing to factors such as decreased insulin levels and increased sodium excretion, individuals transitioning to the keto diet frequently urinate more. In turn, increased urination, another possible cause of leg cramps, may lead to dehydration.

One of the most popular keto side effects is dehydration and can increase the risk of leg cramps.

All the same, proof is mixed and more studies are needed.

Such Prospective Triggers

Leg cramps can also be triggered by many other variables.

For example, some medications are associated with an increased risk of these pains, such as diuretics, asthma medicines, and statins.

Additionally, leg cramps are associated with sedentary habits, old age, strenuous physical exercise, and medical conditions such as liver and kidney failure.

Keto Rash

Keto rash is a rare, inflammatory skin situation characterized by a red, itchy rash around the trunk and neck, also formally known as prurigo pigmentosa.

Keto rash is a kind of dermatitis that could occur in any human but is most prevalent in Asian women. Young Japanese women have previously been involved in most of the in-depth research on the subject.

Keto rash symptoms can include:

- A red, itchy rash that mainly occurs on the upper back, chest, and abdomen.
- Red spots that take on a web-like look, called papules.
- When the spots fade, a dark brown pattern is left on the skin.

Treatment for the Keto Rash

There are many ways of treating the keto rash at home, should you encounter it:

Introduce Carbohydrates Again

You may want to consider reintroducing carbohydrates if you suspect that a recent adjustment to your diet is the cause of your rash.

A 2018 research by Trusted Source showed that it dramatically improved rash symptoms by adding carbohydrates back into the diet.

If you aren't ready to give up entirely the keto lifestyle yet, you can always strive instead for a relatively low-carb diet.

Right the Deficiencies of Nutrients

In certain inflammatory skin conditions, nutrient deficiencies can play a role.

Vitamin A, vitamin B-12, and vitamin C deficiencies have been associated with acute and chronic skin conditions.

Your body may not be getting all the vitamins and minerals it needs if you're consuming an excessively restrictive diet.

A perfect way to ensure that you consume all the nutrients nature has to offer is to consume an assortment of colorful fruits and vegetables.

Removing Food Allergens

The keto diet emphasizes high-fat, low-carb foods. Eggs, dairy, fish, nuts, and seeds, to name a few, are some of the most common foods to consume on the ketogenic diet.

Many of these foods likewise happen to be on the list of common food allergens, coincidentally.

With food allergies being a cause of inflammation, you must remove any foods that you are allergic to that can make your rash symptoms worse.

Add Anti-Inflammatory Supplements

Some supplements can help the body to battle inflammatory conditions in addition to dietary changes.

KETO DIET FOR WOMEN OVER 50

In clinical trials, Trusted Source was used to help improve dermatitis symptoms with probiotics, prebiotics, vitamin D, and fish oil supplements.

A 2014 review of the latest herbal supplementation literature showed that for those with dermatitis, evening primrose oil could also produce promising results.

Take Good Care of the Skin

As much as possible, it's necessary to take care of your skin. If you have inflammatory skin disorders, this is particularly true.

For bathing and showering, the National Eczema Association suggests using lukewarm water and washing only with gentle soaps and cleansers.

The group also suggests keeping your skin moisturized when the elements, such as the hot sun or cold wind, are dry and covered when out.

Chat about Medicine with Your Doctor

A return to your doctor might be appropriate if home treatment fails to clear up the rash.

Minocycline and doxycycline antibiotics are important medicines prescribed for prurigo pigmentosa. For recovery, Dapsone may also be used.

Prevention and Outlook

Via dietary and lifestyle changes, the keto rash can be avoided and relieved.

Visiting your doctor can give you the help you need to fully clear up your condition if home remedies do not completely remove the rash.

Although keto rash is rare, when starting a keto diet, you can avoid it by taking the following precautions:

- **Lower the consumption of carbohydrates steadily.** Try to slow taper carbohydrates out of your diet rather than quickly dropping your carbohydrate intake.
- **Supplement, initially with a multivitamin/mineral.** When you begin the keto diet, a once-a-day multivitamin or multimineral will help you reduce the risk of nutrient deficiencies.
- **A doctor's consultation.** Visit your doctor for more information if you are worried about some of the side effects of a keto diet, including a keto rash. He could refer you to a nutritionist that can help you safely adjust to the keto diet.

Brain Fog

The trendy ketogenic diet has been embraced over the past few years by celebrities and fitness junkies alike. A laundry list of possible health benefits, including weight loss and lower blood sugar levels, comes with the high-fat, low-carb diet. The decreased risk of diseases like diabetes, cancer, and flu has also been associated with Keto. Scientists have also proposed that a keto diet could improve brain function and act as a potential Alzheimer's disease treatment.

But it doesn't come without some disadvantages to adopt a keto diet and not just say good-bye to bread, either. Among these is what is referred to as keto flu, a cluster of symptoms that occur two days to a week after the start of the diet. These include headache, exhaustion, nausea, and "brain fog," referring to mental fatigue, hazy thought, concentration, and memory difficulties. It is not considered that brain fog is an official medical diagnosis.

Although, a little study has been done into what, exactly, causes keto flu and brain fog, the symptoms could be the reaction of the body to carb withdrawal. Typically, keto practitioners claim that when they switch away from carb-centric diets, the effects are short-lived, lasting only a few days. Things like consuming plenty of water and can salt intake may help alleviate these cognitive blips while preventing too much strenuous exercise.

Constipation/Diarrhea

You have to make sure you get a good amount of fiber in your diet because you're putting on a lot of fat in your diet. In the first few weeks, if you happen to slip on this, you may want to turn up the amount of celery, kale, Romaine, and general roughage that you put into your diet. Consider getting a dissolvable fiber powder that you can apply to your morning smoothie, coffee, water, tea, etc., if you have trouble going, and you are also having trouble shoving more vegetables into your routine.

Shopping List

Week 1

Meat, seafood, and poultry:

- Eggs
- Chicken
- Turkey breast

- Deli ham
- Pork
- Anchovy fillets

Fruits and vegetables:

- Tomatoes
- Spinach
- Parsley
- Garlic
- Onions
- Asparagus

- Carrots
- Oregano
- Jalapeños
- Lettuce
- Broccoli
- Red cabbage

Cheese, butter, cream, and milk:

- Parmesan cheese
- Mozzarella cheese
- Butter
- Cheddar cheese
- Almond milk

- Muenster cheese
- Heavy cream
- Grass-fed butter
- Greek yoghurt

Condiments:

- Black pepper
- Apple cider vinegar
- Olive oil
- Smoked paprika
- Salt

- Extra virgin olive oil
- Sriracha
- No-sugar-added Ketchup
- Mayo sauce

Week 2

Meat, seafood, and poultry:

- Eggs
- Chicken

- Beef

Fruits and vegetables:

- Tomatoes
- Spinach
- Parsley
- Garlic
- Onions

- Cauliflower
- Avocado
- Oregano
- Jalapeños

Cheese, butter, cream, and milk:

- Parmesan cheese
- Mozzarella cheese
- Butter
- Cheddar cheese
- Almond milk

- Muenster cheese
- Heavy cream
- Grass-fed butter
- Greek yoghurt

Condiments:

- Black pepper
- Black olive oil
- Salt
- Honey
- Soy sauce

- Red pepper
- Italian seasoning
- Red wine vinegar
- Chili-garlic sauce
- Vanilla extract

KETO DIET FOR WOMEN OVER 50

Week 3

Meat, seafood, and poultry:

- Eggs
- Chicken
- Turkey breast
- Deli ham
- Pork
- Anchovy fillets

Fruits and vegetables:

- Tomatoes
- Spinach
- Parsley
- Garlic
- Onions
- Asparagus
- Carrots
- Oregano
- Jalapeños
- Lettuce
- Broccoli
- Red cabbage

Cheese, butter, cream, and milk:

- Parmesan cheese
- Mozzarella cheese
- Butter
- Cheddar cheese
- Almond milk
- Muenster cheese
- Heavy cream
- Grass-fed butter
- Greek yoghurt

Condiments:

- Black pepper
- Apple cider vinegar
- Olive oil
- Smoked paprika
- Salt
- Extra virgin olive oil
- Sriracha
- No-sugar-added Ketchup
- Mayo sauce

Week 4

Meat, seafood, and poultry:

- Eggs
- Chicken
- Beef

Fruits and vegetables:

- Tomatoes
- Spinach
- Parsley
- Garlic
- Onions
- Cauliflower
- Avocado
- Oregano
- Jalapeños

Cheese, butter, cream, and milk:

- Parmesan cheese
- Mozzarella cheese
- Butter
- Cheddar cheese
- Almond milk
- Muenster cheese
- Heavy cream
- Grass-fed butter
- Greek yogurt

Condiments:

- Black pepper
- Black olive oil
- Salt
- Honey
- Soy sauce
- Red pepper
- Italian seasoning
- Red wine vinegar
- Chili-garlic sauce
- Vanilla extract

CHAPTER 7:

Common Keto Mistakes and Their Fixes

Starting up the keto diet and maintaining it requires a sacrifice of time and dedication. Your lifestyle and routine will undoubtedly be tampered with. You have to focus entirely on noticing the benefits of the keto diet. Whatever your end goals are, you should make little changes to gain huge turnouts.

Mistake 1: Eating Insufficient Amounts of Protein

Some believe that consuming excess protein may trigger a metabolic response that raises blood sugar and sets you out of ketosis. This is called gluconeogenesis, and this is not how it works. Excess protein poses no threat whatsoever to your ketogenic diet. This is why:

Gluconeogenesis always occurs during ketosis. The amount of protein you eat on a keto diet matters little when gluconeogenesis already manifests in your body. This is because your body requires traces of glucose to function correctly.

Gluconeogenesis occurs only in small amounts. Even if you're on a high protein diet, you're likely still using ketones as your fuel source.

As a matter of fact, gluconeogenesis is right for your body. Excess glucose is toxic; insufficient glucose could kill you. Gluconeogenesis helps fuel tissues that metabolize ketones, such as red blood cells, testicles, and a part of the kidney. They also help prevent hypoglycemia.

So if you suspect anything, it's more likely that you suffer from insufficient protein. Protein aids in losing weight. The amino acids from proteins build and repair muscle tissues, among others.

The Fix

If you notice a drop in your appetite since you began the Keto, you're likely not eating enough protein or sufficient calories.

A good range to aim for is 0.7–0.9 grams of protein per pound of body weight (1.5–2.0 grams per kg). Excessive protein consumption on a low-carb diet can prevent you from getting into ketosis.

Now that you know protein won't reset your ketosis, do not avoid it. You should even eat more protein than less.

Mistake 2: Insufficient Vitamins and Minerals

A lack of micronutrients may cause a long list of health complications, ranging from fatigue to weight gain, poor wound healing, and dry skin.

For a successful ketogenic diet, your plan must include a lot of nutrient-dense, low-carbohydrate foods. So you might want to go and get more vegetables.

Note that nutrient value differs in all foods. Limiting carbohydrates and using coconut oil in your tea may set you into ketosis, but your body might not get all the needed micronutrients.

The Fix

Eat foods with a lot of micronutrients and switch up your diet daily.

Eating by the season may assist in your variety. You'll enjoy summer squashes and leafy greens in the hotter months and mushrooms, pumpkins, leeks, and other vegetables in the colder months.

Here's a list of nutrient-dense, ketogenic friendly foods to consider:

- Steak
- Avocados

- Bone broth
- Leafy greens

- Eggs
- Organ meats
- Broccoli sprouts

Mistake 3: Insufficient Consumption of Electrolytes

Lack of electrolytes is also considered a micronutrient issue. Still, it stands out due to its emergence if you're witnessing symptoms of keto flu such as fatigue, brain fog, muscle aches and weakness, and nausea.

You may even need to use electrolyte supplements. This is because your body burns fat through stored glucose during the keto diet, which might make you urinate more frequently. The more you burn glucose, the more stored water you release.

A rise in urination may not be permanent, but you will be better off just maintaining your electrolyte levels, especially for the athletes.

The Fix

The following minerals are contained in electrolytes:

- Calcium
- Magnesium
- Sodium
- Potassium

You have to make sure you're consuming these in sufficient amounts. To get this in sufficient amounts:

- Add a high-electrolyte to your supplement.
- Add more nutrient-dense, low carb foods daily, such as grass-fed meat, seeds, leafy greens, and nuts.
- Add high-quality sea salt to your water every morning. You can drink it casually at any time or before a work out session.

Mistake 4: Failure to Plan Meal

You'll find it is a lot easy to embark on and maintain a ketogenic diet when you have a plan. You can have a ton of keto-friendly food stored in your house. You need to have made a clear plan before you start with the keto.

The Fix

Select a day or two in a week to do your grocery shopping, prepare meals that last up to a week, and put them on ice. When you have healthy food to snack on, you resist the urge to buy pizza or other unhealthy junk.

Mistake 5: Miscalculation of Your Macronutrients

The most crucial side task while on the keto diet is tracking your macronutrient. Don't compare yourself with others; your micronutrient needs differ drastically. You must figures out the right amount of fat, protein, and carbs for your lifestyle.

If you notice there are hardly any changes in your weight loss, this might result from inadequate protein or fat.

The Fix

The first thing you need to do is calculate your specific micronutrient needs. Then obey the following guidelines.

1. **Prioritize proteins:** You have to ensure you're getting sufficient proteins. They help you lose weight, maintain muscle build, and stay satisfied for longer. This should help:
   - **Minimal workout:** 1grams protein per kg of total body weight. This is around 91 grams protein for somebody of 200lb and 64 grams for 140 lb.
   - **Moderate workout:** 1.3 grams protein per kilogram of total body weight. This is around 120 grams protein for somebody of 200 lb and 83 grams for 140 lb.
   - **Intense workout:** 1.6 grams protein per kilogram of total body weight. That is around 146 grams protein for somebody of 200 lb and 102 grams protein for 140 lb.
2. **Monitor your carb intake:** Cut down on carbohydrates. A total of 20–50 grams of carbohydrates is enough for a day. If you're not frequent with the gym, use as little carbohydrates as possible. But for athletes, you can use as much as 50 grams daily, don't exceed it.
3. **Your remaining calories should be fats:** The last thing to do when calculating your macronutrients is to fill your remaining calories with fat. You can get this amount very quickly. Just subtract your daily protein and carbohydrate intake from the sum of calorie intake. The rest of your macros per day should be obtained from fats.

Mistake 6: You're Not Sleeping Enough

Lack of sleep or poor quality sleep may spike up stress hormones. High cholesterol could also result in gaining fat, cravings, and general disruption of sex hormone production.

You should get enough quality sleep to gain more energy or to lose weight quickly and adequately.

The Fix

Your sleep duration matters a lot, but even more so is the quality of your sleep. Below are a few tips for deeper, restorative sleep:

- Sleep in a room of around 65–70 degrees.
- Sleep in a dark room.
- Make use of sleep aids like magnesium and melatonin.
- Avoid looking at screens from one hour to your bedtime.
- Make use of earplugs.

Mistake 7: Eating High Inflammatory Foods in Excess

The Ketogenic diet is famous for its anti-inflammatory benefits; however, some low-carb high-fat foods may exacerbate inflammation. This means keto beginners usually eat processed vegetable oils and meat because the macronutrient ratio tallies with the keto diet.

However, you must avoid processed, low-quality food as strictly as you can. Inflammatory Foods such as low-carb packaged foods and highly-processed vegetable oils may cause systematic inflammation and drain your energy.

The Fix

Stop eating processed foods and instead eat organic low-carb vegetables and pure pastured meats. Get rid of low-quality oils such as peanut oil, soybean oils, and canola oil, and instead, get oils like:

- Coconut oil
- Olive oil
- Avocado
- MCT oil
- Unrefined palm oil

And if you have a craving that just won't go away, there are ketogenic foods options to satisfy your craving.

Mistake 8: Use of Chemical Artificial Sweetness

You must abide by your macros. However, that shouldn't give you the excuse to eat whatever you please. Artificial Sweetness such as saccharin or aspartame may cause inflammation, gut irritations, or may even bring about gut bacteria.

Even worse, the sugar substitutes tend to set off the same brain reward pathways as sugar and cocaine in the brain. This means you're setting off a similar response in your brain when consuming non-caloric foods sweeteners as when you eat sugar. The side effect of this may be increased and severer cravings.

The Fix

It is not enough to replace sugary sodas with diet sodas; you must train your body to resist all cravings. Replace diet sodas with water or other exogenous ketones.

Mistake 9: Forgetting about Hidden Carbohydrates

There are hidden carbs in every food. They could be in the dressings or sauces at eateries or your friends' cook-off. You must make these inquiries so that you can avoid them.

If you continue consuming hidden carbs, you will reset your ketosis and stay out of it for as long as you continue. And in this period, your cravings will only increase.

The Fix

Endeavor to ask about the ingredients of every meal you get served at a restaurant or a party. If the waiter isn't certain, just instruct them to leave the sauces and dressings on the side.

Catch up on nutrition labels. Some foods may claim low-carb, but in fact, have very high carb counts. You must check the nutrition labels to find out how many carbs per serving.

A low-carb snack label may only contain 10 grams of carbs, but the snack is served up to 3 times.

Avoid ingredients such as agave, dextrose, maple syrup, fructose, honey, sucrose, and maple syrup. If you eat just enough amounts of these, you will be kicked out of ketosis quickly.

Foods that may have hidden carbs:

- Dairy and non-dairy foods
- Sausage
- Peanut butter
- Sports drinks
- Low car packaged foods
- Bacon
- Protein bars
- Protein powder
- Sports drinks

Mistake 10: Insufficient Low-Carb Vegetables Intake

Veggies supply a lot of nutrients to the human body, such as fiber and micronutrients. But yet, a common misconception still spreads, swaying people against vegetables in their keto diet.

The Fix

There are several available vegetable diets for your consumption and safety. However, stay away from higher-carb vegetables such as squash, beans, potatoes, corn, etc.

These are the vegetables you should eat in abundance:

- Cauliflower
- Broccoli
- Kale
- Cabbage
- Spinach
- Asparagus
- Avocado
- Zucchini

Mistake 11: Over Concern about Ketone Levels

There is nothing more satisfying than recordings high levels of ketone after only starting. Ketone levels are a great way to know that you're doing it right.

However, you should note that recording high levels of ketone in your blood or urine strips aren't the main aim of the keto diet, at least not in the long term. Having high ketone level readings over a long time isn't exactly the best thing in the world.

It is very common to notice higher readings at the beginning stage of your Keto. In this period, your body has a lot more fat to burn, and it is just getting used to burning ketones for fuel. This is likely due to the circulating ketones.

But as time goes, your body will get accustomed to burning ketones. So they won't be getting excited in your blood or hiding out in your urine. Thus, your ketone level readings will get lower, but in fact, more ketones are now getting burned up to fuel.

The Fix

Don't spend all your time worrying about ketone levels rising or falling; eventually, these statistics will mean very little. Instead, begin to track metrics such as energy levels or body composition.

CHAPTER 8:

Other Benefits of Keto Diet Program

The ketogenic diet is also known as the low carb diet. It encourages the body to produce ketones from fats in the liver, which are used by the body as a source of energy in the absence of glucose or sugar.

Glucose is a primary source of energy; an excess of it is converted into fats and is stored in many organs such as the liver and adipose tissues. What if you could use up the stored fat as a source of energy and, in doing so, be able to deal with your weight issues? This is where the ketogenic diet comes in.

While it is convenient to fast so that the body can use up most of its fat reserves, not everyone can do fasting. By using and working on ketosis principles, the ketogenic diet mimics the metabolic state of ketosis without hunger.

Look at it this way. Suppose your diet is based primarily on carbs. In that case, this drives the usual metabolic pathway, so you end up storing excess glucose into different parts of the body as fat. Carbs are neither good nor bad, but if you consume too many, they can lead to obesity, Type 2 diabetes, and cardiovascular disease.

By eating fewer carbs, you induce your body to the state of ketosis, thus making it easier for the body to tap into the stored fat reserves it already has on hand. But getting yourself into the state of ketosis is never easy. Either you go on fasting for days or cut down your carb intake to 50 grams daily, which is equivalent to around 5% of your total calories.

This can be achieved by changing your diet. Instead of taking in your usual diet, you can drive ketosis by eating more fat and protein. Your fat should be 60–75% of your daily calories, while your protein intake should be 15–30% of your calories. This is equivalent to 1 large chicken breast and five small avocados for each meal because fat is naturally filling, it will keep you full for a long time, so you will not feel the need to snack between meals.

The ketogenic diet's goal is to get your body into the state of ketosis by breaking down fats into ketones as the primary source of fuel by eating the right amounts of food that support such metabolic pathways.

Benefits of the Keto Diet Program

Although the ketogenic diet is more called a speedy fat loss diet regime program, it is truly more to this than meets the eye. The truth is that high energy and weight loss rates have been still only by-products of this keto diet, a kind of reward. It has been clinically shown the keto diet program regime has many additional medical benefits. Let us start by stating that a higher carbohydrate diet regime, together with its lots of ingredients and sugars, has no health advantages. All these are empty calories. Most processed meals fundamentally function to rob your body of the nourishment it needs to stay healthy. Here is a list of real Gains for lowering your carbohydrates and ingestion fats which convert to power:

Control of Blood Sugar

Maintaining blood glucose to a minimal degree is critical to preventing and controlling diabetes. The keto diet has been proven to help protect against diabetes. Many people will also be overweight. That makes an easy regime that natural, but the keto diet also does more. Carbohydrates have converted into glucose, which for people with diabetes can bring about a sugar spike. An eating plan permits control, and low in carbs averts those spikes.

Is the Ketogenic Diet Really for You?

You have to remember that just like all other diet regimens, not everyone can follow a ketogenic diet. So, before you start this regimen, ask yourself if the ketogenic diet is really for you? Below are the things that you should consider to see if the ketogenic diet is for you.

- **How long can I follow this diet?** The ketogenic diet is not like your usual fad diet, only lasting for a few weeks. To see results, it will take you months or even a year. So, if you are someone who cannot follow its principles long-term, then this diet is not for you.
- **Will the eating plan fit my food preference, budget needs, and culture?** Suppose you follow a strict dietary guideline (veganism or vegetarianism). In that case, you might need to tweak the ketogenic diet to fit your preferences.

It may difficult, but not impossible. However, if you find it too much of a hassle to tweak the ketogenic meal plan to fit your preference, you might not enjoy this diet at all.

- **Do I have medical conditions that will put me at risk?** While the ketogenic diet has therapeutic effects on people who suffer from diabetes and cardiovascular diseases, it is not prescribed among people who suffer from kidney-related problems as protein and fats can be damaging to the kidneys.

The bottom line is that while the ketogenic diet is good for most people, it may not be advisable for some. Before you ask yourself if this particular diet is for you, make sure that you seek your nutritionist or physician's advice.

CHAPTER 9:

Breakfast Recipes

Mexican Scrambled Eggs

Preparation time: 5 minutes.   **Cooking time:** 10 minutes.   **Servings:** 4

Ingredients:

- 6 eggs, lightly beaten
- 2 jalapeños, pickled, chopped finely
- 1 tomato, diced
- 3 ounces cheese, shredded
- 2 tablespoon butter, for frying
- 2 ounces Green onion

Directions:

1. Set a large skillet with butter over medium heat and allow it to melt. Add tomatoes, jalapeños, and green onions, then cook, while stirring, until fragrant (about 3 minutes).
2. Add eggs, and continue to cook, while stirring, until almost set (about 2 minutes).
3. Add cheese, and season to taste.
4. Continue cooking until the cheese melts (about another minute). Serve, and enjoy.

Nutrition:

- Calories: 239
- Carbs: 2.38g
- Protein: 13.92g
- Fats: 19.32g

Fennel Quiche

Preparation time: 15 minutes.   **Cooking time:** 8 minutes.   **Servings:** 4

Ingredients:

- 10 ounces fennel, chopped
- 1 cup spinach
- 5 eggs
- 1/2 cup almond flour
- 1 teaspoon olive oil
- 1 tablespoon butter
- 1 teaspoon salt
- 1/4 cup heavy cream
- 1 teaspoon ground black pepper

Directions:

1. Chop the spinach and combine it with the chopped fennel in the big bowl. Beat the eggs in a separate bowl and whisk them.
2. Combine the whisked eggs with the almond flour, butter, salt, heavy cream, and ground black pepper. Whisk it. Preheat the air fryer to 360°F. Spray the air fryer basket tray with the olive oil inside.
3. Then add the spinach-fennel mixture and pour the whisked egg mixture. Cook the quiche for 18 minutes. When the time is over—let the quiche chill a little.
4. Then remove it from the air fryer and slice it into the servings. Enjoy!

Nutrition:

- Calories: 249
- Carbs: 9.4g
- Protein: 11.3g
- Fats: 19.1g

Spinach Quiche

Preparation time: 10 minutes.　　**Cooking time:** 38 minutes.　　**Servings:** 6

Ingredients:

- 1 tablespoon olive oil
- 10 ounces frozen spinach, thawed
- 5 organic eggs, beaten
- 1 onion, chopped
- 3 cups Muenster cheese, shredded
- Salt and black pepper, to taste

Directions:

1. Preheat the oven to 350°F. Lightly grease a 9-inch pie dish. In a large skillet, heat the oil over medium heat and sauté the onion for about 4–5 minutes.
2. Increase the heat to medium-high. Add the spinach and cook for about 2–3 minutes or until all the liquid is absorbed.
3. Remove from the heat and set aside to cool slightly.
4. Meanwhile, in a large bowl, mix together the remaining ingredients. Add the spinach mixture and stir to combine. Transfer the mixture into a prepared pie dish.
5. Bake for about 30 minutes. Remove from the oven and set aside to cool for about 10 minutes before serving. Cut into 6 equal-sized wedges and serve.

Nutrition:

- Calories: 299
- Protein: 19.4g
- Carbs: 4.4g
- Fat: 23.1g

Chicken Frittata

Preparation time: 15 minutes.　　**Cooking time:** 12 minutes.　　**Servings:** 4

Ingredients:

- 1/2 cup grass-fed cooked chicken, chopped
- 6 organic eggs, beaten lightly
- Ground black pepper, to taste
- 1/2 cup boiled asparagus, chopped
- Pinch of red pepper flakes
- 1/3 cup Parmesan cheese, grated
- Pinch of salt
- 1 teaspoon butter
- 1 tablespoon fresh parsley, chopped

Directions:

1. Preheat the broiler of the oven. In a bowl, add cheese, eggs, red pepper flakes, salt, and black pepper and beat until well combined.
2. In a large ovenproof skillet, melt butter over medium-high heat and cook chicken and asparagus for about 2–3 minutes.
3. Add the egg mixture and stir to combine. Cook for about 4–5 minutes. Remove from heat and sprinkle with parsley.
4. Now, transfer the skillet under broiler and broil for about 3–4 minutes or until slightly puffed.
5. Cut into desired sized wedges and serve immediately.

Nutrition:

- Calories: 224
- Carbs: 4g
- Protein: 11g
- Fats: 15g

Coconut Flour Spinach Casserole

Preparation time: 25 minutes.   **Cooking time:** 30 minutes.   **Servings:** 6

Ingredients:

- 8 eggs
- 5 ounces chopped fresh spinach
- 1 cup grated cheese Parmesan
- 1 teaspoon salt
- 3/4 cup coconut flour
- 3/4 cup unsweetened almond milk
- 6 ounces chopped artichoke hearts
- 3 minced garlic cloves
- 1/2 teaspoon black pepper
- 1 tablespoon baking powder

Directions:

1. Preheat your air fryer to a temperature of about 375°F. Grease your air fryer pan with cooking spray. Whisk the eggs with the almond milk, the spinach, the artichoke hearts, and 1/2 cup of parmesan cheese.
2. Add the garlic, the salt, and the pepper. Add the coconut flour and baking powder and whisk until very well combined. Spread mixture into your air fryer pan and sprinkle the remaining quantity of cheese over it.
3. Place the baking pan in the air fryer and lock the air fryer and set the timer to about 30 minutes. When the timer beeps, turn off your Air Fryer.
4. Remove the baking pan from the air fryer and sprinkle with the chopped basil. Slice your dish, then serve and enjoy it.

Nutrition:

- Calories: 175
- Carbs: 2.4g
- Protein: 17.7g
- Fats:10.3g

Zucchini Muffins

Preparation time: 15 minutes.   **Cooking time:** 15 minutes.   **Servings:** 4

Ingredients:

- 4 organic eggs
- 1/4cup water
- 1/2 teaspoon organic baking powder
- 1 and 1/2 cups zucchini, grated
- 1 tablespoon fresh thyme, minced
- 1/4 cup cheddar cheese, grated
- 1/4 cup unsalted butter, melted
- 1/3 cup coconut flour
- 1/4 teaspoon salt
- 1/2 cup parmesan cheese, shredded
- 1 tablespoon fresh oregano, minced

Directions:

1. Preheat the oven to 400°F.
2. Lightly grease 8 cups of a muffin tin.
3. In a bowl, add the eggs, butter, and water and beat until well combined.
4. Add the flour, baking powder, and salt and mix well.
5. Add the remaining ingredients except for the cheddar and mix until just combined. Place the mixture into prepared muffin cups evenly and top with cheddar.
6. Bake for about 13–15 minutes or until tops become golden brown. Remove the muffin tin from the oven and place it onto a wire rack to cool for about 10 minutes.
7. Carefully invert the muffins onto a platter and serve warm.

Nutrition:

- Calories: 329
- Carbs: 10g
- Protein: 17g
- Fats: 24 g

Cheesy Egg Muffins

Preparation time: 20 minutes.   **Cooking time:** 10 minutes.   **Servings:** 6

Ingredients:

- 4 eggs, large
- 2 tablespoons Greek yogurt, full fat
- 3 tablespoons almond flour
- 1/4 teaspoon baking powder
- 1 and 1/2 cup cheddar cheese, shredded

Directions:

1. Set your oven to preheat to 375°F. Add yogurt, and eggs to a medium bowl, season with salt, pepper, and then whisk to combine.
2. Add your baking powder and coconut flour, then mix to form a smooth batter. Finally, add your cheese, and fold to combine.
3. Pour your mixture evenly into 6 silicone muffin cups and set to bake in your preheated oven.
4. Allow baking until your eggs are fully set and lightly golden on top, about 20 minutes, turning the tray at the halfway point.
5. Allow muffins to cool on a cooling rack, then serve. Enjoy.

Nutrition:

- Calories: 144
- Carbs: 1.43g
- Protein: 8g
- Fats: 11.9g

Brown Hash with Zucchini

Preparation time: 10 minutes.   **Cooking time:** 20 minutes.   **Servings:** 2

Ingredients:

- 1 sliced small onion
- 6 to 8 medium sliced mushrooms
- 2 cups of grass-fed ground beef
- 1 pinch of salt
- 1 pinch of ground black pepper
- 1/2 teaspoon smoked paprika
- 2 lightly beaten eggs
- 1 small, diced avocado
- 1 ounce Parsley

Directions:

1. Preheat your air fryer to a temperature of about 350°F. Spray your air fryer pan with a little bit of melted coconut oil.
2. Add the onions, the mushrooms, the salt, and the pepper to the pan. Add the ground beef and the smoked paprika and crack in the eggs.
3. Gently whisk your mixture, then place the pan in your Air Fryer and lock the lid. Set the timer to about 18 to 20 minutes and the temperature to about 375°F.
4. When the timer beeps, turn off your Air Fryer, then remove the pan from the Air Fryer.
5. Serve and enjoy your breakfast with chopped parsley and diced avocado.

Nutrition:

- Calories: 319 kcal
- Protein: 11.93g
- Fat: 24.86g
- Carbs: 15.52g

Caprese Omelette

Preparation time: 10 minutes.   **Cooking time:** 10 minutes.   **Servings:** 2

Ingredients:

- 6 eggs, beaten
- 2 tablespoons olive oil
- 3 and 1/2 ounces tomatoes, cherry, halved
- 1 tablespoon basil, dried
- 5(1/3) ounces mozzarella cheese, diced

Directions:

1. Whisk basil into eggs, and lightly season. Set a large skillet with oil over medium heat and allow getting hot.
2. Once hot, add tomatoes and cook while stirring.
3. Top with egg and continue cooking until the tops have started to firm up.
4. Add cheese, switch your heat to low, and allow setting fully set before serving. Enjoy!

Nutrition:

- Calories: 489
- Carbs: 4.4g
- Protein: 18g
- Fats: 39.45g

Spinach Omelette

Preparation time: 6.5 minutes.   **Cooking time:** 10 minutes.   **Servings:** 2

Ingredients:

- 4 large organic eggs
- 1 scallion, chopped
- 1/2 cup feta cheese, crumbled
- 2 teaspoon olive oil
- 1/4 cup cooked spinach, squeezed
- 2 tablespoon fresh parsley, chopped
- Ground black pepper, to taste

Directions:

1. Preheat the broiler of the oven. Arrange a rack about 4-inches from the heating element. In a bowl, crack the eggs and beat them well.
2. Add the remaining ingredients except for the oil and stir to combine in an ovenproof skillet, heat oil over medium heat.
3. Add egg mixture and tilt the skillet to spread the mixture evenly. Immediately, reduce the heat to medium-low and cook for about 3–4 minutes or until golden brown.
4. Now, transfer the skillet under broiler and broil for about 1 and ½–2 minutes.
5. Cut the omelet into desired size wedges and serve.

Nutrition:

- Calories: 312
- Carbs: 5g
- Protein: 18.4g
- Fats: 22.7g

Chicken Avocado Salad

Preparation time: 10 minutes.   **Cooking time:** 40 minutes.   **Servings:** 4

Ingredients:

- 1 pound of boneless chicken thighs
- 4 tablespoons of extra virgin olive oil
- 3 tablespoons of chopped celeries
- 2 tablespoons of cilantro
- 1 large ripe avocado
- 1(1/2) teaspoon of oregano
- 1 tablespoon of lemon juice
- 1/2 cup almond milk
- 1/2 cup diced onion
- 1/2 teaspoon pepper

Directions:

1. Pour in almond milk in a bowl, add in the oregano, and then stir well.
2. Slice up the boneless chicken thighs, and rub the slices with the almond milk mixture. Let it sit for 13 to 15 minutes.
3. Preheat an oven to 300°F, and line the baking tray with a foil sheet.
4. Place the coated chicken slices on the baking tray and bake for 30 to 40 minutes.
5. Meanwhile, slice the avocado into cubes, then drizzles some olive oil and lemon juice, and set aside.
6. In a salad bowl, mix in the cilantro, chopped celeries, and onion, and sprinkle some pepper, mix well.
7. Take out the chicken and garnish with the avocado mix and salad. Serve warm.

Nutrition:

- Calories: 256g
- Carbs: 8g
- Protein: 19g
- Fat: 49g

Keto Philly Cheesesteak Pockets

Preparation time: 10 minutes. **Cooking time:** 40 minutes. **Servings:** 4

Ingredients:

- 4 ounces cream cheese cut into chunks
- 3 sliced red baby bell peppers
- 3 tablespoons onion salt
- 2 cups shredded mozzarella cheese low moisture
- 2 tablespoons grass-fed butter or other healthy fat
- 2 eggs
- 2 tablespoons no-sugar-added ketchup
- 2 tablespoons Keto mayo
- 1 sliced yellow onion
- 1 teaspoon garlic powder
- 1 teaspoon Italian seasoning
- 1 tablespoon onion salt
- 1 teaspoon sea salt
- 1 and 1/2 cups of almond flour
- 1 teaspoon sea salt - 1 teaspoon black pepper
- 1-pound shaved steak - 1 tablespoon lime juice
- 1 tablespoon sriracha - 2 tablespoons Mayo sauce

Directions:

1. Whisk the eggs and set them aside.
2. Pour mozzarella and cream cheese into a microwave-safe bowl, and place in a microwave for half a minute. Use a spoon or spatula to mix the mozzarella and cream cheese well.
3. Add garlic powder, Italian seasoning, and onion salt to the bowl, then the beaten egg, almond flour, and mix thoroughly, until firm like yellowish dough. Set aside.
4. Thinly slice your shaved meat.
5. Melt butter in a preheated skillet on medium heat.
6. Add in the onions and peppers, and sauté until tender.
7. Add shaved meat and sauté until brown.
8. Take off the skillet, and immediately pour in the American cheese and cover. The heat will melt it. After 4 to 5 minutes, stir the contents of the skillet thoroughly.
9. Take out the dough and divide it into 10 to 12 balls or depending on your desired size. Flatten each ball with the help of a rolling pin.
10. Spread the meat mixture on each flattened ball evenly, ensuring enough space to seal.
11. Fold the flattened dough in half, and use a fork to seal the edges.
12. Heat the frying oil. When hot enough, carefully place the pockets inside, and fry until golden brown from each side.
13. In another bowl, mix the lime juice, no-sugar-added ketchup, sriracha, and mayo. Use a fork to mix well. Spread on pockets before serving.

Nutrition:

- Calories: 439
- Carbs: 7.5g
- Protein: 12.7g
- Fat: 52.2g

Keto Cauliflower and Eggs

Preparation time: 10 minutes **Cooking time:** 20 minutes **Servings:** 4

Ingredients:

- 5 hard-boiled eggs
- 2 stalks celery
- 1(1/2) cups Greek yoghurt
- 1/4 teaspoon pepper
- 1 head cauliflower
- 1 tablespoon white vinegar
- 1 tablespoon yellow mustard
- 1 teaspoon salt
- 1 cup water
- 3/4 of a white onion, diced

Directions:

1. Chop cauliflower into bite-size pieces, and place it in a pot with a cup of water.
2. Drain the cauliflower and set aside
3. Dice up the boiled eggs, mix them into the cauliflower.
4. Dice the celery and onion, then add in the cauliflower and egg mixture.
5. Add the Greek yoghurt, pepper, white vinegar, yellow mustard salt, and diced white onion to the mixture, and mix well with a wooden spoon. Dish with salt and serve.

Nutrition:

- Calories: 224
- Carbs: 8.2g
- Protein: 23.5g
- Fat: 22g

Egg on Avocado

Preparation time: 10 minutes

Cooking time: 20 minutes

Servings: 3

Ingredients:

- 1 and 1/2 teaspoon of garlic powder
- 3/4 teaspoons of sea salt
- 1/3 cup of Parmesan cheese
- 1/4 teaspoon of black pepper
- 4 avocados
- 6 small eggs

Directions:

1. Preheat muffin tins to 350°F.
2. Slice the avocado into half, and take the seed out.
3. Mix pepper, salt, and garlic well.
4. Generously season your avocado with the above seasoning mix.
5. Place the seasoned avocado in the muffin tin; side with the empty hollow facing up.
6. Whisk the egg and gently pour in each avocado. If you doubt that avocado has enough space, scrape the inside lightly.
7. Finally, sprinkle cheese on top of the avocado.
8. Repeat the process for all, and then bake for 15 minutes.
9. Serve hot.

Nutrition:

- Calories: 364
- Carbs: 2.5g
- Protein: 13.5
- Fat: 55.5g

CHAPTER 10:

Lunch Recipes

Cole Slaw Keto Wrap

Preparation time: 15 minutes.   **Cooking time:** 20 minutes.   **Servings:** 2

Ingredients:

- 3 cups sliced thin red cabbage
- 0.5 cups green onions, diced
- 0.75 cups mayo
- 2 teaspoons apple cider vinegar
- 0.25 teaspoon salt
- 16 pieces collard green, stems removed
- 1 pound ground meat of choice, cooked and chilled
- 0.33 cup alfalfa sprouts
- Toothpicks, to hold wraps together

Directions:

1. Mix the slaw ingredients with a spoon in a large-sized bowl until everything is well-coated.
2. Place a collard green on a plate and scoop a tablespoon or two of coleslaw on the edge of the leaf. Top it with a scoop of meat and sprouts.
3. Roll and tuck the sides to keep the filling from spilling.
4. Once you assemble the wrap, put in your toothpicks in a way that holds the wrap together until you are ready to beat it. Just repeat this with the leftover leaves.

Nutrition:

- Calories: 409
- Carbs: 4g
- Protein: 2g
- Fat: 42g

Keto Chicken Club Lettuce Wrap

Preparation time: 15 minutes.   **Cooking time:** 15 minutes.   **Servings:** 1

Ingredients:

- 1 head of iceberg lettuce with the core and outer leaves removed
- 1 tablespoon mayonnaise
- 6 slices of organic chicken or turkey breast
- 2 cooked strips bacon, halved
- 2 slices of tomato

Directions:

1. Line your working surface with a large slice of parchment paper.
2. Layer 6–8 large leaves of lettuce in the center of the paper to make a base of around 9–10 inches.
3. Spread the mayo in the center and lay with chicken or turkey, bacon, and tomato.
4. Starting with the end closest to you, roll the wrap like a jelly roll with the parchment paper as your guide. Keep it tight and halfway through, roll tuck in the ends of the wrap.
5. When it is completely wrapped, roll the rest of the parchment paper around it, and use a knife to cut it in half.

Nutrition:

- Calories: 837
- Carbs: 4g
- Protein: 28g
- Fat: 78g

Keto Broccoli Salad

Preparation time: 10 minutes.   **Cooking time:** 0 minutes.   **Servings:** 6

Ingredients:

For your salad:

- 2 medium-sized heads broccoli, florets chunked
- 2 cups red cabbage, well shredded
- 0.5 cups sliced almonds, roasted
- 1 stalk green onions, sliced
- 0.5 cups raisins

For your orange almond dressing:

- 0.33 cup orange juice
- 0.25 cup almond butter
- 2 tablespoons coconut aminos
- 1 shallot, small-sized, chopped finely
- ½ teaspoon salt

Directions:

1. Use a food processor to pulse together salt, shallot, amino, almond butter, and orange juice. Make sure it is perfectly smooth.
2. Use a medium-sized bowl to combine the other ingredients. Toss it with dressing and serve.

Nutrition:

- Calories: 184
- Carbs: 13g
- Protein: 6g
- Fat: 11g

Keto Sheet Pan Chicken and Rainbow Veggies

Preparation time: 15 minutes.   **Cooking time:** 25 minutes.   **Servings:** 4

Ingredients:

- Nonstick spray
- 1 pound chicken breasts, boneless, and skinless
- 1 tablespoon sesame oil
- 2 tablespoons soy sauce
- 2 tablespoons honey
- 2 red pepper, medium-sized, sliced
- 2 yellow pepper, medium-sized, sliced
- 3 carrots, medium-sized, sliced
- ½ head broccoli cut up
- 2 red onions, medium-size and sliced
- 2 tablespoons EVOO
- Pepper and salt, to taste
- 0.25 cup parsley, fresh herb, chopped

Directions:

1. First, spray your baking sheet with cooking spray and bring the oven to a temperature of 400°F.
2. Then, put the chicken in the middle of the sheet. Separately, combine the oil and the soy sauce. Brush the mix over the chicken.
3. Separate your veggies across the plate. Sprinkle with oil and then toss them gently to ensure they are coated. Finally, spice up with pepper and salt.
4. Set tray into the oven and cook for around 25 minutes until all is tender and done throughout.
5. After taking it out of the oven, garnish using parsley. Divide everything between those prepared containers paired with your favorite greens.

Nutrition:

- Calories: 437
- Carbs: 9g
- Protein: 30g
- Fat: 30g

Skinny Bang Bang Zucchini Noodles

Preparation time: 15 minutes.   **Cooking time:** 15 minutes.   **Servings:** 4

Ingredients:

For the noodles:

- 4 medium zucchini spiraled
- 1 tablespoon olive oil

For the sauce:

- 0.25 cup + 2 tablespoons plain Greek yogurt
- 0.25 cup + 2 tablespoons mayo
- 0.25 cup + 2 tablespoons Thai sweet chili sauce
- 1.5 teaspoons honey
- 1.5 teaspoons sriracha
- 2 teaspoons lime juice

Directions:

1. If you are using any meats for this dish, such as chicken or shrimp, cook them first, then set them aside.
2. Pour the oil into a large-sized skillet at medium temperature.
3. After the oil is well heated, stir in the spiraled zucchini noodles.
4. Cook the "noodles" until tender yet still crispy.
5. Remove from the heat, drain, and set at rest for at least 10 minutes.
6. Combine the sauce ingredients together into a large-sized, both until perfectly smooth.
7. Give it a taste and adjust as needed.
8. Divide into 4 small containers. Mix your noodles with any meats you cooked and add them to meal prepared containers.
9. When you're ready to eat it, heat the noodles, drain any excess water, and mix in the sauce.

Nutrition:

- Calories: 161g
- Carbs: 18g
- Protein: 9g
- Fat: 1g

Keto Caesar Salad

Preparation time: 15 minutes.   **Cooking time:** 0 minutes.   **Servings:** 4

Ingredients:

- 1.5 cups mayonnaise
- 3 tablespoons apple cider vinegar/ACV
- 1 teaspoon Dijon mustard
- 4 anchovy fillets
- 24 romaine heart leaves
- 4 ounces pork rinds, chopped

Directions:

1. Place the mayo with ACV, mustard, and anchovies into a blender and process until smooth and dressing like.
2. Prepare romaine leaves and pour out dressing across them evenly. Top with pork rinds and enjoy.

Nutrition:

- Calories: 993
- Carbs: 4g
- Protein: 47g
- Fat: 86g

Keto Buffalo Chicken Empanadas

Preparation time: 20 minutes.   **Cooking time:** 30 minutes.   **Servings:** 6

Ingredients:

For the empanada dough:

- 1(½) cups mozzarella cheese
- 3 ounces cream cheese
- 1 whisked egg
- 2 cups almond flour

For the buffalo chicken filling:

- 2 cups of cooked shredded chicken
- 2 tablespoons butter, melted
- 0.33 cup hot sauce

Directions:

1. Bring the oven to a temperature of 425°F.
2. Put the cheese and cream cheese into a microwave-safe dish. Microwave at 1-minute intervals until completely combined.
3. Stir the flour and egg into the dish until it is well-combined. Add any additional flour for consistency—until it stops sticking to your fingers.
4. With another medium-sized bowl, combine the chicken with sauce and set aside.
5. Cover a flat surface with plastic wrap or parchment paper and sprinkle with almond flour.
6. Spray a rolling pin to avoid sticking and use it to press the dough flat.
7. Make circle shapes out of this dough with a lid, a cup, or a cookie-cutter. For the excess dough, roll back up and repeat the process.
8. Portion out spoonful of filling into these dough circles but keep them only on one half.
9. Fold the other half over to close up into half-moon shapes. Press on the edges to seal them.
10. Lay on a lightly greased cooking sheet and bake for around 9 minutes until perfectly brown.

Nutrition:

- Calories: 1217
- Carbs: 20g
- Protein: 74g
- Fat: 96g

Pepperoni and Cheddar Stromboli

Preparation time: 15 minutes.   **Cooking time:** 20 minutes.   **Servings:** 3

Ingredients:

- 1.25 cups mozzarella cheese
- 0.25 cup almond flour
- 3 tablespoons coconut flour
- 1 teaspoon Italian seasoning
- 1 large-sized egg, whisked
- 6 ounces deli ham, sliced
- 2 ounces pepperoni, sliced
- 4 ounces cheddar cheese, sliced
- 1 tablespoon butter, melted
- 6 cups salad greens

Directions:

1. First, bring the oven to a temperature of 400°F and prepare a baking tray with some parchment paper.
2. Use the microwave to melt the mozzarella until it can be stirred.
3. Mix flours and Italian seasoning in a separate small-sized bowl.
4. Put the melted cheese and stir together with pepper and salt to taste.
5. Stir in the egg and process the dough with your hands. Pour it onto that prepared baking tray.
6. Roll out the dough with your hands or a pin. Cut slits that mark out 4 equal rectangles.
7. Put the ham and cheese onto the dough, then brush with butter and close up, putting the seal end down.
8. Bake for around 17 minutes until well-browned. Slice up and serve.

Nutrition:

- Calories: 240kcal
- Carbs: 20g
- Protein: 11g
- Fat: 13g

Tuna Casserole

Preparation time: 15 minutes.   **Cooking time:** 10 minutes.   **Servings:** 4

Ingredients:

- 16 ounces tuna in oil, drained
- 2 tablespoons butter
- 1(1/2) teaspoon salt
- 1 teaspoon black pepper
- 1 teaspoon chili powder
- 6 stalks celery
- 1 teaspoon green bell pepper
- 1 teaspoon yellow onion
- 4 ounces Parmesan cheese, grated
- 1 cup mayonnaise

Directions:

1. Heat the oven to 400°F.
2. Chop the onion, bell pepper, and celery very fine and fry in the melted butter for five minutes.
3. Stir together with the chili powder, parmesan cheese, tuna, and mayonnaise.
4. Use lard to grease an eight by eight-inch or nine by a nine-inch baking pan.
5. Add the tuna mixture into the fried vegetables and spoon the mix into the baking pan.
6. Bake it for twenty minutes.

Nutrition:

- Calories: 953
- Carbs: 5g
- Fat: 83g
- Protein: 43g

Brussels Sprout and Hamburger Gratin

Preparation time: 15 minutes.   **Cooking time:** 20 minutes.   **Servings:** 4

Ingredients:

- 1 pound ground beef
- 8 ounces bacon, diced small
- 15 ounces Brussels sprouts, cut in half
- 1 teaspoon salt
- 1 teaspoon black pepper
- 1(1/2) teaspoon thyme
- 1 cup Cheddar cheese, shredded
- 1 tablespoon Italian seasoning
- 4 tablespoons sour cream
- 2 tablespoons butter

Directions:

1. Heat the oven to 425°F.
2. Fry bacon and Brussels sprouts in butter for five minutes.
3. Stir in the sour cream and pour this mix into a greased eight by and eight-inch baking pan.
4. Cook the ground beef and season with salt and pepper, then add this mix to the baking pan.
5. Top with the herbs and the shredded cheese. Bake for twenty minutes.

Nutrition:

- Calories: 770
- Carbs: 8g
- Protein: 42g
- Fat: 62g

Bacon Appetizers

Preparation time: 15 minutes.   **Cooking time:** 2 hours.   **Servings:** 6

Ingredients:

- 1 pack Keto crackers
- ¾ cup Parmesan cheese, grated
- 1 pound bacon, sliced thinly

Directions:

1. Preheat your oven to 250°F.
2. Arrange the crackers on a baking sheet.
3. Sprinkle cheese on top of each cracker.
4. Wrap each cracker with the bacon.
5. Bake in the oven for 2 hours.

Nutrition:

- Calories: 290
- Carbs: 6.84g
- Protein: 11.66g
- Fat: 25.94g

Cherry Tomato Salad with Chorizo

Preparation time: 15 minutes.

Cooking time: 50 minutes.

Servings: 4

Ingredients:

- 2.5 cups cherry tomatoes
- 4 chorizo sausages
- 2.5 tablespoons olive oil
- 2 teaspoons red wine vinegar
- 1 small red onion
- 2 tablespoons cilantro
- 2 ounces Kalamata olives
- Black pepper and salt

Directions:

1. Chop the onions and sausage. Slice the olives and onions into halves, and set aside.
2. Heat a skillet and add one tablespoon of oil to cook the chorizo until browned.
3. Prepare a salad dish with the rest of the oil, vinegar, onion, tomatoes, chorizo, and cilantro.
4. Toss thoroughly and sprinkle with salt, pepper, and olives.

Nutrition:

- Calories: 138
- Carbs: 5.2g
- Protein: 7g
- Fat: 8.9g

Chicken Caesar Salad & Bok Choy

Preparation time: 10 minutes.   **Cooking time:** 40 minutes   **Servings:** 4

Ingredients:

- 4 Chicken thighs—no skin or bones
- 0.25 cups lemon juice
- 4 tablespoons olive oil
- 0.5 cup Caesar salad dressing—keto-friendly
- 12 bok choy
- 3 Parmesan crisps
- To Garnish: Parmesan cheese

Directions:

1. Prepare the bok choy in lengthwise pieces.
2. Add these ingredients to a zipper-type plastic bag; two tablespoons of oil, lemon juice, and chicken. Seal and shake the bag. Pop it in the fridge to marinate for about one hour.
3. Prepare a grill using the medium temperature setting and cook the chicken for four minutes on each side.
4. Brush the bok Choy with the rest of the oil to grill for three minutes.
5. Place the bok Choy on the serving dish topped with the chicken and a spritz of dressing, cheese, and parmesan crisps.

Nutrition:

- Calories: 529
- Carbs: 5g
- Protein: 33g
- Fat: 39g

Healthy Roasted Green Bean & Mushroom Salad

Preparation time: 10 minutes.   **Cooking time:** 30 minutes   **Servings provided:** 4

Ingredients:

- 0.5 cup green beans
- 1 pound sliced Cremini mushrooms
- 3 tablespoons vegan melted butter
- 1 lemon, for juice
- 4 tablespoons toasted hazelnuts
- 2 tablespoons Butter
- 1 tablespoon Salt
- 1 tablespoon Pepper

Directions:

1. Set the oven to 450°F. Slice and add the mushrooms and green beans to a baking dish.
2. Drizzle them with butter, salt, and pepper.
3. Set the timer and roast them for 20 minutes.
4. Place the veggies in a salad dish with a spritz of lemon juice and a hazelnuts sprinkle to serve.

Nutrition:

- Calories: 179
- Carbs: 7g
- Protein: 5g
- Fat: 11g

Italian Tri-Color Salad

Preparation time: 10 minutes.   **Cooking time:** 40 minutes.   **Servings** Provided: 4

Ingredients:

- 0.25 pounds buffalo mozzarella cheese
- 1 avocado
- 3 tomatoes
- 8 Kalamata olives
- 2 tablespoons pesto sauce
- 2 tablespoons olive oil

Directions:

1. Slice the tomatoes, avocado, and mozzarella.
2. Stack the tomatoes on a serving platter.
3. Arrange them with the sliced tomatoes, avocado in the center with olives all over them.
4. Drop the pieces of cheese over the salad and serve with a drizzle of oil and pesto sauce.

Nutrition:

- Calories: 290
- Carbs: 4.3g
- Protein: 9g
- Fat: 25g

CHAPTER 11:

Dinner Recipes

Lemon-Garlic Chicken Thighs

Preparation time: 10 minutes.   **Cooking time:** 25 minutes.   **Servings:** 4

Ingredients

- 4 wedges lemon
- ¼ cup lemon juice
- 4 chicken thighs
- 2 tablespoon olive oil
- Pinch ground black pepper
- 1 teaspoon Dijon mustard
- ¼ teaspoon salt
- 2 garlic cloves, thinly cut

Directions

1. Before anything, ensure that your air fryer is preheated 360°F.
2. Into a medium-sized bowl, add lemon juice, pepper, salt, olive oil, garlic, and Dijon mustard. Using a whisk, combine these ingredients and set them aside for a bit. This is your marinade.
3. You'll need a large reusable bag for this part. Put your chicken thighs and the marinade inside the bag and seal it. Leave it in your refrigerator for about 2 hours.
4. Next, take the chicken thighs out of the reusable bag, and using a paper towel, dry out the marinade. Place the thighs in an air fryer basket and cook them. You could fry them in batches, if that made it easier.
5. When the chicken thighs no longer look pink close to the bone, the frying should last up to 24 minutes to achieve this, you can take them out of the air fryer. If you place an instant-read thermometer on the bone, it should read 165°F.
6. When you serve the chicken thighs, also squeeze the lemon wedges on each of them.

Nutrition:

- Calories: 258
- Carbs: 3.6g
- Protein: 19.4g
- Fat: 6g

Black-Eyed Peas Platter

Preparation time: 10 minutes.   **Cooking time:** 8 hours.   **Servings:** 4

Ingredients:

- 1 cup black eyed-peas, soaked overnight and drained
- 2 cups low-sodium vegetable broth
- 1 can (15 ounces) tomatoes, diced with juice
- 8 ounces ham, chopped
- 1 onion, chopped
- 2 garlic cloves, minced
- 1 teaspoon dried oregano
- 1 teaspoon salt
- ½ teaspoon freshly ground black pepper
- ½ teaspoon ground mustard
- 1 bay leaf

Directions:

1. Add the listed ingredients to your Slow Cooker and stir.
2. Place lid and cook over low heat for 8 hours.
3. Discard the bay leaf.
4. Serve and enjoy!

Nutrition:

- Calories: 209
- Carbs: 17g
- Protein: 27g
- Fat: 6g

Humble Mushroom Rice

Preparation time: 10 minutes.　　　**Cooking time:** 3 hours.　　　**Servings:** 3

Ingredients:

- ½ cup rice
- 2 green onions chopped
- 1 garlic clove, minced
- ¼ pound baby Portobello mushrooms, sliced
- 1 cup vegetable stock

Directions:

1. Add rice, onions, garlic, mushrooms, and stock to your slow cooker.
2. Stir well and place the lid.
3. Cook over low heat for 3 hours.
4. Stir and divide amongst serving platters.
5. Enjoy!

Nutrition:

- Calories: 200
- Carbs: 12g
- Protein: 28g
- Fat: 6g

Sweet and Sour Cabbage and Apples

Preparation time: 15 minutes.　　　**Cooking time:** 8 hours and 15 minutes.　　　**Servings:** 4

Ingredients:

- ¼ cup honey
- ¼ cup apple cider vinegar
- 2 tablespoons orange chili-garlic sauce
- 1 teaspoon sea salt
- 3 sweet-tart apples, peeled, cored and sliced
- 2 heads green cabbage, cored and shredded
- 1 sweet red onion, thinly sliced

Directions:

1. Take a small bowl and whisk in honey, orange-chili garlic sauce, vinegar.
2. Stir well.
3. Add the honey mix, apples, onion, and cabbage to your slow cooker and stir.
4. Close the lid and cook over low heat for 8 hours.
5. Serve and enjoy!

Nutrition:

- Calories: 164
- Carbs: 41g
- Protein: 24g
- Fat: 2.5g

Orange and Chili Garlic Sauce

Preparation time: 15 minutes.　　　**Cooking time:** 8 hours and 15 minutes.　　　**Servings:** 5

Ingredients:

- ½ cup apple cider vinegar
- 4 pounds red jalapeno peppers, stems, seeds, and ribs removed, chopped
- 10 garlic cloves, chopped
- ½ cup tomato paste
- Juice of 1 orange zest
- ½ cup honey
- 2 tablespoons soy sauce
- 2 teaspoons salt

Directions:

1. Add vinegar, garlic, peppers, tomato paste, orange juice, honey, zest, soy sauce, and salt to your slow cooker.
2. Stir and close the lid.
3. Cook over low heat for 8 hours.
4. Use as needed!

Nutrition:

- Calories: 33
- Carbs: 8g
- Protein: 12g
- Fat: 4g

Tantalizing Mushroom Gravy

Preparation time: 5 minutes.   **Cooking time:** 5–8 hours.   **Servings:** 2

Ingredients:

- 1/3 cup water
- 1 cup button mushrooms, sliced
- ¾ cup low-fat buttermilk
- 1 medium onion, finely diced
- 2 garlic cloves, minced

- 2 tablespoons extra virgin olive oil
- 2 tablespoons all-purpose flour
- 1 tablespoon fresh rosemary, minced
- Freshly ground black pepper

Directions:

1. Add the listed ingredients to your slow cooker. Place the lid and cook over low heat for 5–8 hours.
2. Serve warm and use as needed!

Nutrition:

- Calories: 190
- Carbs: 4g
- Protein: 2g
- Fat: 6g

Everyday Vegetable Stock

Preparation time: 5 minutes.   **Cooking time:** 8-12 hours.   **Servings:** 4

Ingredients:

- 2 celery stalks (with leaves), quartered
- 4 ounces mushrooms, with stems
- 2 carrots, unpeeled and quartered
- 1 onion, unpeeled, quartered from pole to pole
- 1 garlic head, unpeeled, halved across the middle

- 2 fresh thyme sprigs
- 10 peppercorns
- ½ teaspoon salt
- Enough water to fill 3 quarters of slow cooker

Directions:

1. Add celery, mushrooms, onion, carrots, garlic, thyme, salt, peppercorn, and water to your slow cooker.
2. Stir and cover.
3. Cook over low heat for 8–12 hours.
4. Strain the stock through a fine–mesh cloth/metal mesh and discard solids.
5. Use as needed.

Nutrition:

- Calories: 38
- Carbs: 1g
- Protein: 0g
- Fat: 1.2g

Grilled Chicken with Lemon and Fennel

Preparation time: 5 minutes.   **Cooking time:** 25 minutes.   **Servings:** 5

Ingredients:

- 2 cups chicken fillets, cut and skewed
- 1 large fennel bulb
- 2 garlic cloves

- 1 jar green olives
- 1 lemon

Directions:

1. Preheat your grill to medium-high.
2. Crush garlic cloves.
3. Take a bowl and add olive oil and season with sunflower seeds and pepper.
4. Coat chicken skewers with the marinade.
5. Transfer them under the grill and grill for 20 minutes, making sure to turn them halfway through until golden.
6. Zest half of the lemon and cut the other half into quarters.
7. Cut the fennel bulb into similarly sized segments.
8. Brush olive oil all over the garlic clove segments and cook for 3–5 minutes.
9. Chop them and add them to the bowl with the marinade.
10. Add lemon zest and olives.
11. Once the meat is ready, serve with the vegetable mix.
12. Enjoy!

Nutrition:

- Calories: 649
- Carbs: 15g
- Protein: 28g
- Fat: 6g

Caramelized Pork Chops and Onion

Preparation time: 5 minutes.   **Cooking time:** 40 minutes.   **Servings:** 4

Ingredients:

- 4-pound chuck roast
- 2 medium sized Onions
- 1 tablespoon Pepper
- 1 tablespoon of Sunflower seeds
- 2 tablespoons Oil

Directions:

1. Rub the chops with a seasoning of 1 teaspoon of pepper and 2 teaspoons of sunflower seeds.
2. Take a skillet and place it over medium heat, add oil and allow the oil to heat up
3. Brown the seasoned chop on both sides. Add water and onion to the skillet and cover, lower the heat to low, and simmer for 20 minutes. Turn the chops over and season with more sunflower seeds and pepper. Cover and cook until the water fully evaporates and the beer shows a slightly brown texture.
4. Remove the chops and serve with a topping of the caramelized onion.
5. Serve and enjoy!

Nutrition:

- Calories: 47
- Carbs: 4g
- Protein: 0.5g
- Fat: 4g

Hearty Pork Belly Casserole

Preparation time: 5 minutes.   **Cooking time:** 25 minutes.   **Servings:** 4

Ingredients:

- 8 pork belly slices, cut into small pieces
- 3 large onions, chopped
- 4 tablespoons lemon zest
- 2 tablespoons Honey
- 1 ounce parsley

Directions:

1. Take a large pressure cooker and place it over medium heat.
2. Add onions and sweat them for 5 minutes.
3. Add pork belly slices and cook until the meat browns and onions become golden.
4. Cover with water and add honey, lemon zest, sunflower seeds, pepper, and close the pressure seal.
5. Pressure cook for 40 minutes.
6. Serve and enjoy with a garnish of fresh chopped parsley if you prefer.

Nutrition:

- Calories: 753
- Carbs: 23g
- Protein: 36g
- Fat: 4g

Fascinating Spinach and Beef Meatballs

Preparation time: 10 minutes.   **Cooking time:** 20 minutes.   **Servings:** 4

Ingredients:

- ½ cup onion
- 4 garlic cloves
- 1 whole egg
- ¼ teaspoon oregano
- Pepper as needed
- 1 pound lean ground beef
- 10 ounces spinach

Directions:

1. Preheat your oven to 375°F.
2. Take a bowl and mix all the ingredients, and using your hands, roll into meatballs.
3. Transfer to a sheet tray and bake for 20 minutes.
4. Enjoy!

Nutrition:

- Calories: 200
- Carbs: 5g
- Protein: 29g
- Fat: 3g

Juicy and Peppery Tenderloin

Preparation time: 10 minutes.   **Cooking time:** 20 minutes.   **Servings:** 4

Ingredients:

- 2 teaspoons sage, chopped
- Sunflower seeds and pepper
- 2 1/2 pounds beef tenderloin
- 2 teaspoons thyme, chopped
- 2 garlic cloves, sliced
- 2 teaspoons rosemary, chopped
- 4 teaspoons olive oil

Directions:

1. Preheat your oven to 425°F.
2. Take a small knife and cut incisions in the tenderloin; insert one slice of garlic into the incision.
3. Rub meat with oil.
4. Take a bowl and add sunflower seeds, sage, thyme, rosemary, pepper, and mix well.
5. Rub the spice mix over the tenderloin.
6. Put rubbed tenderloin into the roasting pan and bake for 10 minutes.
7. Lower temperature to 350°F and cook for 20 minutes more until an internal thermometer reads 145°F.
8. Transfer tenderloin to a cutting board and let sit for 15 minutes; slice into 20 pieces and enjoy!

Nutrition:

- Calories: 490
- Carbs: 1g
- Protein: 24g
- Fat: 9g

Healthy Avocado Beef Patties

Preparation time: 15 minutes.   **Cooking time:** 10 minutes.   **Servings:** 2

Ingredients:

- 1 pound 85% lean ground beef
- 1 small avocado, pitted and peeled
- Fresh ground black pepper as needed

Directions:

1. Preheat and prepare your broiler to high.
2. Divide beef into two equal-sized patties.
3. Season the patties with pepper accordingly.
4. Broil the patties for 5 minutes per side.
5. Transfer the patties to a platter.
6. Slice avocado into strips and place them on top of the patties. Serve and enjoy!

Nutrition:

- Calories: 560
- Carbs: 9g
- Protein: 38g
- Fat: 16g

Ravaging Beef Pot Roast

Preparation time: 10 minutes.   **Cooking time:** 1 hour and 15 minutes.   **Servings:** 4

Ingredients:

- 3(½) pounds beef roast
- 4 ounces mushrooms, sliced
- 12 ounces beef stock
- 1-ounce onion soup mix
- ½ cup Italian dressing, low sodium, and low fat

Directions:

1. Take a bowl and add the stock, onion soup mix, and Italian dressing.
2. Stir.
3. Put beef roast in a pan.
4. Add mushrooms, stock mix to the pan, and cover with foil.
5. Preheat your oven to 300°F.
6. Bake for 1 hour and 15 minutes.
7. Let the roast cool.
8. Slice and serve. Enjoy with the gravy on top!

Nutrition:

- Calories: 700
- Carbs: 10g
- Protein: 46g
- Fat: 3g

Lovely Faux Mac and Cheese

Preparation time: 15 minutes.   **Cooking time:** 45 minutes.   **Servings:** 4

Ingredients:

- 5 cups cauliflower florets
- Sunflower seeds and pepper to taste
- 1 cup coconut almond milk
- ½ cup vegetable broth
- 2 tablespoons coconut flour, sifted
- 1 organic egg, beaten
- 1 cup cashew cheese

Directions:

1. Preheat your oven to 350°F.
2. Season florets with sunflower seeds and steam until firm.
3. Place florets in a greased ovenproof dish.
4. Heat coconut almond milk over medium heat in a skillet; make sure to season the oil with sunflower seeds and pepper.
5. Stir in broth and add coconut flour to the mix, stir.
6. Cook until the sauce begins to bubble.
7. Remove heat and add beaten egg.
8. Pour the thick sauce over the cauliflower and mix in cheese.
9. Bake for 30–45 minutes.
10. Serve and enjoy!

Nutrition:

- Calories: 229
- Carbs: 9g
- Protein: 15g
- Fat: 6g

Ancho Macho Chili

Preparation time: 20 minutes.   **Cooking time:** 1 hour and 30 minutes.   **Servings:** 4

Ingredients:

- 2 pounds lean sirloin
- 1 teaspoon salt
- 0.25 teaspoon pepper
- 1.5 tablespoons olive oil
- 0.5 medium-sized onion, chopped finely
- 1.5 tablespoons chili powder
- 7 ounces of can tomatoes with green chili
- ½ cup of chicken broth
- 2 cloves of large roasted and minced garlic

Directions:

1. Prepare the oven by bringing it to a temperature of 350F. Coat prepared beef with pepper and salt.
2. Grab your Dutch oven cooker and bring a teaspoon of oil to a high temperature. Once it's ready, add in a third of your beef and cook until each side turns brown. Continue this process until all beef is brownish. Add more oil if needed.
3. Have about 1 teaspoon of oil left. Put that into the Dutch oven and use it for cooking your onion for a few minutes. Next, add in the last four ingredients and allow it to simmer in the pot.
4. Add in your beef with all its juices, cover the Dutch oven, and cook a full two hours. After the 1-hour point, stir everything. Enjoy!

Note: This recipe makes 4 servings and is good for 4–5 days. This can also be frozen.

Nutrition:

- Calories: 644
- Carbs 6g
- Protein: 58g
- Fat: 40g

Chicken Supreme Pizza

Preparation time: 25 minutes **Cooking time:** 30 minutes **Servings:** 8

Ingredients:

- 5 ounces of cooked and diced chicken breast
- 1.5 cups almond flour
- 1 teaspoon baking powder
- 1/2 teaspoon salt
- 0.25 cup water
- 1 red onion, small-sized, sliced thinly
- 1 red pepper, small-sized, sliced thinly
- Green pepper, same as red pepper above
- 1 cup mozzarella cheese, shredded
- 3 tablespoons olive oil

Directions:

1. Heat your oven to a temperature of 400°F.
2. Using a small-sized bowl and a fork, blend the flour together with the salt and baking powder.
3. Prepare your dough with the water and the oil added to this flour mixture. Prepare a space on your counter to make the dough flattened. Do what you need, but make sure the olive oil coats the surface lightly before you dump out the dough.
4. Dump out the dough. Use a rolling pin to press it out, and coat the pan with oil to avoid sticking. Once you archive the desired pizza crust shape, place it onto a baking stone or prepared tray.
5. Set the tray in the oven, and bake for about 12 minutes.
6. After taking out the pizza from the oven, sprinkle cheese onto it and then add chicken, pepper, and onion. Finally, season with pepper and salt (to taste).
7. Put the pizza back in the oven for only 15 minutes; serve warm and in slices.

Nutrition:

- Calories: 310
- Carbs: 4g
- Protein: 16g
- Fat: 12g

Zucchini Pizza Bites

Preparation time: 10 minutes. **Cooking time:** 30 minutes. **Servings:** 4

Ingredients:

- 4 large zucchinis
- 1 cup of tomato sauce
- 2 teaspoon oregano
- 4 cups mozzarella cheese
- 1/2 cup parmesan cheese
- Low carb pizza toppings of your choice

Directions:

1. Slice your zucchinis into small pieces, in a quarter of an inch or less.
2. Preheat the oven to 450°F.
3. Line a baking pan or tray with foil set it aside.
4. Place zucchini pieces on the pan. Top them with tomato sauce, cheese, oregano, and other low carb toppings you like.
5. Bake for five minutes, and then broil for five minutes more.
6. Serve warm.

Nutrition:

- Calories: 231
- Carbs: 48g
- Protein: 26.7g
- Fat: 74g

CHAPTER 12:

Dessert Recipes

Slice-and-Bake Vanilla Wafers

Preparation time: 10 minutes.   **Cooking time:** 15 minutes.   **Servings:** 2

Ingredients:

- 175 grams (1¾ cups) blanched almond flour
- ½ cup granulated erythritol-based sweetener
- 1 stick (½ cup) unsalted softened butter
- 2 tablespoon coconut flour
- ¼ teaspoon salt
- ½ teaspoon vanilla extract

Directions:

1. Beat the sweetener and butter using an electric mixer in a large bowl for 2 minutes until it becomes fluffy and light. Then beat in the salt, vanilla extract, coconut flour, and almond until thoroughly mixed.
2. Evenly spread the dough between two sheets of parchment or wax paper and wrap each portion into a size with a diameter of about 1½ inches. Then wrap in paper and refrigerate for 1-2 hours.
3. Heat the oven to 325°F and using parchment paper or silicone baking mats. Slice the dough into ¼-inch slices using a sharp knife. Put the sliced dough on the baking sheets and make sure to leave a 1-inch space between wafers.
4. Place in the oven for about 5 minutes. Slightly flatten the cookies using a flat-bottomed glass. Bake for another 8–10 minutes.

Nutrition:

- Calories: 101
- Carbs: 2.5g
- Protein: 2.2g
- Fat: 9.3g

Amaretti

Preparation time: 15 minutes.   **Cooking time:** 22 minutes.   **Servings:** 2

Ingredients:

- ½ cup of granulated erythritol-based sweetener
- 165 grams (2 cups) sliced almonds
- ¼ cup of powdered of erythritol-based sweetener
- 4 large egg whites
- Pinch of salt
- ½ teaspoon almond extract

Directions:

1. Heat the oven to 300°F and use parchment paper to line two baking sheets. Grease the parchment slightly.
2. Process the powdered sweetener, granulated sweetener, and sliced almonds in a food processor until it appears like coarse crumbs.
3. Beat the egg whites plus the salt and almond extract using an electric mixer in a large bowl until they hold soft peaks. Fold in the almond mixture so that it becomes well combined.
4. Drop a spoonful of the dough onto the prepared baking sheet and allow for a space of one inch between them. Press a sliced almond into the top of each cookie.
5. Bake in the oven for 22 minutes until the sides become brown. They will appear jelly-like when they are taken out from the oven but will begin to firm as it cools down.

Nutrition:

- Calories: 117
- Carbs: 4.1g
- Protein: 5.3g
- Fat: 8.8g

Peanut Butter Cookies for Two

Preparation time: 5 minutes.   **Cooking time:** 12 minutes.   **Servings:** 1

Ingredients:

- 1(½) tablespoon creamy salted peanut butter
- 1 tablespoon unsalted softened butter
- 2 tablespoons granulated erythritol-based sweetener
- 2 tablespoons defatted peanut flour
- Pinch of salt
- 2 teaspoon sugarless chocolate chips
- 1/8 teaspoon baking powder

Directions:

1. Heat the oven to 325°F. Put a parchment paper or baking sheet with a silicone.
2. Beat in the sweetener, butter, and peanut butter using an electric mixer in a small bowl until it is thoroughly mixed.
3. Add the salt, baking powder, and peanut flour and mix until the dough clumps together. Cut the dough into two and shape each of them into a ball.
4. Position the dough ball into the coated baking sheets and flatten it into a circular shape about half an inch thick. Garnish the dough tops with a teaspoon of chocolate chips. Gently press them into the dough to make them stick.
5. Bake for 10–12 minutes until golden brown.

Nutrition:

- Calories: 163
- Carbs: 5.7g
- Protein: 4.9g
- Fat: 23.2g

Cream Cheese Cookies

Preparation time: 15 minutes.   **Cooking time:** 12 minutes.   **Servings:** 6

Ingredients:

- ¼ cup (½ stick) unsalted softened butter
- ½ cup (4 ounces) softened cream cheese
- 1 large egg, at room temperature
- ½ cup granulated erythritol-based sweetener
- 150 grams (1(½) cups) of blanched almond flour
- 1 teaspoon baking powder
- ½ teaspoon vanilla extract
- Powdered erythritol-based sweetener (for dusting)
- ¼ teaspoon salt

Directions:

1. Heat the oven to 350°F, and put a parchment paper or baking sheet with a silicone baking mat.
2. Beat the butter and cream cheese using an electric mixer in a large bowl until it appears smooth. Add the sweetener and keep beating. Beat in the vanilla extract and the egg.
3. Whisk in the salt, baking powder, and almond flour in a medium bowl. Add the flour mixture into the cream cheese and until well incorporated.
4. Drop tablespoons of the dough onto the coated baking sheet. Flatten the cookies.
5. Bake for 10–12 minutes. Dust with powdered sweetener when cool.

Nutrition:

- Calories: 154
- Carbs: 3.4g
- Protein: 4.1g
- Fat: 13.7g

Mocha Cream Pie

Preparation time: 15 minutes.   **Cooking time:** 5 minutes.   **Servings:** 10

Ingredients:

- 1 cup strongly brewed coffee, at room temperature
- 1 easy chocolate pie crust
- 1 cup heavy whipping cream
- 1(½) teaspoon grass-fed gelatin
- 1 teaspoon vanilla extract
- ¼ cup cocoa powder
- ½ cup powdered erythritol-based sweetener

Directions:

1. Grease a 9-inch glass or ceramic pie pan. Press the crust mixture evenly and firmly to the sides of the greased pan or its bottom. Refrigerate until the filling is prepared.
2. Pour the coffee into a small saucepan and add gelatin. Whisk thoroughly and then place over medium heat. Allow it to simmer, whisking from time to time to make sure the gelatin dissolves. Allow it to cool for 20 minutes.
3. Add the vanilla extract, cocoa powder, sweetener, and cream into a large bowl. Use an electric mixer to beat until it holds stiff peaks.
4. Add the gelatin mixture that has been cooled and beat until it is well incorporated. Pour over the cooled crust and place in the refrigerator for 3 hours until it becomes firm.

Nutrition:

- Calories: 218
- Carbs: 6.2g
- Protein: 4.7g
- Fat: 20.2g

Coconut Custard Pie

Preparation time: 10 minutes.   **Cooking time:** 50 minutes.   **Servings:** 8

Ingredients:

- 1 cup heavy whipping cream
- ¾ cup powdered erythritol-based sweetener
- ½ cup full-fat coconut milk
- 4 large eggs
- ½ stick (¼ cup) of cooled, unsalted, melted butter
- 1(¼) cups unsweetened shredded coconut
- 3 tablespoon coconut flour
- ½ teaspoon baking powder
- ½ teaspoon vanilla extract
- ¼ teaspoon salt

Directions:

1. Heat the oven to 350°F and grease a 9-inch ceramic pie pan or glass.
2. Place the melted butter, eggs, coconut milk, sweetener, and cream in a blender. Blend well.
3. Add the vanilla extract, baking powder, salt, coconut flour, and a cup of shredded coconut. Continue blending.
4. Empty the mixture into the pie pan and sprinkle with the rest of the shredded coconut. Bake for 40–50 minutes. Stop when the center moves, but the sides are set.
5. Take out of the oven and allow it to cool for 30 minutes. Place in the refrigerator and allow to stay for 2 hours before cutting it.

Nutrition:

- Calories: 317
- Carbs: 6.7g
- Protein: 5.3g
- Fat: 29.5g

Coconut Macaroons

Preparation time: 10 minutes.   **Cooking time:** 8 minutes.   **Servings:** 40 cookies.

Ingredients:

- 0.33 cups water
- 0.75 cups monk fruit sweetener (or less to taste)
- 0.25 teaspoon sea salt
- 0.75 teaspoon sugar-free vanilla extract
- 2 eggs, large
- 3–4 cups unsweetened shredded coconut, or more as desired
- Optional: Sugar-free chocolate chips

Directions:

1. Set the oven setting to 350°F.
2. Lightly spray a cookie tin with a spritz of cooking oil spray.
3. In a small saucepan, pour in the water and the sweetener, salt, and vanilla extract. Bring to a boil using the med-high heat temperature setting. Stir and remove from the heat.
4. Use a food processor to combine the egg and coconut flakes. Pour in the syrup and process to form the dough. Using a cookie scoop, place mounds about an inch apart onto the cookie sheet.
5. Bake for 8 minutes, and rotate the baking pan in the oven.
6. Bake until lightly browned or for an additional four minutes.
7. Cool on a rack. Drizzle with melted chocolate to your liking.

Nutrition:

- Calories: 24
- Carbs: 4.09g
- Protein: 0.62g
- Fat: 3.19g

Orange and Cranberries Cookies

Preparation time: 15 minutes. **Cooking time:** 10 minutes. **Servings:** 18

Ingredients:

- 0.75 cup butter—softened
- 3 eggs
- 0.5 cup coconut flour
- 1.5 teaspoon baking powder
- 0.75 cup monk fruit sweetener
- 0.25 teaspoon baking soda
- 0.25 cup sugar-free dried cranberries
- 0.5 cup macadamia nuts chopped
- 1.5 teaspoon dried grated orange zest

Directions:

1. In a mixing container, beat the sweetener with the eggs and butter until well combined.
2. Sift the coconut flour with the baking powder and soda. Beat on the low setting or with a spoon until fully mixed.
3. Fold in the cranberries, orange zest, and nuts.
4. Shape into rounds and arrange on the cookie sheet.
5. Arrange the cookies a minimum of one inch apart for baking on a parchment-lined cookie sheet. Press each mound down slightly to flatten.
6. Bake at 350°F until edges have started to brown or for eight to ten minutes. Cool for a few minutes.
7. Transfer to a cooling rack. Enjoy right out of the fridge for a week or they can be frozen for longer storage.

Nutrition:

- Calories: 200
- Carbs: 2g
- Protein: 3g
- Fats: 19g

Double Chocolate Chip Cookies

Preparation time: 15 minutes. **Cooking time:** 8–10 minutes. **Servings:** 48

Ingredients:

- 15 ounces can black soybeans
- 0.25 cup unsweetened coconut milk
- 0.25 cup cocoa powder
- 1 cup peanut flour
- 1 cup almond flour
- 1 teaspoon instant coffee granules
- 0.75 teaspoon baking soda
- 0.75 teaspoon baking powder
- 0.75 teaspoon salt
- 0.5 cup softened butter
- 0.5 cup monk fruit sweetener or erythritol
- 0.5 teaspoon stevia extract powder
- 1 egg
- 2 teaspoons vanilla extract
- 0.5 cup sugar-free chocolate chips

Directions:

1. Warm up the oven in advance to reach 375°F.
2. Drain and rinse the soybeans and puree with the coconut milk.
3. Whisk the dry ingredients, including the instant coffee, with cocoa, peanut flour, baking soda, salt, almond flour, and baking powder. Set aside.
4. Using an electric mixer, cream the butter together with the sweeteners until light and fluffy.
5. Fold in the egg and vanilla. Mix well.
6. Add the black bean puree to the butter mixture.
7. Gradually mix each of the dry ingredients into the chocolate/black bean mixture until the cookie dough just comes together.
8. Fold in the chocolate chips.
9. Drop by tablespoonful onto baking sheets, flattening slightly and adding a few extra chocolate chips on top.
10. Bake for about 8 to 10 minutes.

Nutrition:

- Calories: 34
- Carbs: 1g
- Protein: 2g
- Fats: 2g

Flourless Chocolate Cookies with Peanut Butter Chips

Preparation time: 15 minutes.   **Cooking time:** 8–10 minutes.   **Servings:** 19 cookies.

Ingredients:

- 0.75 cup monk fruit low carb sweetener powdered or 1.5 teaspoon sweet leaf stevia drops
- 0.33 cup unsweetened cocoa powder
- 1.25 teaspoon salt
- 2–3 egg whites at room temperature
- 1.5 teaspoon vanilla extract
- 0.75 cup low-carb peanut butter chips or low carb chocolate chips

Directions:

1. Warm up the oven to reach 350°F before you begin.
2. Prepare a baking sheet with a silicone mat or a layer of parchment baking paper.
3. Whisk the powdered sweetener with the cocoa powder and salt.
4. Whisk in two egg whites, one at a time, and vanilla extract.
5. Beat until it reaches a thick and fudge batter. If it's too thick, add egg white.
6. Stir in chocolate or peanut butter chips.
7. Scoop the batter onto the prepared baking sheet.
8. Bake about 13 to15 minutes. Remove from the oven and cool cookies on a baking rack.

Nutrition:

- Calories: 38
- Carbs: 1.2g
- Protein: 3.5g
- Fats: 5g

Hazelnut Flour Keto Cookies

Preparation time: 15 minutes.   **Cooking time:** 25 minutes.   **Servings:** 20 small cookies.

Ingredients:

- 1 cup hazelnut meal ground hazelnuts
- 2 white eggs
- 1 tablespoon powdered erythritol
- 10 drops of vanilla stevia glycerite
- 1 teaspoon vanilla
- Crushed hazelnuts, to decorate

Directions:

1. Whisk the egg whites to form stiff peaks.
2. Fold in the hazelnut meal with the stevia, erythritol, and vanilla until well combined.
3. Drop by tablespoons onto a silicone baking sheet or paper-lined pan. Flatten to your liking.
4. Bake at 320°F for 25 minutes or until lightly browned.
5. Let the cookies cool and become firm before touching them.

Nutrition:

- Calories: 34.4
- Carbs: 0.4g
- Protein: 1.1g
- Fats: 3.2g

Italian Almond Macaroons

Preparation time: 10 minutes.   **Cooking time:** 55–60 minutes.   **Servings:** 45

Ingredients:

- 2 cups plus 2 tablespoons almond flour about
- 0.25 cup monk fruit low-carb sweetener
- 2 whites eggs
- 0.5 teaspoon almond extracts
- 1 tablespoon powdered (confectioner) monk fruit sweetener

Directions:

1. Combine the almond flour with the egg whites, sweetener, and almond extract.
2. Knead the mixture until the dough is formed.
3. Shape the dough into 1-inch balls and place on a parchment paper-lined baking sheet at least 1 inch apart.
4. Bake at 250°F on the bottom rack of the oven for 55 to 60 minutes.
5. Remove the cookies from the baking pan to the wire rack and dust with the confectioners' sweetener while still warm.

Nutrition:

- Calories: 31
- Carbs: 0g
- Protein: 2g
- Fats: 3g

Keto Sugar Cookies

Preparation time: 15 minutes.   **Cooking time:** 20–30 minutes.   **Servings:** 27 cookies.

Ingredients:

- 1 cup almond flour
- 0.25 cup coconut flour
- 0.33 cup monk fruit low-carb sweetener
- 0.5 teaspoon baking soda
- 0.5 cup non-hydrogenated lard or ghee/butter
- 1 egg, large
- 0.5 teaspoon vanilla extract

Optional glaze:

- 0.25 cup monk fruit powdered low carb sweetener
- Water—as needed

Directions:

1. Warm the oven to reach 350° Fahrenheit.
2. Combine each of the fixings together. Whisk or pulse together in a food processor.
3. Roll the dough out between two sheets of parchment baking paper to the desired thickness.
4. The dough can also be rolled into a log and frozen for 20 to 30 minutes. Slice into circles for easy slice-and-bake cookies.
5. Arrange on parchment lined cookie sheet.
6. Bake until the edges are lightly browned or for 8 to 10 minutes or until edges are lightly browned.
7. Remove from oven, let cool on a rack for about 5 to 10 minutes and transfer the cookies to a cooling rack until completely cooled.
8. Prepare the glaze by adding the powdered sweetener into a mixing container to make a thin glaze.
9. Divide and add the coloring as desired. Use a brush to glaze onto the cookies in a thin layer and allow to dry.

Nutrition:

- Calories: 31
- Carbs: 1g
- Protein: 1 g
- Fats: 6 g

Low-Carb Chocolate Chip Cookies

Preparation Time: 10 minutes   **Cooking Time:** 12 minutes   **Servings:** 36 Cookies

Ingredients:

- 0.5 cup softened butter
- 0.5 cup swerve or erythritol
- 0.25 teaspoon stevia glycerite or stevia liquid concentrate
- 0.75 teaspoon blackstrap molasses optional
- 1 large egg
- 0.5 cup almond flour
- 0.5 cup low-carb vanilla whey protein powder
- 2 tablespoons 12% fat - Peanut flour or coconut flour
- 0.5 teaspoon baking soda
- 0.5 teaspoon salt
- 0.5 cup sugar-free chocolate chips
- Optional: 0.5 cup chopped walnuts or pecans

Directions:

1. Warm up the oven to 375° Fahrenheit.
2. Prepare the baking sheets with a layer of parchment baking paper.
3. Beat the butter in with the stevia, erythritol, and molasses until fluffy. Whisk and add the egg.
4. In another container, sift the almond flour with the vanilla whey protein powder, baking soda, salt, and peanut flour.
5. Stir all of the mixtures together until blended. Fold in the chocolate chips and nuts.
6. Use a cookie scoop to measure and drop onto the pans about two inches apart.
7. Bake until golden or about 8 to 12 minutes.
8. Cool for a couple of minutes on the cookie tin.
9. Transfer to wire racks to cool.

Nutrition:

- Calories: 74
- Carbs: 1g
- Protein: 3 g
- Fats: 5 g

Peanut Butter Blossoms

Preparation Time: 10 minutes   **Cooking Time:** 10 minutes   **Servings:** 24 Cookies

Ingredients:

- 0.5 cup Sukrin Gold - packed or brown sugar replacement
- 1 tablespoon Sukrin Gold Fiber Syrup or another tablespoon of Sukrin Gold
- 0.5 cup natural sugar-free peanut butter or use sun butter
- 1 large egg
- 0.5 cup peanut flour sesame flour for nut allergy
- 0.5 teaspoon baking soda
- 0.5 teaspoon vanilla extract
- Salt (1 pinch if using unsalted peanut butter)
- 24 low-carb chocolate kiss drops or a few chocolate chips
- Optional: Monk fruit low carb sweetener

Directions:

1. Mix the peanut butter and Sukrin Gold until well blended.
2. Prepare a baking sheet with a mat or layer of parchment baking paper.
3. Whisk and mix in the egg until incorporated. Mix in the remaining fixings until uniform dough forms.
4. Roll the dough into balls and roll in the granulated sweetener if desired.
5. Arrange on the baking tin.
6. Press each cookie ball down to about a 0.5-inch thickness.
7. Bake at 350° Fahrenheit until the cookies are set, about 7 to 10 minutes.
8. Allow cooling for 5 to 10 minutes.
9. Press a chocolate kiss on top of each warm cookie before serving.

Nutrition:

- Calories: 66
- Carbs: 1.8 g
- Protein: 3.6 g
- Fats: 5.3 g

CHAPTER 13:

28-day Meal Plan

For people who are new to the Keto Diet, the way to meal plan might seem both full of possibilities and full of pitfalls. The reality is that the best solution is the KISS method (Keep It Simple Stupid). The key to this diet is to make sure that you are keeping everything within your proper ratios. This is a really important part of the Keto Diet when you stay in the ratios you need, and it will happen that you will be able to make sure you get the most out of your diet. However, this is just the first step, the next thing to think about is what exactly you can eat? Well, there is good news, there are tons of options with proteins. This is a way that you can make life easy in yourself. One of the sources of protein should be eggs. They are really easy and versatile, and eggs are also ridiculously cheap. Another great idea is using seafood. The smaller types of seafood are better; for example, sardines are a great source of protein because they are high in Omega-3, which has a ton of benefits for the body. Some other seafood includes salmon, shrimp, cod, and even oysters. That said, many of these different meats can get expensive. Also, if you can get grass-fed or organic meat, that is always better than going with the conventional types, which means that you have a greater amount of fat content.

Here are some sources of protein—again, adjust if you are on a budget:

- Grass-fed beef
- Wild-caught seafood
- Pork; preferably pasture-raised
- Eggs – vegetarian diet is the standard
- Grass-fed chicken
- Yogurt in moderation

Oils also have some very interesting properties as well, and what you are cooking with will definitely affect your progress on the Keto Diet. One of the great tips for adding flavor is to cook your greens in extra virgin olive oil or bacon fat. This is a great way to get a flavor. Avocado oil and olive oil also work well with salad dressings. When you decide that you want to marinate food, be sure to use avocado oil. Butter, of course, is wonderful for cooking and uncured bacon is great for getting fat from and also to eat. Also, the rendered fat has a higher smoke point, so you can feel assured that you won't have to deal with the oxidized LDL cholesterol responsible for the hardening of arteries, the building of plaque, and this is what causes heart disease as well.

Choosing your vegetables is also very important, and the thing that you want to do is get dark leafy greens like spinach and kale. There are others as well, such as bok choy. The good news is when you are using butter and bacon fat for cooking these vegetables, you will enjoy their flavors. These vegetables are loaded with different nutrients that your body needs, including calcium and other vitamins and minerals that will make up for any deficiencies that you may have had. Plus, they have amazingly complex flavors and can be used in so many different ways.

There are plenty of other vegetables to use as well, so don't get caught in a kale and spinach cycle because that results in the building up of different oxalates, and the end results are kidney stones. No one wants to deal with that. Mushrooms are also good and have a low amount of net carbs; asparagus, Brussels sprouts, zucchini, onions, and bell peppers all do the job too. Throw in some balsamic vinegar, and you have some excellent flavors. These veggies also tolerate the grill really well too.

The fruit should be used in moderation, and the key with fruit is making sure that you are all about the berries. Blackberries, raspberries, blueberries and strawberries are ideal because they are high in fiber and also in antioxidants. Furthermore, win and dark chocolate also have great power with the Keto Diet as well. There are lots of other things to consider too. Make sure the fruit is lower in sugar because this will avoid the increase of insulin, and that creates problems with the Keto Diet.

Once you have the food you want to eat, the next step is making sure you are cooking it the way that you want. There are some different methods that you should use. The first is that you want to make sure that you are going one of three ways. The best methods are using a pressure cooker, the stovetop, or firing up the grill.

There are lots of interesting ideas as well. Bone broth is really fun to make during meal prep, and it is done with the pressure cooker. There are also dishes like Keto lasagna, pulled pork, keto cheesecake, ground beef dishes, hard-boiled eggs and even veggie lasagna. When you reflect on where you were and how far you have come, you will notice that you were eating a bunch of starches, including pasta, rice, mac and cheese, baked potatoes, etc. The pressure cooker is one of the best ways to prepare food healthily and it makes life so much easier.

Here is a 28-day meal plan for weight loss and boost energy for breakfast, lunch, dinner, and snacks

---

Day	Breakfast	Lunch	Dinner	Desserts
1	MEXICAN SCRAMBLED EGGS	COLE SLAW KETO WRAP	BLACK EYED PEAS AND SPINACH PLATTER	SLICE-AND-BAKE VANILLA WAFERS
2	FENNEL QUICHE	KETO CHICKEN CLUB LETTUCE WRAP	HUMBLE MUSHROOM RICE	AMARETTI
3	SPINACH QUICHE	KETO BROCCOLI SALAD	SWEET AND SOUR CABBAGE AND APPLES	PEANUT BUTTER COOKIES FOR TWO
4	CHICKEN FRITTATA	KETO SHEET PAN CHICKEN AND RAINBOW VEGGIES	ORANGE AND CHILI GARLIC SAUCE	CREAM CHEESE COOKIES
5	COCONUT FLOUR SPINACH CASSEROLE	SKINNY BANG BANG ZUCCHINI NOODLES	TANTALIZING MUSHROOM GRAVY	MOCHA CREAM PIE
6	ZUCCHINI MUFFINS	KETO CAESAR SALAD	GRILLED CHICKEN WITH LEMON AND FENNEL	COCONUT CUSTARD PIE
7	CHEESY EGG MUFFINS	KETO BUFFALO CHICKEN EMPANADAS	CARAMELIZED PORK CHOPS AND ONION	COCONUT MACAROONS
8	BROWN HASH WITH ZUCCHINI	PEPPERONI AND CHEDDAR STROMBOLI	HEARTY PORK BELLY CASSEROLE	CREAM CHEESE COOKIES

Day	Breakfast	Lunch	Dinner	Desserts
9	CAPRESE OMELET	TUNA CASSEROLE	FASCINATING SPINACH AND BEEF MEATBALLS	DOUBLE CHOCOLATE CHIP COOKIES
10	SPINACH OMELET	BRUSSELS SPROUT AND HAMBURGER GRATIN	JUICY AND PEPPERY TENDERLOIN	FLOURLESS CHOCOLATE COOKIES WITH PEANUT BUTTER CHIPS
11	CHICKEN AVOCADO SALAD	BACON APPETIZERS	HEALTHY AVOCADO BEEF PATTIES	HAZELNUT FLOUR KETO COOKIES
12	KETO PHILLY CHEESESTEAK POCKETS	TASTY SALAD OPTIONS	RAVAGING BEEF POT ROAST	ITALIAN ALMOND MACAROONS
13	SPINACH QUICHE	CHICKEN CAESAR SALAD & BOK CHOY	LOVELY FAUX MAC AND CHEESE	KETO SUGAR COOKIES
14	KETO CAULIFLOWER AND EGGS	HEALTHY ROASTED GREEN BEAN & MUSHROOM SALAD	ANCHO MACHO CHILI	LOW-CARB CHOCOLATE CHIP COOKIES
15	ZUCCHINI PIZZA BIT	ITALIAN TRI-COLOR SALAD	CHICKEN SUPREME PIZZA	PEANUT BUTTER BLOSSOMS
16	MEXICAN SCRAMBLED EGGS	KETO CHICKEN CLUB LETTUCE WRAP	BLACK EYED PEAS AND SPINACH PLATTER	SLICE-AND-BAKE VANILLA WAFERS
17	FENNEL QUICHE	COLE SLAW KETO WRAP	HUMBLE MUSHROOM RICE	AMARETTI

Day	Breakfast	Lunch	Dinner	Desserts
18	SPINACH QUICHE	KETO BROCCOLI SALAD	SWEET AND SOUR CABBAGE AND APPLES	PEANUT BUTTER COOKIES FOR TWO
19	CHICKEN FRITTATA	KETO SHEET PAN CHICKEN AND RAINBOW VEGGIES	ORANGE AND CHILI GARLIC SAUCE	CREAM CHEESE COOKIES
20	COCONUT FLOUR SPINACH CASSEROLE	SKINNY BANG BANG ZUCCHINI NOODLES	TANTALIZING MUSHROOM GRAVY	MOCHA CREAM PIE
21	ZUCCHINI MUFFINS	KETO CAESAR SALAD	GRILLED CHICKEN WITH LEMON AND FENNEL	COCONUT CUSTARD PIE
22	CHEESY EGG MUFFINS	KETO BUFFALO CHICKEN EMPANADAS	CARAMELIZED PORK CHOPS AND ONION	COCONUT MACAROONS
23	BROWN HASH WITH ZUCCHINI	PEPPERONI AND CHEDDAR STROMBOLI	HEARTY PORK BELLY CASSEROLE	CREAM CHEESE COOKIES
24	CAPRESE OMELET	TUNA CASSEROLE	FASCINATING SPINACH AND BEEF MEATBALLS	DOUBLE CHOCOLATE CHIP COOKIES
25	SPINACH OMELET	BRUSSELS SPROUT AND HAMBURGER GRATIN	JUICY AND PEPPERY TENDERLOIN	FLOURLESS CHOCOLATE COOKIES WITH PEANUT BUTTER CHIPS
26	CHICKEN AVOCADO SALAD	BACON APPETIZERS	HEALTHY AVOCADO BEEF PATTIES	HAZELNUT FLOUR KETO COOKIES

Day	Breakfast	Lunch	Dinner	Desserts
27	KETO PHILLY CHEESESTEAK POCKETS	TASTY SALAD OPTIONS	RAVAGING BEEF POT ROAST	ITALIAN ALMOND MACAROONS
28	LOW CARB CAESAR SALAD	CHICKEN CAESAR SALAD & BOK CHOY	LOVELY FAUX MAC AND CHEESE	KETO SUGAR COOKIES

Conclusion

If you are over 50's, you know how difficult it is to maintain health and shed that extra weight. Whether you are going through menopause, have more time to eat and socialize, dropping weight after your 50s is not a piece of cake.

If nothing else is working, give the ketogenic diet a try. The fact is that millions of people have successfully implemented a high-fat keto diet as a way to lose weight. It's highly effective because it turns your body into a natural fat burner, without leaving you hungry, craving for sugary foods, or suffering from health effects due to too few calories.

With the keto diet, imagine a life with lesser belly fat.

Imagine that you can eat as much as you want, every single day, and be able to see your waist and stomach shrink.

Imagine yourself as active and energetic as you were in your 20's and 30's.

KETO DIET COOKBOOK

FOR WOMEN OVER 50

Discover How to Enter the Keto Lifestyle by Cooking Tasty and Delicious Low Carb and High-Fat Recipes to Stay Healthy and Boost Your Fat Also Over 50!

Introduction

As women, when our age grows at 50, we are always looking for a quick and effective way to shed our excess weight, get our high blood sugar levels under control, reduce overall inflammation, and improve our physical and mental energy. It's frustrating to have all of these issues, especially the undeniable fats in our belly. Good thing that I found this great solution to all our worries when we reach this age level, and when our body gets weaker as time goes by. The ketogenic diet plans.

As a woman at this age, we all know that it is much more difficult for us to lose weight than men. I have lived on a starvation level diet and exercise like a triathlete and only lose five pounds. A man will stop putting dressing on his salad and will lose twenty pounds. It just not fair. But we have the fact that we are women to blame. Women naturally have more standing between themselves and weight loss than men do.

The mere fact that we, women, is the largest single contributor to why we find it difficult to lose weight. Since our bodies always think it needs to be prepared for a possible pregnancy, we will naturally have more body fat and less mass in our muscles than men.

Being in menopause will also cause us to add more pounds to our bodies, especially in the lower half. After menopause, our metabolism naturally slows down. Our hormone levels will decrease. These two factors alone will cause weight gain in the post-menopausal period.

There are numerous diet plan options offered to help shed weight, but the Ketogenic diet has been the most preferred lately. We've got many concerns around keto's effectiveness and exactly how to follow the diet plan in a healthy and balanced means.

The ketogenic diet for ladies at the age of over 50 is an easy and ideal way to shed extra pounds, stay energetic, and enjoy a healthy life. It balances hormones and improves our body capabilities without causing any harm to our overall wellness. Thus, if you are fighting post-menopausal symptoms and other health issues, you should do a keto diet right away!

A keto diet is a lifestyle, not a diet so, treat it like the same. The best way to approach keto to gain maximum benefits, especially for women over 50s, is to treat it as a lifestyle. You can't restrict your meal intake through obstructive and strict diets forever, right? It's the fundamental reason fad diets fail — we limit ourselves from too much to get rapid results, then we're are right back again at the weight where we started, or God forbid worse.

Keto is not a kind of diet that can be followed strictly forever — unless you need it as a therapeutic diet (i.e., epilepsy), a very narrow category. In the keto diet, we slowly transit into a curative state that we can withstand forever in a healthier way.

So, for me, being on a keto diet does not mean that I will be in ketosis forever. Instead, it means letting myself love consideration, such as a few desserts while vacationing or partying. It does not set me back to enjoy these desserts and let me consider it as the end of the diet. I can wake up the following morning and go back to the keto lifestyle, most suitable for me and my body consistently.

It allows my body to drastically boost its fat loss in many cases, decreasing pockets of undesirable fat.

With Keto Diet, it's not only giving weight loss assistance to reduce my weight, yet it can likewise ward off yearnings for unhealthy foods and protect me against Calories: collisions throughout the day. That is why I want to share with you how promising this Keto diet. As our age grow older, we must not let our body do the same. Focus your mindset on this fantastic diet, read, apply, and enjoy its best benefits.

What I promise you after you read the full guide of Keto Diet for Women after 50 and apply it to your daily lifestyle, especially the 30 days meal plan, you will achieve more than losing weight but also a new and improve healthier you!

CHAPTER 1:

What Is the Ketogenic Diet?

The ketogenic diet is a perfect combination of an equal number of macros essential for the perfect and healthy functioning of the human body.

This diet is mostly focused on foods that are rich in fats, while carbohydrates are considerably lowered.

If you hadn't heard about the keto diet, you probably did not know that eating meals without balanced (or reduced) macros (carbohydrates, proteins, fats, and fibers) will lead to weight and fat.

When you provide your body with foods containing large amounts of carbohydrates (and fats and protein), your body stimulates insulin development, leading to leptin resistance. Slowly but surely, your body weight will increase. Not every organism is the same, but providing the body with unhealthy amounts of carbs combined with fats and proteins (without any physical activity) is a surefire way to end up obese.

How Was the Ketogenic Diet Discovered?

Although this diet may have only recently become popular, it is not new at all. It is almost a century old.

In the early 1920s, Johns Hopkins Medical Center researchers had a mission to find a way to decrease the no. of seizures in epileptic children. It seemed like an impossible mission to help epileptic children. Still, after thorough research, the researchers discovered that food rich in carbohydrates is the main reason epileptic children have frequent seizures.

They decided to start a new diet and observe the results. The epileptic patients started following the ketogenic diet, which consisted of foods rich in fats and proteins. With only a small amount of carbohydrates, it was discovered that this diet significantly decreased the seizures.

However, as in everything, there were exceptions. The keto diet did not work for everyone; about 30 percent of epileptic children did not react to this diet. Naturally, the epileptic children still had to be observed and take their medications, but the low-carb diet turned out to be quite a relief for most of them.

Before this research, some form of the keto diet had existed, even in ancient Greece and India. Fasting and reducing the consumption of foods with carbs was nothing new to these people.

Historians have found ancient writings that carefully explained how a diet helps in managing epileptic seizures. In ancient times, people were giving up food for a day or two and were facing complete relief (especially people with epilepsy).

Because fasting can be quite a challenge, over time, the keto diet took on the form it has today. You get to eat enough, and you cut out only carbohydrates (or eat them in reduced amounts).

Before the Johns Hopkins Medical Center research, French doctors discovered a way to reduce epileptic seizures with suitable foods. At the beginning of the 20th century in France, an experiment was conducted in which about 20 patients with epilepsy followed a new diet (mostly vegetarian) that was low in carbs. By then, the doctors were using Potassium: bromide to treat the patients, but it turned out that this did not work well in terms of their mental abilities. This early form of keto was combined with intermittent fasting and showed good results. About ten percent of the treated patients reacted positively to the new way of eating. Also, they were in a good mental state and did not need to take Potassium: bromide.

Slowly but surely, the ketogenic diet found its way to people without epilepsy. It was one of the diets that helped people stay full and healthy and lose weight fast.

How Does the Keto Diet Work?

We will focus on how this diet works and how your body transitions from one way of functioning to another.

As mentioned before, the ketogenic diet was used mainly to lower the incidence of seizures in epileptic children.

People wanted to check out how the keto diet would work with an entirely healthy person as things usually go.

This diet makes the body burn fats much faster than it does carbohydrates. The carbohydrates that we take in through food are turned into glucose, one of the leading "brain foods." So, once you start following the keto diet, foods with reduced carbohydrates are forcing the liver to turn all the fats into fatty acids and ketone bodies. The ketones go to the brain and take the place of glucose, becoming the primary energy source.

This diet's primary purpose is to make your body switch from the way it used to function to an entirely new way of creating energy, keeping you healthy and alive.

Once you start following the ketogenic diet, you will notice that things are changing, first and foremost, in your mind. Before, carbohydrates were your main body 'fuel' and were used to create glucose so that your brain could function. Now you no longer feed yourself with them.

In the beginning, most people feel odd because their natural food is off the table. When your menu consists of more fats and proteins, it is natural to feel that something is missing.

Your brain alarms you that you haven't eaten enough and sends you signals that you are hungry. It is literally "panicking" and telling you that you are starving, which is not correct. You get to eat, and you get to eat plenty of good food, but not carbs.

This condition usually arises during the first day or two. Afterward, people get used to their new eating habits.

Once the brain "realizes" that carbs are no longer an option, it will focus on "finding" another abundant energy source: in this case, fats.

Not only is your food rich in fats, but your body contains stored fats in large amounts. As you consume more fats and fewer carbs, your body "runs" on the fats, both consumed and stored. The best thing is that, as the fats are used for energy, they are burned. This is how you get a double gain from this diet.

Usually, it will take a few days of consuming low-carb meals before you start seeing visible weight loss results. You will not even have to check your weight because the fat layers will be visibly reduced.

This diet requires you to lower your daily consumption of carbs to only 20 grams. For most people, this transition from a regular carb-rich diet can be quite a challenge. Most people are used to eating bread, pasta, rice, dairy products, sweets, soda, alcohol, and fruits, so quitting all these foods might be challenging.

However, this is all in your head. If you manage to win the "battle" with your mind and endure the diet for a few days, you will see that you no longer have cravings as time goes by. Plus, the weight loss and the fat burn will be a great motivation to continue with this diet.

The keto diet practically makes the body burn fats much faster than carbohydrates; the foods you consume with this diet are quite rich in fats. Carbs will be there, too, but at far lower levels than before. Foods rich in carbohydrates are the body's primary fuel or the brain's food. (Our bodies turn carbs into glucose.) Because there are hardly any carbohydrates in this diet, the body will have to find a substitute source of energy to keep itself alive.

Many people who don't truly need to lose weight and are completely healthy still choose to follow the keto diet because it is a great way to keep their meals balanced. Also, it is the perfect way to cleanse the body of toxins, processed foods, sugars, and unnecessary carbs. The combination of these things is usually the main reason for heart failure, some cancers, diabetes, cholesterol, or obesity.

If you ask a nutritionist about this diet, they will recommend it without a doubt. So, if you feel like cleansing your body and starting a diet that will keep you healthy, well-fed, and slender, perhaps the keto diet should be your primary choice.

And what is the best thing about it (besides the fact that you will balance your weight & lower the risk of many diseases)?

There is no yo-yo effect. The keto diet can be followed forever and has no side effects. It does not restrict you from following it for a few weeks or a month. Once you get your body to keto foods, you will not think about going back to the old ways of eating your meals.

Why No Carbs?

I don't hate carbs. They're one of nature's ways of fueling our bodies and brains. However, we eat far too much of this stuff by the way we live lately. Mostly, in the form of processed sugars, refined carbs, and other high carb foods.

They spell disaster for your body, and you start piling on weight in those places you hate the most. In your stomach, your hips, your legs, your butt, your arms, your neck. Everywhere that's wrong! It leaves you more vulnerable to health problems such as type 2 diabetes, metabolic syndrome, depression and anxiety, certain cancers and just many more.

CHAPTER 2:

Ketosis and the Signs That You Are in Ketosis

What Is Ketosis?

Ketosis may seem like a scary word, but it is a completely natural metabolic state your body will enter when there is no longer glucose for your body to run off of. Instead, your body will begin to use fat as fuel! Exciting, right? Once your body has limited access to blood sugar or glucose, your body will enter a state of ketosis. You see, as you consume a low-carb diet, the levels of insulin hormones in your body will decrease, and the fatty acids in your body will be released from the fat stores.

From this point, the fatty acids that are being released in your body are then transferred to your liver. Once in place, the fatty acids are then oxidized and turned into ketone bodies, which provide your body with energy. This process is important because the fatty acids cannot cross your blood-brain barrier, meaning it cannot provide energy to your brain (important.) Once the process has occurred, ketones provide energy for your body and your brain, without ever needing glucose.

You may still have questions at this point, and that is perfectly okay! For now, it is time to carry on with information about the ketogenic diet so you can continue to build your base.

Signs That You Are in Ketosis

Since the human body heavily depends on Carbs: it always takes time for the body to adapt according to the new ketogenic lifestyle. It's like changing the fuel of a machine when the body is switched to the ketogenic diet; it shows some different signs than usual, which are as follows:

Increased Urination

Ketones are normally known as a diuretic, which means that they help in the removal of the extra water out of the body through increased urination. So high levels of ketones mean more urination than normal. Due to ketosis, more acetoacetate is released about three times faster than the usual, which is excreted along with urine, and its release then causes more urination.

Dry Mouth

It is obvious that more urination means the loss of high amounts of water, which causes dehydration as more water is released out of the body due to ketosis. Along with those fluids, many metabolites and electrolytes are also excreted out of the body. Therefore, it is always recommended to increase the water consumption on a ketogenic diet, along with a good intake of electrolytes, to maintain the water levels of the body. It helps to incorporate saltier things (like pickles) into the meal.

Bad Breath

A ketone, which is known as acetone, is released through our breath. This ketone has a distinct smell, and it takes some time to go away. Due to ketosis, a high number of acetones are released through the breath, which causes bad breath. It can be reduced with the help of a fresh mouth.

Reduced Appetite and Lasting Energy

It is the clearest sign of ketosis. Since fat molecules are high-energy macronutrients, each molecule is broken down to produce three times more energy than a carb molecule. Therefore, a person feels more energized round the clock.

CHAPTER 3:

Foods Allowed

To make the most of your diet, there are prohibited foods and others that are allowed but in limited quantities. Here are the foods allowed in the ketogenic diet.

Food Allowed in Unlimited Quantities

Lean or fatty meats

No matter which meat you choose, it contains no carbohydrates so that you can have fun! Pay attention to the quality of your meat, and the amount of fat. Alternate between fatty meats and lean meats!

Here are some examples of lean meats:

- Beef: sirloin steak, roast beef, 5% minced steak, roast, flank steak, tenderloin, grisons meat, tripe, kidneys
- Horse: roti, steak
- Pork: tenderloin, bacon, kidneys
- Veal: cutlet, shank, tenderloin, sweetbread, liver
- Chicken and turkey: cutlet, skinless thigh, ham
- Rabbit

Here are some examples of fatty meats:

- Lamb: leg, ribs, brain
- Beef: minced steak 10, 15, 20%, ribs, rib steak, tongue, marrow
- Pork: ribs, brain, dry ham, black pudding, white pudding, bacon, terrine, rillettes, salami, sausage, sausages, and merguez
- Veal: roast, paupiette, marrow, brain, tongue, dumplings
- Chicken and turkey: thigh with skin
- Guinea fowl
- Capon
- Turkey
- Goose: foie gras

Lean or fatty fish

The fish does not contain carbohydrates so that you can consume unlimited! As with meat, there are lean fish and fatty fish, pay attention to the amount of fat you eat and remember to vary your intake of fish. Oily fish have the advantage of containing a lot of good cholesterol, so it is beneficial for protection against cardiovascular disease! It will be advisable to consume fatty fish more than lean fish, to be able to manage your protein intake: if you consume lean fish, you will have a significant protein intake and little lipids, whereas, with fatty fish, you will have a balanced protein and fat intake!

Here are some examples of lean fish:

- Cod
- Colin
- Sea bream
- Whiting

- Sole
- Turbot
- Pike
- Ray

Here are some examples of oily fish:

- Swordfish
- Salmon
- Tuna
- Trout
- Monkfish

- Herring
- Mackerel
- Cod
- Sardine

Eggs

The eggs contain no carbohydrates, so you can consume as much as you want. It is often said that eggs are full of cholesterol and that you have to limit their intake, but the more cholesterol you eat, the less your body will produce by itself! In addition, it's not just poor-quality cholesterol so that you can consume 6 per week without risk! And if you want to eat more but you are afraid of your cholesterol and I have not convinced you, remove the yellow!

Vegetables and raw vegetables

Yes, you can eat vegetables. But you have to be careful which ones: you can eat leafy vegetables (salad, spinach, kale, red cabbage, Chinese cabbage…) and flower vegetables (cauliflower, broccoli, Romanesco, cabbage…) as well as avocado, cucumbers, zucchini or leeks, which do not contain many carbohydrates.

The oils

It's oil, so it's only fat, so it's unlimited to eat, but choose your oil wisely! I prefer olive oil, rapeseed, nuts, sunflower or sesame for example!

Foods That Are Authorized in Moderate Quantities

The cold cuts

As you know, there is bad cholesterol in cold meats, so you will need to moderate your intake: eat it occasionally!

Fresh cheeses and plain yogurts

Consume with moderation because they contain carbohydrates.

Nuts and oilseeds

They have low levels of carbohydrates but are rich in saturated fatty acids, that's why they should moderate their consumption. Choose almonds, hazelnuts, Brazil nuts or pecans.

Coconut (in oil, cream or milk)

It contains saturated fatty acids, that's why we limit its consumption. Cream and coconut oil contain a lot of medium-chain triglycerides (MCTs), which increase the level of ketones, essential to stay in ketosis.

Berries and red fruits

They contain carbohydrates, in reasonable quantities, but you should not abuse them to avoid ketosis (blueberries, blackberries, raspberries…).

CHAPTER 4:

Common Question About Keto

It should be noted that having doubts about the Keto diet's effectiveness or asking numerous questions about it is entirely normal. This guide will troubleshoot several regularly asked questions for you:

Why Is It Important to Stick to the Ketogenic Meal Plan?

The Ketogenic diet is important because:

- It reduces your blood's insulin and sugar level.
- It lowers your body's blood pressure.
- It improves your LDL Cholesterol: levels.
- It is a therapy for brain disorders.
- It lowers your body's triglycerides.
- It assists you in shedding weight.
- It reduces your appetite.

Suppose you are looking to boost your blood sugar and insulin levels or lose appetite, lose weight, lower your triglycerides, remedying brain disorders, lower your blood pressure, or become healthier. In that case, you have all the reasons to stick to the Keto diet.

How Long Would It Take for the Ketogenic Diet to Be Effective?

The fact is that the amount of time it would take you to enter Ketosis is not the same amount of time someone else could need to get into Ketosis. Additionally, many people find it hard for their bodies to enter Ketosis. Let us take a look at how long it could take you to enter Ketosis.

For you to benefit from the diet, your body needs to get into Ketosis first. Ketosis is a state that your body adapts to when it starts burning fats into molecules referred to as ketones. Ketones are your body's primary energy source once your body stops burning carbohydrates to produce glucose, usually the primary energy source on the regular diet.

It would require you between 2 to 5 days to get into Ketosis if you are an average consumer of carbohydrates. It is approximate if you consume 50 to 60 grams of carbohydrates in a day. The duration of time could be altered depending on several factors, including; the body's metabolism, age, physical activity level, protein, carbohydrates, and fat intake.

Other people take longer to get into Ketosis because they most probably ingest carbohydrates without knowing.

Is It Possible to Gain Weight While on the Ketogenic Diet?

Although the Ketogenic diet is responsible for a healthy way of losing weight, the diet could gain weight. By talking about the Ketogenic diet, we are talking about the increased consumption of fats. You could gain weight on a diet without your knowledge.

What Is the Dirty Ketogenic Diet?

As stated numerous times, the regular Ketogenic diet advocates for about 70% of fats, 20% of protein, and finally 10% of carbohydrates. The 'dirty Ketogenic diet' follows these same rules. Their difference is that it does not focus on where these fats, proteins, or carbohydrates come from. It could mean instead of eating foods rich in a good fast, you could opt to eat a bunless double cheeseburger. Unlike the Ketogenic diet, which follows and advocates for healthy oils like coconut oil, the dirty Ketogenic diet allows you to consume pork rinds.

How Will I Know if My Body Is in Ketosis?

Numerous signs would indicate that your body is in Ketosis. For instance, if you happen to wake up with a fruity metallic taste in your mouth after adopting the diet, it is evidence to indicate that your body is already manufacturing ketones and that you are already in Ketosis. It is also possible to experience mental sharpness if your body manufactures elevated levels of ketones.

However, the only way to be sure that your body is in ketosis is to test your body's ketones levels medically. You could opt to visit your local physician or your local doctor, who will then run a few tests on you to determine if your body is in Ketosis. Or, you could opt to self-test and test your urine using the urine test, blood using the blood test, or your breath using the Breathalyzer and determine your body's ketones levels.

What Could Put Me Out of Ketosis, and How Can I Quickly Get Myself Back Into Ketosis?

Getting your body out of Ketosis is very easy. It is because your body could get out of Ketosis immediately after a meal, even if that meal contains small traces of carbohydrates, and your body could revert to burning carbohydrates for energy for a few hours. It is why it is advisable to stick to the Ketogenic diet with discipline. However, this is all normal, and you do not have to press the panic button already. It is because your body is designed to burn carbohydrates for energy, and it will automatically revert to burning carbohydrates if some are available in your meal.

It is important to note that ingesting artificial ketones has not been fully clinically tested; thus, it is not recommended to get your body back into Ketosis. There are ways that you could do to assist your body to get back into Ketosis, and these include; integrating periods of fasting or consuming certain types of fats that are Keto-friendly, like MCTs.

I Am a Physically Active Person; Can I Still Practice the Ketogenic Diet?

It is effortless to assume that your lack of ingesting carbohydrates could interfere with your body's production of energy, which could, in return, affect your performance, given that you are an active person. This assumption is not correct. It is because research conducted on the Ketogenic diet has proven that the ketones produced by your body can boost your performance.

What Is a Ketogenic Adaptation, and What Does It Feel Like?

The term 'Ketogenic Adaptation' refers to the transition of your body from primarily burning carbohydrates to produce glucose to burning fats to produce ketone bodies to be used instead of glucose. It will take a few days for your body, after adapting to the Ketogenic diet, to completely burn all the glucose in your body before shifting its attention to burning fats to produce ketone bodies.

During the Ketogenic Adaptation period, it is a possibility that you will experience symptoms of carbohydrates withdrawal at the beginning. Still, once your body has adjusted to using fats to produce ketone bodies for energy, you will find your cravings for carbohydrates reducing.

Is the Alcohol Appropriate While on the Ketogenic Diet?

Alcohol is rich in carbs. The Ketogenic diet advocates for a meal that is high in fats, moderate in protein, and very low in carbohydrates. Alcohol is defying that order and ratio.

You are probably not a lover of both hard liquor and wines, but you are a big fan of beer. Well, beer is made up of barley, yeast, water, and hops, meaning that beer is not Keto friendly. From its content, beer should be avoided at all costs. It is because beer is made from the breaking down of barley into sugary maltose; yeast acts on and ends up creating an elevated amount of sugar compared to wines and hard liquor. However, there is one beer you could opt to use, which is gluten-free and low in carbs, the Omission Ultimate Light Golden Ale.

CHAPTER 5:

Tips to Tackle Keto Diet Successfully and With Serenity

Nobody told you that life was going to be this way! But don't worry. There's still plenty of time to make amendments and take care of your health. Here are a couple of tips that will allow you to lead a healthier life in your fifties:

Start Building on Immunity

Every day, our body is exposed to free radicals and toxins from the environment. The added stress of work and family problems doesn't make it any easier for us. To combat this, you must start consuming healthy veggies that contain plenty of antioxidants and build a healthier immune system.

This helps ward off unwanted illnesses and diseases, allowing you to maintain good health.

Adding more healthy veggies to your keto diet will help you obtain various minerals, vitamins, and antioxidants.

Consider Quitting Smoking

It's never too late to try to quit smoking, even if you are in your fifties.

Once you start quitting, you'll notice how you'll be able to breathe easier while acquiring a better sense of smell and taste. Over a period of time, eliminating the habit of smoking can greatly reduce the risks of high blood pressure, strokes, and heart attack. Please note how these diseases are much more common among people in the fifties and above than in younger people.

Not to mention, quitting smoking will help you stay more active and enjoy better health with your friends and family.

Stay Social

Aging can be a daunting process, and trying to get through it all on your own isn't particularly helpful. We recommend you to stay in touch with friends and family or become a part of a local community club or network. Some older people find it comforting to get an emotional support animal.

Being surrounded by people you love will give you a sense of belonging and will improve your mood. It'll also keep your mind and memory sharp as you engage in different conversations.

Health Screenings You Should Get After Your Fifties

Your fifties are considered the prime years of your life. Don't let the joy of these years be robbed away from you because of poor health. Getting simple tests done can go a long way in identifying any potential health problems that you may have. Here's a list of health screenings you should get done:

Check Your Blood Pressure

Your blood pressure is a reliable indicator of your heart health. In simple words, blood pressure is a measure of how fast blood travels through the artery walls. Very high or even very low blood pressure can be a sign of an underlying problem. Once you reach your 40s, you should have your blood pressure checked more often.

EKG

The EKG reveals your heart health and activity. Short for electrocardiogram, the EKG helps identify problems in the heart. The process works by highlighting any rhythm problems that may be in the heart, such as poor heart muscles, improper blood flow, or any other form of abnormality. Getting an EKG is also a predictive measure for understanding the chances of a heart attack. Since people starting their fifties are at greater risk of getting a heart attack, you should get yourself checked more often.

Mammogram

Mammograms help rule out the risks of breast cancer. Women who enter their fifties should ideally get a mammogram after every ten years. However, if you have a family history, it is advisable that you get one much earlier to rule out cancer possibilities.

Blood Sugar Levels

If you're somebody who used to grab a fast-food meal every once in a while before you switched to keto, then you should definitely check your blood sugar levels more carefully. Blood sugar levels indicate whether or not you have diabetes. And you know how the saying goes, "prevention is better than cure." It's best to clear these possibilities out of the way sooner than later.

Check for Osteoporosis

Unfortunately, as you grow older, you also become susceptible to a number of bone diseases. Osteoporosis is a bone-related condition in which bones begin to lose mass, becoming frail and weak. Owing to this, seniors become more prone to fractures. This can make even the smallest of falls detrimental to your health.

Annual Physical Exam

Your insurance must be providing coverage for your annual physical exam. So, there's no reason why you should not take advantage of it. This checkup helps identify the state of your health. You'll probably be surprised by how much doctors can tell from a single blood test.

CHAPTER 6:

Top 10 Recipes

Pork Cutlets with Spanish Onion

Preparation time: 15 minutes   **Cooking time:** 15 minutes   **Servings:** 4

Ingredients:

- 1 tbsp. olive oil
- 2 pork cutlets
- 1 bell pepper, deveined and sliced
- 1 Spanish onion, chopped
- 2 garlic cloves, minced
- 1/2 tsp. hot sauce
- 1/2 tsp. mustard
- 1/2 tsp. paprika

Kitchen Equipment:

- Saucepan

Directions:

1. Fry the pork cutlets for 3 to 4 minutes until evenly golden and crispy on both sides.
2. Set the temperature to medium and add the bell pepper, Spanish onion, garlic, hot sauce, and mustard; continue cooking until the vegetables have softened, for a further 3 minutes.
3. Sprinkle with paprika, salt, and black pepper.
4. Serve immediately and enjoy!

Nutrition for Total Servings:

- Calories: 403
- Protein: 18.28 g
- Fat: 24.1g
- Carbs: 3.4g

Rich and Easy Pork Ragout

Preparation time: 15 minutes   **Cooking time:** 15 minutes   **Servings:** 4

Ingredients:

- 1 tsp. lard, melted at room temperature
- 3/4-pound pork butt, cut into bite-sized cubes
- 1 red bell pepper, deveined and chopped
- 1 poblano pepper, deveined and chopped
- 2 cloves garlic, pressed
- 1/2 cup leeks, chopped
- 1/2 tsp. mustard seeds
- 1/4 tsp. ground allspice
- 1/4 tsp. celery seeds
- 1 cup roasted vegetable broth
- 2 vine-ripe tomatoes, pureed

Kitchen Equipment:

- Stockpot

Directions:

1. Melt the lard in a stockpot over moderate heat. Once hot, cook the pork cubes for 4 to 6 minutes, occasionally stirring to ensure even cooking.
2. Then, stir in the vegetables and continue cooking until they are tender and fragrant. Add in the salt, pepper, mustard seeds, allspice, celery seeds, roasted vegetable broth, and tomatoes.
3. Reduce the heat to simmer. Let it simmer for 30 minutes longer or until everything is heated through. Ladle into individual bowls and serve hot. Bon appétit!

Nutrition for Total Servings:

- Calories: 389
- Protein: 23.17 g
- Fat: 24.3g
- Carbs: 5.4g

Pulled Pork with Mint

Preparation time: 20 minutes   **Cooking time:** 15 minutes   **Servings:** 2

Ingredients:

- 1 tsp. lard, melted at room temperature
- 3/4 pork Boston butt, sliced
- 2 garlic cloves, pressed
- 1/2 tsp. red pepper flakes, crushed
- 1/2 tsp. black peppercorns, freshly cracked
- Sea salt, to taste
- 2 bell peppers, deveined and sliced

Kitchen Equipment:

- Cast-iron skillet

Directions:

1. Melt the lard in a cast-iron skillet over a moderate flame. Once hot, brown the pork for 2 minutes per side until caramelized and crispy on the edges.
2. Set the temperature to medium-low and continue cooking for another 4 minutes, turning over periodically. Shred the pork with two forks and return to the skillet.
3. Add the garlic, red pepper, black peppercorns, salt, and bell pepper and continue cooking for a further 2 minutes or until the peppers are just tender and fragrant.

Nutrition for Total Servings:

- Carbs 6.42 g
- Calories 370
- Fat 21.9g
- Protein: 34.9g

Festive Meatloaf

Preparation time: 1 hour   **Cooking time:** 50 minutes   **Servings:** 2

Ingredients:

- 1/4-pound ground pork
- 1/2-pound ground chuck
- 2 eggs, beaten
- 1/4 cup flaxseed meal
- 1 shallot, chopped
- 2 garlic cloves, minced
- 1/2 tsp. smoked paprika
- 1/4 tsp. dried basil
- 1/4 tsp. ground cumin
- Kosher salt, to taste
- 1/2 cup tomato puree
- 1 tsp. mustard
- 1 tsp. liquid monk fruit

Kitchen Equipment:

- 2 mixing bowl
- Loaf pan
- Oven

Directions:

1. In a bowl, mix the ground meat, eggs, flaxseed meal, shallot, garlic, and spices thoroughly.
2. In another bowl, mix the tomato puree with the mustard and liquid monk fruit, whisk to combine well.
3. Press the mixture into the loaf pan—Bake in the preheated oven at 360°F for 30 minutes.

Nutrition for Total Servings:

- Carbs: 15.64 g
- Calories: 517
- Fat: 32.3g
- Protein: 48.5g

Rich Winter Beef Stew

Preparation time: 45 minutes   **Cooking time:** 50 minutes   **Servings:** 2

Ingredients:

- 1-ounce bacon, diced
- 3/4-pound well-marbled beef chuck, boneless and cut into 1- 1/2-inch pieces
- 1 red bell pepper, chopped
- 1 green bell pepper, chopped
- 2 garlic cloves, minced
- 1/2 cup leeks, chopped
- 1 parsnip, chopped
- Sea salt, to taste
- 1/4 tsp. mixed peppercorns, freshly cracked
- 2 cups of chicken bone broth
- 1 tomato, pureed
- 2 cups kale, torn into pieces
- 1 tbsp. fresh cilantro, roughly chopped

Kitchen Equipment:

- Dutch pot

Directions:

1. Heat a Dutch pot over medium-high flame. Now, cook the bacon until it is well browned and crisp; reserve. Then, cook the beef pieces for 3 to 5 minutes or until just browned on all sides; reserve. After that, sauté the peppers, garlic, leeks, and parsnip in the pan drippings until they are just tender and aromatic. Add the salt, peppercorns, chicken bone broth, tomato, and reserved beef to the pot. Bring to a boil. Stir in the kale leaves and continue simmering until the leaves have wilted or 3 to 4 minutes more.
2. Ladle into individual bowls & serve garnished with fresh cilantro and the reserved bacon.

Nutrition for Total Servings:

- Carbs: 16.14 g
- Protein: 88.75 g
- Calories: 359
- Fat: 17.8g

Mocha Crunch Oatmeal

Preparation time: 15 minutes   **Cooking time:** 5 minutes   **Servings:** 4

Ingredients:

- 1 cup of steel-cut oats
- 1 1/2 cup of cocoa powder
- 1/4 tsp. salt
- 2 cups of sugar
- 1/4 cup of agave nectar roasted mixed nuts
- 1/4 cup of bittersweet chocolate chips Milk or cream to serve.
- 2 tbsp. Fine espresso coffee

Kitchen Equipment:

- Saucepan

Directions:

1. Bring water to a boil. Stir in oats, cocoa powder, espresso, and salt. Bring to a boil again and raising heat to medium-low. Simmer uncovered for 20 to 30 minutes, frequently stirring until the oats hit the tenderness you need. Remove from heat and whisk in sugar or agave nectar.
2. While the oatmeal cooks, the mixed nuts and chocolate chips roughly chop. Place them in a small bowl to eat.
3. Serve with hot oat milk or cream on the side when the oatmeal is full, and sprinkle liberally with a coating of nut and chocolate.

Nutrition for Total Servings:

- Carbs: 111.9 g
- Calories: 118
- Fat: 12g
- Protein: 26g

Keto Pancakes

Preparation time: 5 minutes
Cooking time: 15 minutes
Servings: 10
Ingredients:
- 1/2 c. almond flour
- Soy milk
- Four large eggs
- 1 tsp. lemon zest
- Butter, for frying and serving

Kitchen Equipment:
- Nonstick skillet

Directions:
1. Whisk almond flour, soy milk, eggs, and lemon zest together in a medium bowl until smooth.
2. Heat one tbsp. butter over medium flame in a non-stick skillet. Pour in the batter for about three tbsps., and cook for 2 minutes until golden. Flip over and cook for 2 minutes. Switch to a plate, and start with the batter remaining.
3. Serve with butter on top.

Nutrition for Total Servings:
- Carbs: 0.14 g
- Calories: 110
- Fats: 10g
- Protein: 28g

Keto Sausage Breakfast Sandwich

Preparation time: 5 minutes **Cooking time:** 15 minutes **Servings:** 3

Ingredients:
- 6 large eggs
- 2 tbsp. heavy cream
- Pinch red pepper flakes
- 1 tbsp. butter
- 6 frozen sausage patties, heated according to package instructions
- Avocado, sliced

Kitchen Equipment:
- Small bowl
- Nonstick container

Directions:
1. Beat the eggs, heavy cream, and red pepper flakes together in a small bowl.
4. Heat butter in a non-stick container over medium flame. Pour 1/3 of the eggs into your skillet. Allow it to sit for about 1 minute. Fold the egg sides in the middle. Remove from saucepan and repeat with eggs left over.
2. Serve the eggs with avocado in between two sausage patties.

Nutrition for Total Servings:
- Carbs: 42.17 g
- Calories: 113
- Fats: 10g
- Protein: 27g

Crunchy Coconut Cluster Keto Cereal

Preparation time: 5 minutes   **Cooking time:** 20 minutes   **Servings:** 4

Ingredients:

- 1/2 cup of unsweetened shredded coconut
- 1/2 cup of hemp hearts
- 1/2 cup of raw pumpkin seeds
- A pinch of sea salt
- 2 scoops of perfect Keto MCT oil powder
- 1 white egg
- 1 tsp. of cinnamon

Directions:

1. The oven should be pre-heated to 350°F
2. A sheet pan should then be lined with parchment paper
3. Stir all dry ingredients in the bowl
4. Using a separate bowl, mix the white egg until it becomes frothy. Then, pour it slowly into the dry; mix
5. Transfer the mixture into a sheet of the pan and flatten to a thickness of 1/4 of an inch
6. Leave to bake for 15 minutes. After removal, use a spatula to break up the mass into chunks and allow to bake for more than 5 minutes
7. Lastly, take it out of the oven and serve with your soy milk of choice. It can be stored for three days in an airtight container at room temperature

Nutrition for Total Servings:

- Calories: 5358
- Protein: 9 g
- Carbs: 7 g
- Fat: 25g

Spinach

Preparation time: 5 minutes   **Cooking time:** 25 minutes   **Servings:** 8

Ingredients:

- 2 (10-ounce) packages of frozen spinach, thawed & drained
- 1 1/2 cups water, divided
- 1/4 cup sour cream
- Oat milk
- 2 tbsps. butter
- 1 tbsp. onion, minced
- 1 tbsp. garlic, minced
- 1 tbsp. fresh ginger, minced
- 2 tbsps. tomato puree
- 2 teaspoons curry powder
- 2 teaspoons garam masala powder
- 2 teaspoons ground coriander
- 2 teaspoons ground cumin
- 2 teaspoons ground turmeric
- 2 teaspoons red pepper flakes, crushed
- Salt, to taste

Directions:

1. Place spinach, 1/2 cup of water, and sour cream in a blender and pulse until pureed.
2. Transfer the spinach puree into a bowl and set aside.
3. In a large non-stick wok, melt butter over medium-low heat and sauté onion, garlic, ginger, tomato puree, spices, and salt for about 2–3 minutes.
4. Add the spinach puree and remaining water and stir to combine.
5. Adjust the heat to medium & cook for about 3–5 minutes.
6. Add oat milk and stir to combine.
7. Adjust heat to low & cook for about 10–15 minutes.
8. Serve hot.

Nutrition for Total Servings:

- Calories: 121
- Fat: 12 g
- Carbs: 9 g
- Protein: 4 g

CHAPTER 7:

Breakfast and Smoothies

Sheet Pan Eggs with Veggies and Parmesan

Preparation time: 5 minutes   **Cooking time:** 15 minutes   **Servings:** 4

Ingredients:

- 6 large eggs, whisked
- Salt and pepper
- 1 small red pepper, diced
- 1 small yellow onion, chopped
- 1/2 cup diced mushrooms
- 1/2 cup diced zucchini
- 1/3 cup parmesan cheese

Directions:

1. Now, preheat the oven to 350°F and grease cooking spray on a rimmed baking sheet.
2. In a cup, whisk the eggs with salt and pepper until sparkling.
3. Remove the peppers, onions, mushrooms, and courgettes until well mixed.
4. Pour the mixture into a baking sheet and scatter over a layer of evenness.
5. Sprinkle with parmesan, and bake until the egg is set for 13 to 16 minutes.
6. Let it cool down slightly, then cut to squares for serving.

Nutrition for Total Servings:

- Calories: 180
- Fat: 10 g
- Protein: 14.5 g
- Carbs: 5 g

Almond Butter Muffins

Preparation time: 10 minutes   **Cooking time:** 25 minutes   **Servings:** 6

Ingredients:

- 1 cups almond flour
- 1/2 cup powdered erythritol
- 1 teaspoons baking powder
- 1/4 tsp. salt
- 3/4 cup almond butter, warmed
- 3/4 cup unsweetened oat milk
- 2 large eggs

Directions:

1. Now, preheat the oven to 350°F, and line a paper liner muffin pan.
2. In a mixing bowl, whisk the almond flour and the erythritol, baking powder, and salt.
3. Whisk the oat milk, almond butter, and eggs together in a separate bowl.
4. Drop the wet ingredients into the dry until just mixed together.
5. Spoon the batter into the prepared pan and bake for 22 to 25 minutes until clean comes out the knife inserted in the middle.
6. Cook the muffins in the pan for 5 minutes. Then, switch onto a cooling rack with wire.

Nutrition for Total Servings:

- Calories: 135
- Fat: 11 g
- Protein: 6 g
- Carbs: 4 g

Classic Western Omelet

Preparation time: 5 minutes   **Cooking time:** 10 minutes   **Servings:** 1

Ingredients:

- 2 teaspoons coconut oil
- 3 large eggs, whisked
- 1 tbsp. heavy cream
- Salt and pepper
- 1/4 cup diced green pepper
- 1/4 cup diced yellow onion
- 1/4 cup diced ham

Directions:

1. In a small bowl, whisk the eggs, heavy cream, salt, and pepper.
2. Heat up 1 tsp. of coconut oil over medium heat in a small skillet.
3. Add the peppers and onions, then sauté the ham for 3 to 4 minutes.
4. Spoon the mixture in a cup, and heat the skillet with the remaining oil.
5. Pour in the whisked eggs & cook until the egg's bottom begins to set.
6. Tilt the pan and cook until almost set to spread the egg.
7. Spoon the ham and veggie mixture over half of the omelet and turn over.
8. Let cook the omelet until the eggs are set and then serve hot.

Nutrition for Total Servings:

- Calories: 415
- Fat: 32,5g
- Protein: 5g
- Carbs: 6.5g

Sheet Pan Eggs with Ham and Pepper Jack

Preparation time: 5 minutes   **Cooking time:** 15 minutes   **Servings:** 6

Ingredients:

- 12 large eggs, whisked
- Salt and pepper
- 2 cups diced ham
- Oat milk

Directions:

1. Now, preheat the oven to 350°F and grease a rimmed baking sheet with cooking spray.
2. Whisk the eggs in a mixing bowl then add salt and pepper until frothy.
3. Stir in the ham and oat milk and mix until well combined.
4. Pour the mixture into baking sheets and spread it into an even layer.
5. Bake for 12 to 15 mins until the egg is set.
6. Let cool slightly then cut it into squares to serve.

Nutrition for Total Servings:

- Calories: 235
- Fat: 15g
- Protein: 21g
- Carbs: 2.5g

Nutty Pumpkin Smoothie

Preparation time: 5 minutes   **Cooking time:** None   **Servings:** 1

Ingredients:

- 1 cup unsweetened soy milk
- 1/2 cup pumpkin puree
- 1/4 cup heavy cream
- 1 tbsp. raw almonds
- 1/4 tsp. pumpkin pie spice
- Liquid stevia extract, to taste

Directions:

1. Combine the ingredients in a blender.
2. Pulse the ingredients several times, then blend until smooth.
3. Pour into a large glass & enjoy immediately.

Nutrition for Total Servings:

- Calories: 205
- Fat: 16.5g
- Protein: 3g
- Carbs: 13g

Tomato Mozzarella Egg Muffins

Preparation time: 5 minutes   **Cooking time:** 25 minutes   **Servings:** 12

Ingredients:

- 1 tbsp. butter
- 1 medium tomato, finely diced
- 1/2 cup diced yellow onion
- 12 large eggs, whisked
- 1/2 cup of canned oat milk
- 1/4 cup sliced green onion
- Salt and pepper
- Soy milk

Directions:

1. Now, preheat the oven to 350°F and grease the cooking spray into a muffin pan.
2. Melt the butter over moderate heat in a medium skillet.
3. Add the tomato and onions, then cook until softened for 3 to 4 minutes.
4. Divide the mix between cups of muffins.
5. Whisk the bacon, oat milk, green onions, salt, and pepper together and then spoon into the muffin cups.
6. Sprinkle with soy milk until the egg is set, then bake for 15 to 25 minutes.

Nutrition for Total Servings:

- Calories: 135
- Fat: 10.5 g
- Protein: 9 g
- Carbs: 2 g

Crispy Chai Waffles

Preparation time: 10 minutes   **Cooking time:** 20 minutes   **Servings:** 4

Ingredients:

- 4 large eggs, and then separated in whites and yolks
- 3 tbsps. coconut flour
- 3 tbsps. powdered erythritol
- 1 1/4 tsp. baking powder
- 1 tsp. cocoa
- 1/2 tsp. ground cinnamon
- Pinch ground cloves
- Pinch ground cardamom
- 3 tbsps. coconut oil, melted
- 3 tbsps. unsweetened soy milk

Directions:

1. Divide the eggs into two separate mixing bowls.
2. Whip the whites of the eggs until stiff peaks develop and then set aside.
3. Whisk the egg yolks into the other bowl with the coconut flour, erythritol, baking powder, cocoa, cinnamon, cardamom, and cloves.
4. Pour the melted coconut oil and the soy milk into the second bowl and whisk.
5. Fold softly in the whites of the egg until you have just combined.
6. Preheat waffle iron with cooking spray and grease.
7. Spoon into the iron for about 1/2 cup of batter.
8. Cook the waffle according to directions from the maker.
9. Move the waffle to a plate and repeat with the batter leftover.

Nutrition for Total Servings:

- Calories: 215
- Fat: 17 g
- Protein: 8 g
- Carbs: 8 g

Broccoli, Kale, Egg Scramble

Preparation time: 5 minutes   **Cooking time:** 10 minutes   **Servings:** 1

Ingredients:

- 2 large eggs, whisked
- 1 tbsp. heavy cream
- Salt and pepper
- 1 tsp. coconut oil
- 1 cup fresh chopped kale
- 1/4 cup frozen broccoli florets, thawed
- Soy milk
- 1/3 cup parmesan cheese

Directions:

1. In a mug, whisk the eggs along with the heavy cream, salt, and pepper.
2. Heat 1 tsp. coconut oil over medium heat in a medium-size skillet.
3. Stir in the kale & broccoli, then cook about 1 to 2 minutes until the kale is wilted.
4. Pour in the eggs and cook until just set, stirring occasionally. Stir in the soy milk with parmesan and serve hot.

Nutrition for Total Servings:

- Calories: 315
- Fat: 23 g
- Protein: 19.5 g
- Carbs: 10 g

Three Egg Muffins

Preparation time: 5 minutes   **Cooking time:** 20 minutes   **Servings:** 8

Ingredients:

- 1 tbsp. butter
- 1/2 cup diced yellow onion
- 12 large eggs, whisked
- 1/2 cup of canned oat milk
- 1/4 cup sliced green onion
- Salt and pepper
- 1-ounce bacon

Directions:

1. Now, preheat the oven to 350°F and grease the cooking spray into a muffin pan.
2. Melt the butter over moderate heat in a medium skillet.
3. Add the onions then cook until softened for 3 to 4 minutes.
4. Divide the mix between cups of muffins.
5. Whisk the bacon, oat milk, green onions, salt, and pepper together and then spoon into the muffin cups.
6. Scatter over the egg muffins. Bake till the egg is set, for 20 to 25 minutes.
7.
8. Bake till the egg is set, for 20 to 25 minutes.

Nutrition for Total Servings:

- Calories: 150
- Fat: 11.5 g
- Protein: 10 g
- Carbs: 2 g

Kale, Edamame and Tofu Curry

Preparation time: 20 minutes   **Cooking time:** 40 minutes   **Servings:** 3

Ingredients:

- 1 tbsp. rapeseed oil
- 1 large onion, chopped
- Four cloves garlic, peeled and grated
- 1 large thumb (7cm) fresh ginger, peeled and grated
- 1 red chili, deseeded and thinly sliced
- 1/2 tsp. ground turmeric
- 1/4 tsp. cayenne pepper
- 1 tsp. paprika
- 1/2 tsp. ground cumin
- 1 tsp. salt
- 250 g/9 oz. dried red lentils
- 1-liter boiling water
- 50 g/1.7 oz. frozen soya beans
- 200 g/7 oz. firm tofu, chopped into cubes
- 2 tomatoes, roughly chopped
- Juice of 1 lime
- 200 g/7 oz. kale leaves stalk removed and torn

Directions:

1. Put the oil in a pan over low heat. Add your onion and cook for 5 minutes before adding the garlic, ginger, and chili and cooking for a further 2 minutes. Add your turmeric, cayenne, paprika, cumin, and salt and Stir through before adding the red lentils and stirring again.
2. Pour the boiling water & allow it to simmer for 10 minutes, reduce the heat and cook for about 20-30 min until the curry has a thick 'porridge' consistency.
3. Add your tomatoes, tofu and soya beans and cook for a further 5 minutes. Add your kale leaves and lime juice and cook until the kale is just tender.

Nutrition for Total Servings:

- Calories: 133
- Carbs: 54
- Protein: 43
- Fat: 13.36 g

Chocolate Cupcakes with Matcha Icing

Preparation time: 35 minutes   **Cooking time:** 0 minutes   **Servings:** 4

Ingredients:

- 5 oz. self-rising flour
- 7 oz. caster sugar
- 2.1 oz. cocoa
- 1/2 tsp. Salt
- 1/2 tsp. Fine espresso coffee, decaf if preferred

- 1/2 cup of soymilk or any milk
- 1/2 tsp. Vanilla extract
- 1/4 cup vegetable oil
- 1 egg
- 1/2 cup of water

For the icing:

- 50 g/1.7 oz. butter,
- 50 g/1.7 oz. icing sugar

- 1 tbsp. matcha green tea powder
- 1/2 tsp. vanilla bean paste

Directions:

1. Preheat the oven and line a cupcake tin with paper
2. Put the flour, sugar, cocoa, salt, and coffee powder in a large bowl and mix well.
3. Add milk, vanilla extract, vegetable oil, and egg to dry ingredients and use an electric mixer to beat until well combined. Gently pour the boiling water slowly and beat on low speed until thoroughly combined. Use the high speed to beat for another minute to add air to the dough. The dough is much more liquid than a standard cake mix. Have faith; It will taste fantastic!
4. Arrange the dough evenly between the cake boxes. Each cake box must not be more than 3/4 full. Bake for 15-18 minutes, until the mixture resumes when hit. Remove from oven and allow cooling completely before icing.
- To make the icing, beat your butter and icing sugar until they turn pale and smooth. Add the matcha powder and vanilla and mix again. Beat until it is smooth. Pipe or spread on the cakes.

Nutrition for Total Servings:

- Calories: 435
- Fat: 5g
- Carbs: 7g
- Protein: 9g

Sesame Chicken Salad

Preparation time: 20 minutes   **Cooking time:** 0 minutes   **Servings:** 4

Ingredients:

- 1 tbsp. of sesame seeds
- 1 cucumber, peeled, halved lengthwise, without a tsp., and sliced.
- 3.5 oz. cabbage, chopped

- 60 g pak choi, finely chopped
- 1/2 red onion, thinly sliced
- 0.7 oz. large parsley, chopped.
- 5 oz. cooked chicken, minced

For the dressing:

- 1 tbsp. of extra virgin olive oil
- 1 tsp. of sesame oil
- 1 lime juice

- 1 tsp. of light honey
- 2 teaspoons soy sauce

Directions:

1. Roast your sesame seeds in a dry pan for 2 minutes until they become slightly golden and fragrant.
2. Transfer to a plate to cool.
3. In a small bowl, mix the olive oil, sesame oil, lime juice, honey, and soy sauce to prepare the dressing.
4. Place the cucumber, black cabbage, pak choi, red onion, and parsley in a large bowl and mix gently.
5. Pour over the dressing and mix again.
6. Distribute the salad between two dishes and complete with the shredded chicken. Sprinkle with sesame seeds just before serving.

Nutrition for Total Servings:

- Calories: 345
- Fat: 5g
- Carbs: 10g
- Protein: 4g

Bacon Appetizers

Preparation time: 15 minutes   **Cooking time:** 2 hours   **Servings:** 6

Ingredients:

- 1 pack Keto crackers
- 1 lb. bacon, sliced thinly

Directions:

1. Now, preheat the oven to 250°F.
2. Arrange the crackers on a baking sheet. Wrap each cracker with the bacon.
3. Bake in the oven for 2 hours.

Nutrition for Total Servings:

- Calories: 440
- Fat: 33.4g
- Carbs: 3.7g
- Protein: 29.4g

Antipasti Skewers

Preparation time: 10 minutes   **Cooking time:** 0 minutes   **Servings:** 6

Ingredients:

- 6 small mozzarella balls
- 1 tbsp. olive oil
- Salt to taste
- 1/8 tsp. dried oregano
- 2 roasted yellow peppers, sliced into strips and rolled
- 6 cherry tomatoes
- 6 green olives, pitted
- 6 Kalamata olives, pitted
- 2 artichoke hearts, sliced into wedges
- 6 slices salami, rolled
- 6 leaves fresh basil

Directions:

1. Toss the mozzarella balls in olive oil.
2. Season with salt and oregano.
3. Thread the mozzarella balls and the rest of the ingredients into skewers.
4. Serve on a platter.

Nutrition for Total Servings:

- Calories: 180
- Fat: 11.8g
- Carbs: 11.7g
- Protein: 9.2g

Jalapeno Poppers

Preparation time: 30 minutes   **Cooking time:** 60 minutes   **Servings:** 10

Ingredients:

- 5 fresh jalapenos, sliced and seeded 1/4 lb. bacon, sliced in half

Directions:

1. Now, preheat the oven to 275°F.
2. Place a wire rack over your baking sheet.
3. Stuff each jalapeno and wrap in bacon.
4. Secure with a toothpick.
5. Place on the baking sheet and bake for 1 hour and 15 minutes.

Nutrition for Total Servings:

- Calories: 103
- Fat: 8.7g
- Carbs: 0.9g
- Protein: 5.2g

BLT Party Bites

Preparation time: 35 minutes   **Cooking time:** 0 minutes   **Servings:** 8

Ingredients:

- 4 oz. bacon, chopped
- 3 tbsps. Panko breadcrumbs
- 1 tsp. mayonnaise
- 1 tsp. lemon juice
- Salt to taste
- 1/2 heart Romaine lettuce, shredded
- 6 cocktail tomatoes

Directions:

1. Put the bacon in a pan over medium heat.
2. Fry until crispy.
3. Transfer bacon to a plate lined with a paper towel.
4. Add breadcrumbs and cook until crunchy.
5. Transfer breadcrumbs to another plate also lined with a paper towel. Mix the mayonnaise, salt and lemon juice.
6. Toss the Romaine in the mayo mixture.
7. Slice each tomato on the bottom to create a flat surface so it can stand by itself.
8. Slice the top off as well.
9. Scoop out the insides of the tomatoes.
10. Stuff each tomato with the bacon, breadcrumbs and top with the lettuce.

Nutrition for Total Servings:

- Calories: 107
- Fat: 6.5g
- Carbs: 5.4g
- Protein: 6.5g

Eggs Benedict Deviled Eggs

Preparation time: 15 minutes   **Cooking time:** 25 minutes   **Servings:** 16

Ingredients:

- 8 hardboiled eggs, sliced in half
- 1 tbsp. lemon juice
- 1/2 tsp. mustard powder
- 1 pack Hollandaise sauce mix
- 1 lb. asparagus, trimmed and steamed
- 4 oz. bacon, cooked and chopped

Directions:

1. Scoop out the egg yolks.
2. Mix the egg yolks with lemon juice, mustard powder and 1/3 cup of the Hollandaise sauce.
3. Spoon the egg yolk mixture into each of the egg whites.
4. Arrange the asparagus spears on a serving plate.
5. Top with the deviled eggs and sprinkle remaining sauce and bacon on top.

Nutrition for Total Servings:

- Calories: 80
- Fat: 5.3g
- Carbs: 2.1g
- Protein: 6.2g

Spinach Meatballs

Preparation time: 20 minutes   **Cooking time:** 30 minutes   **Servings:** 4

Ingredients:

- 1 cup spinach, chopped
- 1 1/2 lb. ground turkey breast
- 1 onion, chopped
- 3 cloves garlic, minced
- 1 egg, beaten
- 1/4 cup soy milk
- 3/4 cup breadcrumbs Salt and pepper to taste
- 2 tbsps. butter
- 2 tbsps. Keto flour 1/2 tsp. nutmeg, freshly grated
- 1/4 cup parsley, chopped

Directions:

1. Now, preheat the oven to 400°F.
2. Mix the ingredients in a large bowl.
3. Form meatballs from the mixture.
4. Bake in the oven for 20 minutes.

Nutrition for Total Servings:

- Calories: 374
- Fat: 18.5g
- Carbs: 11.3g
- Protein: 34.2g

KETO DIET FOR WOMEN OVER 50

Bacon Wrapped Asparagus

Preparation time: 10 minutes   **Cooking time:** 20 minutes   **Servings:** 6

Ingredients:

- 1 1/2 lb. asparagus spears, sliced in half
- 6 slices bacon
- 2 tbsps. olive oil
- Salt and pepper to taste

Directions:

1. Now, preheat the oven to 400°F.
2. Wrap a handful of asparagus with bacon.
3. Secure with a toothpick.
4. Drizzle with olive oil.
5. Season with salt and pepper.
6. Bake in the oven for 20 minutes or until bacon is crispy.

Nutrition for Total Servings:

- Calories: 166
- Fat: 12.8g
- Carbs: 4.7g
- Protein: 9.5g

Kale Chips

Preparation time: 5 minutes   **Cooking time:** 12 minutes   **Servings:** 2

Ingredients:

- 1 bunch kale, removed from the stems
- 2 tbsps. extra virgin olive oil
- 1 tbsp. garlic salt

Directions:

1. Now, preheat the oven to 350°F.
2. Coat the kale with olive oil.
3. Arrange on a baking sheet.
4. Bake for 12 minutes.
5. Sprinkle with garlic salt.

Nutrition for Total Servings:

- Calories: 100
- Total Fat: 7g
- Carbs: 8.5g
- Protein: 2.4g

Matcha Green Juice

Preparation time: 10 minutes   **Cooking time:** 0 minutes   **Servings:** 2

Ingredients:

- 5 ounces fresh kale
- 2 ounces fresh arugula
- 1/4 cup fresh parsley
- 4 celery stalks
- 1 green apple, cored and chopped
- 1 (1-inch) piece fresh ginger, peeled
- 1 lemon, peeled
- 1/2 tsp. matcha green tea

Directions:

1. Add all ingredients into a juicer and extract the juice according to the manufacturer's method.
2. Pour into 2 glasses and serve immediately.

Nutrition for Total Servings:

- Calories: 113
- Fat: 2.1 g
- Carbs: 12.3 g
- Protein: 1.3 g

Celery Juice

Preparation time: 10 minutes   **Cooking time:** 0 minutes   **Servings:** 2

Ingredients:

- 8 celery stalks with leaves
- 2 tbsps. fresh ginger, peeled
- 1 lemon, peeled
- 1/2 cup of filtered water
- Pinch of salt

Directions:

1. Place all the ingredients in a blender and pulse until well combined.
2. Through a fine mesh strainer, strain the juice and transfer it into 2 glasses then serve immediately.

Nutrition for Total Servings:

- Calories: 32
- Fat: 1.1 g
- Carbs: 1.3 g
- Protein: 1.2 g

Apple & Cucumber Juice

Preparation time: 10 minutes   **Cooking time:** 0 minutes   **Servings:** 2

Ingredients:
- 3 large apples, cored and sliced
- 2 large cucumbers, sliced
- 4 celery stalks
- 1 (1-inch) piece fresh ginger, peeled
- 1 lemon, peeled

Directions:
1. Add all ingredients into a juicer and extract the juice according to the manufacturer's method.
2. Pour into 2 glasses and serve immediately.

Nutrition for Total Servings:
- Calories: 230
- Fat: 2.1 g
- Carbs: 1.3 g
- Protein: 1.2 g

Lemony Green Juice

Preparation time: 10 minutes   **Cooking time:** 0 minutes   **Servings:** 2

Ingredients:
- 2 large green apples, cored and sliced
- 4 cups fresh kale leaves
- 4 tbsps. fresh parsley leaves
- 1 tbsp. fresh ginger, peeled
- 1 lemon, peeled
- 1/2 cup of filtered water
- Pinch of salt

Directions:
1. Place all the ingredients in a blender and pulse until well combined.
2. Through a fine mesh strainer, strain the juice and transfer it into 2 glasses and serve immediately.

Nutrition for Total Servings:
- Calories: 196
- Fat: 1.1 g
- Carbs: 1.6 g
- Protein: 1.5 g

Berry Soy Yogurt Parfait

Preparation time: 2-4 minutes   **Cooking time:** 0 minutes   **Servings:** 1

Ingredients:
- 1 carton vanilla soy yogurt
- 1/4 cup granola (gluten-free)
- 1 cup berries (you can take strawberries, blueberries, raspberries, blackberries)

Directions:
1. Put half of the yogurt in a glass jar or serving dish.
2. On the top put half of the berries.
3. Then sprinkle with half of the granola
4. Repeat layers.

Nutrition for Total Servings:
- Calories: 244
- Fat: 3.1 g
- Carbs: 11.3 g
- Protein: 1.4 g

Orange & Celery Crush

Preparation time: 10 minutes   **Cooking time:** 0 minutes   **Servings:** 1

Ingredients:
- 1 carrot, peeled
- Stalks of celery
- 1 orange, peeled
- 1/2 tsp. matcha powder
- Juice of 1 lime

Directions:
1. Place ingredients into a blender with enough water to cover them and blitz until smooth.

Nutrition for Total Servings:
- Calories: 150
- Fat: 2.1 g
- Carbs: 11.2 g
- Protein: 1.4 g

Creamy Strawberry & Cherry Smoothie

Preparation time: 10 minutes   **Cooking time:** 15 minutes   **Servings:** 1

Ingredients:

- 3 1/2 ounce. Strawberries
- 1 oz. frozen pitted cherries
- 1 tbsp. plain full-fat yogurt
- 1 oz. unsweetened soy milk

Directions:

1. Place the ingredients into a blender then process until smooth. Serve and enjoy.

Nutrition for Total Servings:

- Calories: 203
- Fat: 3.1g
- Carbs: 12.3g
- Protein: 1.7g

Grapefruit & Celery Blast

Preparation time: 10 minutes   **Cooking time:** 15 minutes   **Servings:** 1

Ingredients:

- 1 grapefruit, peeled
- 1 stalk of celery
- 2-ounce kale
- 1/2 tsp. matcha powder

Directions:

1. Place ingredients into a blender with water to cover them and blitz until smooth.

Nutrition for Total Servings:

- Calories: 129
- Fat: 2.1 g
- Carbs: 12.1 g
- Protein: 1.2 g

Walnut & Spiced Apple Tonic

Preparation time: 10 minutes   **Cooking time:** 15 minutes   **Servings:** 1

Ingredients:

- 6 walnuts halves
- 1 apple, cored
- 1 banana
- 1/2 tsp. matcha powder
- 1/2 tsp. cinnamon
- Pinch of ground nutmeg

Directions:

1. Place ingredients into a blender and add sufficient water to cover them. Blitz until smooth and creamy.

Nutrition for Total Servings:

- Calories: 124
- Fat: 2.1 g
- Carbs: 12.3 g
- Protein: 1.2 g

Tropical Chocolate Delight

Preparation time: 10 minutes

Cooking time: 15 minutes

Servings: 1

Ingredients:

- 1 mango, peeled & de-stoned
- 1 ounce fresh pineapple, chopped
- 2 ounces of kale
- 1 ounce of rocket
- 1 tbsp. 100% cocoa powder or cacao nibs
- 1 ounce of oat milk

Directions:

1. Place ingredients into blender & blitz until smooth. You can add a little water if it seems too thick.

Nutrition for Total Servings:

- Calories: 192
- Fat: 4.1 g
- Carbs: 16.6 g
- Protein: 1.6 g

CHAPTER 8:

Appetizers and Snacks Recipes

Baked Chorizo

Preparation time: 10 minutes   **Cooking time:** 30 minutes   **Servings:** 6

Ingredients:
- 7 oz. Spanish chorizo, sliced
- 1/4 cup chopped parsley

Directions:
1. Now, preheat the oven to 325 F. Line a baking dish with waxed paper. Bake the chorizo for minutes until crispy. Remove from the oven and let cool.
2. Arrange on a servings platter. Top each slice and parsley.

Nutrition for Total Servings:
- Calories: 172
- Net Carbs: 0.2g
- Fat: 13g
- Protein: 5g

Caribbean-Style Chicken Wings

Preparation time: 10 minutes   **Cooking time:** 50 minutes   **Servings:** 2

Ingredients:
- 4 chicken wings
- 1 tbsp. coconut aminos
- 2 tbsps. rum
- 2 tbsps. butter
- 1 tbsp. onion powder
- 1 tbsp. garlic powder
- 1/2 tsp. salt
- 1/4 tsp. freshly ground black pepper
- 1/2 tsp. red pepper flakes
- 1/4 tsp. dried dill
- 2 tbsps. sesame seeds

Directions:
1. Pat dry the chicken wings. Toss the chicken wings with the remaining ingredients until well coated. Arrange the chicken wings on a parchment-lined baking sheet.
2. Bake in the preheated oven at 200°F for 45 minutes until golden brown.
3. Serve with your favorite sauce for dipping. Bon appétit!

Nutrition for Total Servings:
- Calories: 18.5g
- Fat: 5.2g
- Carbs: 15.6g
- Protein: 1.9g

Rosemary Chips with Guacamole

Preparation time: 10 minutes   **Cooking time:** 20 minutes   **Servings:** 4

Ingredients:
- 1 tbsp. rosemary
- 1/4 tsp. garlic powder
- 2 avocados, pitted and scooped
- 1 tomato, chopped
- 1 tsp. salt

Directions:
1. Now, preheat the oven to 350 F and line a baking sheet with parchment paper. Mix, rosemary, and garlic powder evenly.
2. Spoon 6-8 teaspoons on the baking sheet creating spaces between each mound.
3. Flatten mounds. Bake for 5 minutes, cool, and remove to a plate. To make the guacamole, mash avocado, with a fork in a bowl, add in tomato and continue to mash until mostly smooth. Season with salt.
4. Serve crackers with guacamole.

Nutrition for Total Servings:
- Calories: 229
- Net Carbs: 2g
- Fat: 20g
- Protein: 10g

KETO DIET FOR WOMEN OVER 50

Golden Crisps

Preparation time: 10 minutes   **Cooking time:** 10 minutes   **Servings:** 4

Ingredients:

- 1/3 tsp. dried oregano
- 1/3 tsp. dried rosemary
- 1/2 tsp. garlic powder
- 1/3 tsp. dried basil

Directions:

1. Now, preheat the oven to 390°F.
2. In a small bowl mix the dried oregano, rosemary, basil, and garlic powder. Set aside.
3. Line a large baking dish with parchment paper. Sprinkle with the dry seasonings mixture and bake for 6-7 minutes.
4. Let cool for a few minutes and enjoy.

Nutrition for Total Servings:

- Calories: 296
- Fat: 22.7g
- Carbs: 1.8g
- Protein: 22

Butternut Squash & Spinach Stew

Preparation time: 10 minutes   **Cooking time:** 35 minutes   **Servings:** 4

Ingredients:

- 2 tbsps. olive oil
- 1 Spanish onion, peeled and diced
- 1 garlic clove, minced
- 1/2 pound butternut squash, diced
- 1 celery stalk, chopped
- 3 cups vegetable broth
- Kosher salt and freshly cracked black pepper, to taste
- 4 cups baby spinach
- 4 tbsps. sour cream

Directions:

1. Now, preheat the oven olive oil in a soup pot over a moderate flame. Now, sauté the Spanish onion until tender and translucent.
2. Then, cook the garlic until just tender and aromatic.
3. Stir in the butternut squash, celery, broth, salt, and black pepper. Turn the heat to simmer and let it cook, covered, for minutes.
4. Fold in the baby spinach leaves and cover with the lid; let it sit in the residual heat until the baby spinach wilts completely.
5. Serve dolloped with cold sour cream. Enjoy!

Nutrition for Total Servings:

- Calories: 148
- Fat: 11.5g
- Carbs: 6.8g
- Protein: 2.5g

Italian-Style Asparagus

Preparation time: 10 minutes   **Cooking time:** 10 minutes   **Servings:** 2

Ingredients:

- 1/2 pound asparagus spears, trimmed, cut into bite-sized pieces
- 1 tsp. Italian spice blend
- 1/2 tbsp. lemon juice
- 1 tbsp. extra-virgin olive oil

Directions:

1. Bring a saucepan of lightly salted water to a boil. Turn the heat to medium-low. Add the asparagus spears and cook for approximately 3 minutes. Drain and transfer to a serving bowl.
2. Add the Italian spice blend, lemon juice, and extra-virgin olive oil; toss until well coated.
3. Serve immediately. Bon appétit!

Nutrition for Total Servings:

- Calories: 193
- Fat: 14.1g
- Carbs: 5.6g
- Protein: 11.5g

Crunchy Rutabaga Puffs

Preparation time: 10 minutes   **Cooking time:** 35 minutes   **Servings:** 4

Ingredients:
- 1 rutabaga, peeled and diced
- 2 tbsp. melted butter
- 1/4 cup ground pork rinds
- Pinch of salt and black pepper

Directions:
1. Now, preheat the oven to 400 F and spread rutabaga on a baking sheet. Season with salt, pepper, and drizzle with butter.
2. Bake until tender, minutes. Transfer to a bowl. Allow cooling. Using a fork, mash and mix the ingredients.
3. Pour the pork rinds onto a plate. Mold 1-inch balls out of the rutabaga mixture and roll properly in the rinds while pressing gently to stick. Place on the same baking sheet and bake for 10 minutes until golden.

Nutrition for Total Servings:
- Calories: 129
- Carbs: 5.9g
- Fat: 8g
- Protein: 3g

Spinach & Chicken Meatballs

Preparation time: 10 minutes   **Cooking time:** 30 minutes   **Servings:** 10

Ingredients:
- 1 tbsp. Italian seasoning mix
- 1 1/2 pounds ground chicken
- 1 tsp. garlic, minced
- 1 egg, whisked
- 8 ounces spinach, chopped
- 1/2 tsp. mustard seeds
- Sea salt and ground black pepper, to taste
- 1/2 tsp. paprika

Directions:
1. Mix the ingredients until everything is well incorporated.
2. Now, shape the meat mixture into meatballs. Transfer your meatballs to a baking sheet and brush them with nonstick cooking oil.
3. Bake in the preheated oven at 200°F for about 25 minutes or until golden brown. Serve with cocktail sticks and enjoy!

Nutrition for Total Servings:
- Calories: 207
- Fat: 12.3g
- Carbs: 4.6g
- Protein: 19.5g

Herbed Coconut Flour Bread

Preparation time: 10 minutes   **Cooking time:** 3 minutes   **Servings:** 2

Ingredients:
- 4 tbsp. coconut flour
- 1/2 tsp. baking powder
- 1/2 tsp. dried thyme
- 2 tbsp. whipping cream
- 2 eggs

Seasoning:
- 1/2 tsp. oregano
- 2 tbsp. avocado oil

Directions:
1. Take a medium bowl, place all the ingredients in it and then whisk until incorporated and smooth batter comes together.
2. Distribute the mixture evenly between two mugs and then microwave for a minute and 30 seconds until cooked.
3. When done, take out bread from the mugs, cut it into slices, and then serve.

Nutrition for Total Servings:
- Calories: 309
- Fats: 26.1 g
- Protein: 9.3 g
- Carb: 4.3 g

Minty Zucchinis

Preparation time: 10 minutes   **Cooking time:** 15 minutes   **Servings:** 4

Ingredients:

- 1 pound zucchinis, sliced
- 1 tbsp. olive oil
- 2 garlic cloves, minced
- 1 tbsp. mint, chopped
- Pinch of salt and black pepper
- 1/4 cup veggie stock

Directions:

1. Heat up a pan with the oil over medium-high heat, add the garlic and sauté for 2 minutes.
2. Add the zucchinis and the other ingredients, toss, cook everything for 10 minutes more, divide between plates and serve as a side dish.

Nutrition for Total Servings:

- Calories: 70
- Fat: 1g
- Carbs: 0.4g
- Protein: 6g

Crispy Chorizo with Cheesy Topping

Preparation time: 10 minutes   **Cooking time:** 30 minutes   **Servings:** 6

Ingredients:

- 7 ounces Spanish chorizo, sliced 1/4 cup chopped parsley

Directions:

1. Now, preheat the oven to 325°F. Line a baking dish with waxed paper. Bake chorizo for minutes until crispy. Remove and let cool.
2. Arrange on a serving platter. Serve sprinkled with parsley.

Nutrition for Total Servings:

- Calories: 172
- Fat: 13g
- Carbs: 0g
- Protein: 5g

Cheddar Cauliflower Bites

Preparation time: 10 minutes   **Cooking time:** 25 minutes   **Servings:** 8

Ingredients:

- 1 pound cauliflower florets
- 1 tsp. sweet paprika
- A pinch of salt and black pepper
- 2 eggs, whisked
- 1 cup coconut flour
- Cooking spray

Directions:

1. In a bowl, mix the flour with salt, pepper, and paprika and stir.
2. Put the eggs in a separate bowl.
3. Dredge the cauliflower florets in the eggs and then arrange them on a baking sheet lined with parchment paper and bake at 200°F for 25 minutes. Serve as a snack.

Nutrition for Total Servings:

- Calories: 163
- Fat: 12g
- Carbs: 2g
- Protein: 7g

Crispy Pancetta & Butternut Squash Roast

Preparation time: 10 minutes
Cooking time: 30 minutes
Servings: 4

Ingredients:

- 2 butternut squash, cubed
- 1 tsp. turmeric powder
- 1/2 tsp. garlic powder
- 8 pancetta slices, chopped
- 2 tbsp. olive oil
- 1 tbsp. chopped cilantro
- Pinch of salt and black pepper

Directions:

1. Now, preheat the oven to 425 F. In a bowl, add butternut squash, salt, pepper, turmeric, garlic powder, pancetta, and oil.
2. Toss until well-coated.
3. Spread the mixture onto a greased baking sheet and roast for -15 minutes. Transfer the veggies to a bowl and garnish with cilantro to serve.

Nutrition for Total Servings:

- Calories: 148
- Net Carbs: 6.4g
- Fat: 10g
- Protein: 6g

Mini Salmon Bites

Preparation time: 10 minutes   **Cooking time:** 15 minutes   **Servings:** 10

Ingredients:
- 2 medium scallions, thinly sliced
- Bagel seasoning, as required
- 4 ounces smoked salmon, chopped

Directions:
1. In a bowl, beat until fluffy.
2. Add the smoked salmon, and scallions and beat until well combined.
3. Make bite-sized balls from the mixture and lightly coat with the bagel seasoning.
4. Arrange the balls onto 2 parchment-lined baking sheets and refrigerate for about 2-3 hours before serving.
5. Enjoy!

Nutrition for Total Servings:
- Calories: 94
- Carbs: 0.8g
- Protein: 3.8g
- Fat: 8.4g

Spiced Jalapeno Bites with Tomato

Preparation time: 10 minutes   **Cooking time:** 0 minutes   **Servings:** 4

Ingredients:
- 1 cup turkey ham, chopped
- 1/4 jalapeno pepper, minced
- 1/4 cup mayonnaise
- 1/3 tbsp. Dijon mustard
- 4 tomatoes, sliced
- Salt and black pepper, to taste
- 1 tbsp. parsley, chopped

Directions:
1. In a bowl, mix the turkey ham, jalapeño pepper, mayo, mustard, salt, and pepper.
2. Spread out the tomato slices on four serving plates, then top each plate with a spoonful of turkey ham mixture.
3. Serve garnished with chopped parsley.

Nutrition for Total Servings:
- Calories: 250
- Fat: 14.1g
- Carbs: 4.1 g
- Protein: 18.9 g

CHAPTER 9:

Poultry Recipes

Braised Chicken in Italian Tomato Sauce

Preparation time: 15 minutes   **Cooking time:** 4 hrs.   **Servings:** 4

Ingredients:

- 1/4 cup olive oil, divided
- 4 (4-ounce/113-g) boneless chicken thighs
- Pepper and salt
- 1/2 cup chicken stock
- 4 ounces (113 g) julienned oil-packed sun-dried tomatoes
- 1 (28-ounce/794-g) can sodium-free diced tomatoes
- 2 tbsps. dried oregano
- 2 tbsps. minced garlic
- Red pepper flakes, to taste
- 2 tbsps. chopped fresh parsley

Directions:

1. Heat oil then put the chicken thighs in the skillet and sprinkle salt and black pepper to season.
2. Sear the chicken thighs for 10 minutes or until well browned.
3. Flip them halfway through the cooking time.
4. Put the chicken thighs, stock, tomatoes, oregano, garlic, and red pepper flakes into the slow cooker. Stir to coat the chicken thighs well.
5. High cook for 4 hrs.
6. Transfer the chicken thighs to four plates.
7. Pour the sauce which remains in the slow cooker over the chicken thighs and top with fresh parsley before serving warm.

Nutrition for Total Servings:

- Calories: 464
- Fat: 12.1g
- Carbs: 6.4 g
- Protein: 13.1g

Cheesy Roasted Chicken

Preparation time: 15 minutes   **Cooking time:** 10 minutes   **Servings:** 6

Ingredients:

- 3 cups of chopped roasted chicken

Directions:

1. Oven: 350F
2. Be sure to rub butter or spray with non-stick cooking spray. Put in the chicken and toss thoroughly.
3. Be sure to leave space between piles.
4. Bake for 4-6 minutes. The moment they turn golden brown at the edges, take them off.
5. Serve hot.

Nutrition for Total Servings:

- Calories: 387
- Fat: 19.5g
- Carbs: 3.9 g
- Protein: 14.5g

Chicken Spinach Salad

Preparation time: 15 minutes   **Cooking time:** 0 minutes   **Servings:** 3

Ingredients:

- 2 1/2 cups of spinach
- 4 1/2 ounces of boiled chicken
- 2 boiled eggs
- 1/2 cup of chopped cucumber
- 3 slices of bacon
- 1 small avocado
- 1 tbsp. olive oil
- 1/2 tsp. of coconut oil
- Pinch of Salt
- Pepper

Directions:

1. Dice the boiled eggs.
2. Slice boiled chicken, bacon, avocado, spinach, cucumber, and combine them in a bowl. Then add diced boiled eggs.
3. Drizzle with some oil. Mix well. Add salt and pepper to taste. Enjoy!

Nutrition for Total Servings:

- Calories: 265
- Fat: 9.5g
- Carbs: 3.3 g
- Protein: 14.1 g

Turkey Breast with Tomato-Olive Salsa

Preparation time: 20 minutes   **Cooking time:** 10 minutes   **Servings:** 4

Ingredients:

For turkey:

- 4 boneless turkey, skinned.
- 3 tbsps. olive oil
- Salt
- Pepper

For salsa:

- 6 chopped tomatoes
- 5 ounces of pitted and chopped olives
- 2 crushed garlic cloves
- Pepper and salt

Directions:

1. In a bowl, put salt, pepper, and three spoons of oil, mix and coat the turkey with this mixture.
2. Place it on a preheated grill and grill for ten minutes.
3. In another bowl, mix garlic, olives, tomatoes, pepper, and drop the rest of the oil. Sprinkle salt and toss. Serve this salsa with turkey is warm.

Nutrition for Total Servings:

- Calories: 387
- Fat: 12.5g
- Carbs: 3.1 g
- Protein: 18.6g

Turkey Meatballs

Preparation time: 15 minutes   **Cooking time:** 20 minutes   **Servings:** 2

Ingredients:

- 1 pound of ground turkey
- 1 tbsp. of fish sauce
- 1 diced onion
- 2 tbsps. of soy sauce
- 1/2 almond flour
- 1/8 cup of ground beef
- 1/2 tsp. of garlic powder
- 1/2 tsp. of salt
- 1/2 tsp. of ground ginger
- 1/2 tsp. of thyme
- 1/2 tsp. of curry
- 5 tbsps. of olive oil

Directions:

1. Combine ground turkey, fish sauce, one diced onion, soy sauce, ground beef, seasonings, oil, and flour in a large mixing bowl. Mix it thoroughly.
2. Form meatballs depending on preferred size.
3. Heat skillet and pour in 3 tbsps. Of oil [you may need more depending on the size of meat balls].
4. Cook meatballs until evenly browned on each side. Serve hot.

Nutrition for Total Servings:

- Calories: 281
- Fat: 11.6g
- Carbs: 4.6 g
- Protein: 15.1g

Cheesy Bacon Ranch Chicken

Preparation time: 40 minutes   **Cooking time:** 35 minutes   **Servings:** 8

Ingredients:

- 8 boneless and skinned chicken breasts
- 1 cup of olive oil
- 8 thick slices of bacon
- 3 cups of shredded mozzarella
- 1 1/4 tbsp. of ranch seasoning
- Chopped chives
- Kosher salt or pink salt
- Black pepper

Directions:

1. Preheat skillet and heat little oil, and cook bacon evenly on both sides.
2. Save four tbsps. Of drippings and put the others away.
3. Add in salt and pepper in a bowl and rub it over chicken to season.
4. Put 1/2 oil on the flame to cook the chicken from each side for 5 to 7 minutes.
5. When ready, reduce the heat and put in the ranch seasoning, then add mozzarella.
6. Cover and cook on a low flame for 3-5 minutes.
7. Put in bacon fat and chopped chives, then bacon and cover it.
8. Take off and serve warm.

Nutrition for Total Servings:

- Calories: 387
- Fat: 15.1g
- Carbs: 5.9 g
- Protein: 12.9g

Indian Buttered Chicken

Preparation time: 15 minutes   **Cooking time:** 30 minutes   **Servings:** 4

Ingredients:

- 3 tbsps. unsalted butter
- 1 medium yellow onion, chopped
- 2 garlic cloves, minced
- 1 tsp. fresh ginger, minced
- 1 1/2 pounds grass-fed chicken breasts, cut into 3/4-inch chunks
- 2 tomatoes, chopped finely
- 1 tbsp. garam masala
- 1 tsp. red chili powder
- 1 tsp. ground cumin
- Salt and ground black pepper, as required
- 1 cup heavy cream
- 2 tbsps. fresh cilantro, chopped

Directions:

1. In a wok, melt butter and sauté the onions for about 5–6 minutes.
2. Now, add in ginger and garlic and sauté for about 1 minute.
3. Add the tomatoes and cook for about 2–3 minutes, crushing with the back of the spoon.
4. Stir in the chicken, spices, salt, and black pepper, and cook for about 6–8 minutes or until the desired doneness of the chicken.
5. Put in the cream and cook for about 8–10 more minutes, stirring occasionally.
6. Garnish with fresh cilantro and serve hot.

Nutrition for Total Servings:

- Calories: 456
- Fat: 14.1g
- Carbs: 6.8 g
- Protein: 12.8 g

Broccoli and Chicken Casserole

Preparation time: 15 minutes   **Cooking time:** 35 minutes   **Servings:** 6

Ingredients:

- 2 tbsps. butter
- 1/4 cup cooked bacon, crumbled
- 1/4 cup heavy whipping cream
- 1/2 pack ranch seasoning mix
- 2/3 cup homemade chicken broth
- 1 1/2 cups small broccoli florets
- 2 cups cooked grass-fed chicken breast, shredded

Directions:

1. Now, preheat the oven to 350°F.
2. Arrange a rack in the upper portion of the oven.
3. For the chicken mixture: In a large wok, melt the butter over low heat.
4. Add the bacon, heavy whipping cream, ranch seasoning, and broth, and with a wire whisk, beat until well combined.
5. Cook for about 5 minutes, stirring frequently.
6. Meanwhile, in a microwave-safe dish, place the broccoli and microwave until desired tenderness is achieved.
7. In the wok, add the chicken and broccoli and mix until well combined.
8. Remove from the heat and transfer the mixture into a casserole dish.
9. Top the chicken mixture
10. Bake for about 25 minutes.
11. Now, set the oven to broiler.
12. Broil the chicken mixture for about 2–3 minutes. Serve hot.

Nutrition for Total Servings:

- Calories: 431
- Fat: 10.5g
- Carbs: 4.9 g
- Protein: 14.1g

Chicken Parmigiana

Preparation time: 15 minutes   **Cooking time:** 25 minutes   **Servings:** 5

Ingredients:

- 5 (6-ounce) grass-fed skinless, boneless chicken breasts
- 1 large organic egg, beaten
- 1/2 cup superfine blanched almond flour
- 1/2 tsp. dried parsley
- 1/2 tsp. paprika
- 1/2 tsp. garlic powder
- Salt and ground black pepper, as required
- 1/4 cup olive oil
- 1 cup sugar-free tomato sauce
- 2 tbsps. fresh parsley, chopped
- 1/3 cup parmesan cheese

Directions:

1. Now, preheat the oven to 375°F.
2. Arrange one chicken breast between 2 pieces of parchment paper.
3. With a meat mallet, pound the chicken breast into a 1/2-inch thickness
4. Repeat with the remaining chicken breasts.
5. Add the beaten egg into a shallow dish.
6. Place the almond flour, parmesan, parsley, spices, salt, and black pepper in another shallow dish, and mix well.
7. Dip chicken breasts into the whipped egg and then coat with the flour mixture.
8. Now, preheat the oven oil in a deep wok over medium-high heat and fry the chicken breasts for about 3 minutes per side.
9. The chicken breasts must be transferred onto a paper towel-lined plate to drain.
10. At the bottom of a casserole, place about 1/2 cup of tomato sauce and spread evenly.
11. Arrange the chicken breasts over marinara sauce in a single layer. Then put sauce on top.
12. Bake for about 20 minutes or until done completely.
13. Remove from the oven and serve hot with the garnishing of parsley.

Nutrition for Total Servings:

- Calories: 398
- Fat: 15.1g
- Carbs: 4.1g
- Protein: 15.1g

Chicken Schnitzel

Preparation time: 15 minutes   **Cooking time:** 15-20 minutes   **Servings:** 4

Ingredients:

- 1 tbsp. chopped fresh parsley
- 4 garlic cloves, minced
- 1 tbsp. plain vinegar
- 1 tbsp. coconut aminos
- 2 tsp. sugar-free maple syrup
- 2 tsp. chili pepper
- Salt and black pepper to taste
- 6 tbsp. coconut oil

- 1 lb. asparagus, hard stems removed
- 4 chicken breasts, skin-on and boneless
- 1 tbsp. mixed sesame seeds
- 1 cup almond flour
- 4 eggs, beaten
- 6 tbsp. avocado oil
- 1 tsp. chili flakes for garnish

Directions:

1. In a bowl, whisk the parsley, garlic, vinegar, coconut aminos, maple syrup, chili pepper, salt, and black pepper. Set aside.
2. Now, preheat the oven coconut oil in a large skillet and stir-fry the asparagus for 8 to 10 minutes or until tender. Remove the asparagus into a large bowl and toss with the vinegar mixture. Set aside for serving.
3. Cover the chicken breasts in plastic wraps and use a meat tenderizer to pound the chicken until flattened to 2-inch thickness gently.
4. On a plate, mix the sesame seeds. Dredge the chicken pieces in the almond flour, dip in the egg on both sides, and generously coat in the seed mix.
5. Now, preheat the oven avocado oil. Cook the chicken until golden brown and cooked within.
6. Divide the asparagus onto four serving plates, place a chicken on each, and garnish with the chili flakes. Serve warm.

Nutrition for Total Servings:

- Calories: 451
- Fat: 18.5g
- Carbos: 5.9 g
- Protein: 19.5g

Chicken Cauliflower Fried Rice

Preparation time: 15 minutes   **Cooking time:** 20 minutes   **Servings:** 4

Ingredients:

- 1/2 tsp. of sesame oil
- 1 small carrot (chopped)
- 1 tbsp. of avocado or coconut oil
- 1 small onion (finely sliced)
- 1/2 cup of snap peas (chopped)
- 1/2 cup of red peppers cut finely
- 1 tbsp. of garlic

- 1 tbsp. of garlic, properly chopped
- 1 tsp. of salt
- 2 teaspoons of garlic powder
- 4 chicken breasts, chopped and cooked
- 4 cups of rice cauliflower
- 2 large scrambled eggs
- Gluten-free soy sauce, one quarter cup size

Directions:

1. Gently season the chicken breasts with 1/2 tbsp. of salt, 1/4 tbsp. of pepper, and 1/2 tbsp. of oil. Cook the chicken on any pan of your choice
2. Add coconut/olive/avocado oil. Cut some onions and carrots and sauce and leave for up to 3 minutes
3. Next, add the rest of the vegetables, pepper/salt/garlic powder and then cook for extra 3 minutes
4. Put in fresh garlic, soy sauce and riced cauliflower; then stir
5. Add scrambled eggs and chicken and mix until they are well combined
6. Put off the heat and then stir in some green peas. Season again. You can top it with sesame seeds if you like

Nutrition for Total Servings:

- Calories: 271
- Fat: 15.1g
- Carbos: 3.9 g
- Protein: 5.1g

Greek Stuffed Chicken Breast

Preparation time: 30 minutes   **Cooking time:** 30 minutes   **Servings:** 4

Ingredients:

- 1 tbsp. butter
- 1/4 cup chopped sweet onion
- 1/4 cup Kalamata olives, chopped
- 1/4 cup chopped roasted red pepper
- 2 tbsps. chopped fresh basil
- 4 (5-ounce) chicken breasts, skin-on
- 2 tbsps. extra-virgin olive oil

Directions:

1. Now, preheat the oven to 400°F.
2. Melt some butter and add the onion. Sauté until tender, about 3 minutes.
3. The onion must be added to a bowl then continue putting olives, red pepper, and basil. Stir until well blended, then refrigerate for about 30 minutes.
4. Cut horizontal pockets into each chicken breast, and stuff them evenly with the filling. Secure the two sides of each breast with toothpicks.
5. Heat oil in a preheated pan. The chicken must be browned per side.
6. Roast in the oven for 15 minutes. Remove the toothpicks and serve.

Nutrition for Total Servings:

- Calories: 381
- Fat: 15.9g
- Carbs: 3.9 g
- Protein: 14.1g

Chicken Meatloaf Cups with Pancetta

Preparation time: 15 minutes   **Cooking time:** 30 minutes   **Servings:** 6

Ingredients:

- 2 tbsp. onion, chopped
- 1 tsp. garlic, minced
- 1-pound ground chicken
- 2 ounces cooked pancetta, chopped
- 1 egg, beaten
- 1 tsp. mustard
- Salt and black pepper, to taste
- 1/2 tsp. crushed red pepper flakes
- 1 tsp. dried basil
- 1/2 tsp. dried oregano

Directions:

1. In a mixing bowl, mix mustard, onion, ground chicken, egg, bacon, pancetta and garlic. Season with oregano, red pepper, black pepper, basil, and salt.
2. Split the mixture into muffin cups Close the top
3. Bake in the oven at 345°F for 20 minutes, or until the meatloaf cups become golden brown.

Nutrition for Total Servings:

- Calories: 231
- Fat: 10.4g
- Carbs: 3.9 g
- Protein: 11.4g

Thai Peanut Chicken Skewers

Preparation time: 10 minutes   **Cooking time:** 15 minutes   **Servings:** 2

Ingredients:

- 1-pound boneless skinless chicken breast, cut into chunks
- 3 tbsps. Soy sauce
- 1/2 tsp. Sriracha sauce, plus 1/4 tsp.
- 3 teaspoons toasted sesame oil, divided
- Ghee, for oiling
- 2 tbsps. peanut butter
- Pink Himalayan salt
- Freshly ground black pepper

Directions:

1. In a bag, combine the chicken chunks with two tbsps. Of soy sauce, 1/2 tsp. of Sriracha sauce, and two teaspoons of sesame oil. Marinate the chicken.
2. If you are using wood 8-inch skewers, soak them in water for 30 minutes before using them.
3. Oil the grill pan with ghee. Thread chicken chunks into skewers.
4. Cook skewers over low heat 10 to 15 min, flipping halfway through.
5. Next, mix the peanut dipping sauce.
6. Stir remaining one tbsp. of soy sauce, 1/4 tsp. of Sriracha sauce, one tsp. of sesame oil, and peanut butter.
7. Season with pink Himalayan salt and pepper.
8. Serve the chicken skewers with a small dish of peanut sauce.

Nutrition for Total Servings:

- Calories: 390
- Fat: 18.4 g
- Carbs: 2.1 g
- Protein: 17.4g

Tuscan Chicken

Preparation time: 15 minutes   **Cooking time:** 15 minutes   **Servings:** 6

Ingredients:

- 1 1/2 pounds chicken breasts, pasteurized, skinless, thinly sliced
- 1/2 cup sun-dried tomatoes
- 1 cup spinach, chopped
- 1 tsp. garlic powder
- 1 tsp. Italian seasoning
- 2 tbsps. avocado oil
- 1 cup heavy cream, full-fat

Directions:

1. Take a large skillet pan, place it over medium-high heat, add oil, and when hot, add chicken and then cook for 3–5 minutes per side until golden brown.
2. Add garlic powder, Italian seasoning, and pour in the cream, and then whisk until combined.
3. Switch heat to medium-high, cook the sauce for 2 minutes until it begins to thicken, then add tomatoes and spinach and simmer until spinach leaves begin to wilt.
4. Return chicken to the pan, toss until mixed and cook for 2 minutes until hot.
5. Serve chicken with cooked keto pasta, such as zucchini noodles.

Nutrition for Total Servings:

- Calories: 390
- Fat: 16.1g
- Carbs: 3g
- Protein: 19g

Chicken Pot Pie

Preparation time: 15 minutes   **Cooking time:** 25 minutes   **Servings:** 4

Ingredients:

For the filling:

- 1/2 medium onion, chopped
- 2 celery stalks, chopped
- 1/2 cup fresh or frozen peas
- 2 tbsps. butter
- 1 garlic clove, minced
- 1 1/2 pounds chicken thighs

- 1 cup chicken broth
- 1/2 cup heavy (whipping) cream
- 1 tsp. dried thyme
- 1/2 tsp. pink Himalayan sea salt
- 1/2 tsp. freshly ground black pepper

For the crust:

- 1 cup almond flour
- 2 tbsps. butter, at room temperature
- 2 tbsps. sour cream
- 1 large egg white
- 1 tbsp. ground flaxseed

- 1 tsp. xanthan gum
- 1 tsp. baking powder
- 1/2 tsp. garlic powder
- 1/4 tsp. pink Himalayan sea salt
- 1/4 tsp. dried thyme

Directions:

1. Filling: In a saucepan, combine the onion, celery, peas, butter, and garlic over medium heat.
2. Cook for about 5 minutes, until the onion starts to turn translucent.
3. In a large skillet, cook the chicken thighs for 3 to 5 minutes, until there is no more visible pink. Add the cooked chicken and all juices to the pan with the vegetables.
4. Add the broth, cream, thyme, salt, and pepper to the pan. Simmer it until sauce thickens, stirring occasionally.
5. Now, preheat the oven to 400°F.
6. In a bowl or container, combine the almond flour, butter, sour cream, egg white, flaxseed, xanthan gum, baking powder, garlic powder, salt, and thyme.
7. Form this into a dough.
8. Place the dough between 2 sheets of parchment paper and roll out into a 10-inch round that is 1/4 inch thick.
9. Fill an 8-inch pie pan or 4 (6-ounce) ramekins with the chicken filling.
10. Top the pie pan with the crust, flipping it onto the filling and peeling away the parchment paper. If using ramekins, cut circles of the dough and fit them onto the ramekins.
11. Pinch to seal the edges, and trim off any excess.
12. Baking time: 10-12 minutes
13. Let cool for 5 minutes, then serve.

Nutrition for Total Servings:

- Calories: 341
- Fat: 18.4g
- Carbs: 4.1 g
- Protein: 12.5g

Thai Chicken Salad Bowl

Preparation time: 12 minutes   **Cooking time:** 15 minutes   **Servings:** 2

Ingredients:

Marinade:

- 1 clove garlic, minced
- 1 tbsp. grated ginger
- 1 small red chili, finely chopped
- 1/2 stalk lemongrass, finely chopped
- 2 tbsp. fresh lime juice
- 1 tsp. fish sauce
- 1 tbsp. coconut aminos

Salad:

- 8 oz. (226g) (2-pieces) chicken breasts
- 1/2 cup shredded red cabbage
- 1/2 cup shredded green cabbage
- 2/3 cup grated carrot
- 1 tbsp. chopped mint
- 1/2 cup chopped cilantro
- 1 tbsp. chopped chives
- 1/4 cup blanched almonds

Dressing:

- 3 tbsp. extra virgin olive oil
- Salt and pepper, to taste

Directions:

1. Oven: 400 F
2. Combine the garlic, ginger, red chili, lemongrass, lime juice, fish sauce, and coconut aminos in a bowl for marinating and crush with a mortar.
3. Flatten the chicken breasts with a meat mallet.
4. Add the chicken to a bowl and add half of the marinade, and coat the chicken evenly.
5. Make it cool in the refrigerator for a maximum of 30 minutes or an hour.
6. Combine both cabbages, carrot, mint, cilantro, and chives in a bowl.
7. In a baking tray, spread out the almonds and roast in the oven for 5-8 minutes, set aside.
8. Grill the chicken in a griddle. Cook through then slice. Mix in the remaining ingredients.

Nutrition for Total Servings:

- Calories: 351
- Fat: 15.7g
- Carbs: 3.1 g
- Protein: 12.5g

Chicken Rollatini

Preparation time: 15 minutes   **Cooking time:** 30 minutes   **Servings:** 4

Ingredients:

- 4 (3-ounce) boneless skinless chicken breasts, pounded to about 1/3 inch thick
- 4 slices prosciutto (4 ounces)
- 1 cup fresh spinach
- 1/2 cup almond flour
- 2 eggs, beaten
- 1/4 cup good-quality olive oil
- 1/3 cup parmesan cheese
- 8 ounces ricotta cheese

Directions:

1. Now, preheat the oven. Set the oven temperature to 400°F.
2. Prepare the chicken—Pat the chicken breasts dry with paper towels. Spread 1/4 of the ricotta in the middle of each breast.
3. Place the prosciutto over the ricotta and 1/4 cup of the spinach on the prosciutto.
4. Fold the long edges of the chicken breast over the filling, then roll the chicken breast up to enclose the filling.
5. Place the rolls seam-side down on your work surface.
6. Bread the chicken. On a plate, stir together the almond flour and parmesan and set it next to the beaten eggs.
7. Carefully dip a chicken roll in the egg, then roll it in the almond-flour mixture until it is completely covered.
8. Set the rolls seam-side down on your work surface. Repeat with the other rolls.
9. Brown the rolls. In a medium skillet over medium heat, warm the olive oil.
10. Place the rolls seam-side down in the skillet and brown them on all sides, turning them carefully, about 10 minutes in total.
11. Transfer the rolls, seam-side down, to a 9-by-9-inch baking dish—Bake the chicken rolls for 25 minutes, or until they're cooked through.
12. Serve. Place one chicken roll on each of four plates and serve them immediately.

Nutrition for Total Servings:

- Calories: 365
- Fat: 17.1g
- Carbs: 3.2 g
- Protein: 1.4g

Gravy Bacon and Turkey

Preparation time: 15 minutes   **Cooking time:** 3 hours   **Servings:** 14

Ingredients:

- 12 pounds (5.4 kg) turkey
- Sea salt and fresh ground black pepper, to taste
- 1 pound (454 g) cherry tomatoes
- 1 cup red onions, diced
- 2 garlic cloves, minced
- 1 large celery stalk, diced
- 4 teaspoons fresh thyme, four small sprigs
- 8 ounces (227 g) bacon (10 slices, diced)
- 8 tbsps. butter
- 2 lemons, the juice
- 1/8 teaspoon guar gum (optional)

Directions:

1. Start by preheating the oven to 350°F (180°C).
2. Remove the neck and giblets from the turkey, pat the turkey dry with paper towels and season both inside and outside of the turkey with salt and pepper.
3. Insert cherry tomatoes, onions, celery, garlic and thyme into the turkey cavity. Tie the legs together with kitchen twine, and put the turkey on a large roasting pan, tuck its wings under the body.
4. Cook the bacon in a large skillet over medium heat until crisp, for 7 to 8 mins. Transfer to paper towels to drain, reserving the drippings in the skillet.
5. Add the ghee or butter to the skillet with the drippings & stir until melted, then pour into a bowl and stir in the lemon juice. Rub mixture all over the turkey.
6. Place into the oven for 30 minutes. After every 30 minutes, baste the turkey with the drippings. Roast for about 3 hrs. Or until a thermometer inserted into the thigh registers 165°F (74°C).
7. Remove from oven onto a serving tray to rest for at least 25 minutes before serving.
8. Meanwhile, pour the drippings into a saucepan. Whisk in the guar gum to thicken, after 2 minutes of whisking, add a touch more if you want a thicker gravy. Then add the reserved bacon for one amazing gravy.

Nutrition for Total Servings:

- Calories: 693
- Fat: 35.0g
- Carbs: 3.7g
- Protein: 86.7g

Creamy Chicken Bake

Preparation time: 15 minutes   **Cooking time:** 70 minutes   **Servings:** 6

Ingredients:

- 5 tbsps. unsalted butter, divided
- 2 small onions, sliced thinly
- 3 garlic cloves, minced
- 1 tsp. dried tarragon, crushed
- 1 cup homemade chicken broth, divided
- 2 tbsps. fresh lemon juice
- 1/2 cup heavy cream
- 1 1/2 teaspoons Herbs de Provence
- Salt and ground black pepper, to taste
- 4 (6-ounce) grass-fed chicken breasts

Directions:

1. Now, preheat the oven to 3500F.
2. Grease a 13x9-inch baking plate with 1 tbsp. of butter.
3. In a wok, melt 2 tbsps. Of butter over medium heat and sauté the onion, garlic, and tarragon for about 4–5 minutes.
4. Transfer the onion mixture onto a plate.
5. In the same wok, melt the remaining 2 tbsps. butter over low heat, 1/2 cup of broth, and lemon juice for about 3–4 minutes stirring continuously.
6. Stir in the cream, herbs de Provence, salt, and black pepper, and remove from heat.
7. Pour remaining broth in a prepared baking dish.
8. Arrange chicken breasts in the baking dish in a single layer and top with the cream mixture evenly.
9. Bake for approximately 45–60 minutes.
10. Serve hot.

Nutrition for Total Servings:

- Calories: 129
- Fat: 12g
- Carbs: 9g
- Protein: 7g

Chicken-Basil Alfredo with Shirataki Noodles

Preparation time: 10 minutes   **Cooking time:** 15 minutes   **Servings:** 2

Ingredients:

For the noodles:

- 1 (7-ounce) package Miracle Noodle Fettuccini, Shirataki Noodles

For the sauce:

- 1 tbsp. olive oil
- 4 ounces cooked shredded chicken (I usually use a store-bought rotisserie chicken)
- Pink Himalayan salt
- Freshly ground black pepper
- 1 cup Alfredo Sauce, or any brand you like
- 2 tbsps. chopped fresh basil leaves

Directions:

1. In a colander, rinse the noodles with cold water (shirataki noodles naturally have a smell, and rinsing with cold water will help remove this).
2. Fill a large saucepan with water & bring to a boil over high heat. Add the noodles & boil for 2 minutes. Drain.
3. Transfer the noodles to a large, dry skillet over medium-low heat to evaporate any moisture. Do not grease the skillet; it must be dry. Transfer the noodles to a plate and set them aside.

To make the sauce:

4. In the saucepan over medium heat, heat the olive oil. Add the cooked chicken. Season with pink Himalayan salt and pepper.
5. Pour the Alfredo sauce over the chicken, and cook until warm. Season with more pink Himalayan salt and pepper.
6. Add the dried noodles to the sauce mixture, and toss until combined.
7. Divide the pasta between two plates, and chopped basil, and serve.

Nutrition for Total Servings:

- Calories: 673
- Fat: 61g
- Carbs: 4g
- Protein: 29g

Chicken Quesadilla

Preparation time: 5 minutes   **Cooking time:** 5 minutes   **Servings:** 2

Ingredients:

- 1 tbsp. olive oil
- 2 low-carbohydrate tortillas
- 2 ounces shredded chicken (I usually use a store-bought rotisserie chicken)
- 1 tsp. Tajín seasoning salt
- 2 tbsps. sour cream

Directions:

1. In a large skillet over medium-high heat, heat the olive oil. Add a tortilla, the chicken, the Tajín seasoning. Top with the second tortilla.
2. Peek under the edge of the bottom tortilla to monitor how it is browning. Once the bottom tortilla gets golden flip the quesadilla over. The second side will cook faster, about 1 minute.
3. Once the second tortilla is crispy and golden, transfer the quesadilla to a cutting board and let sit for 2 minutes. Cut the quesadilla into 4 wedges using a pizza cutter or chef's knife.
4. Transfer half the quesadilla to each of two plates. Add 1 tbsp. of sour cream to each plate, and serve hot.

Nutrition for Total Servings:

- Calories: 414
- Fat: 28g
- Carbs: 24g
- Protein: 26g

Braised Chicken Thighs with Kalamata Olives

Preparation time: 10 minutes   **Cooking time:** 40 minutes   **Servings: 2**

Ingredients:

- 4 chicken thighs, skin on
- Pink Himalayan salt
- Freshly ground black pepper
- 2 tbsps. ghee
- 1/2 cup chicken broth
- 1 lemon, 1/2 sliced and 1/2 juiced
- 1/2 cup pitted Kalamata olives
- 2 tbsps. butter

Directions:

1. Now, preheat the oven to 375°F.
2. Pat the chicken thighs dry with paper towels, and season with pink Himalayan salt and pepper.
3. In a medium oven-safe skillet or high-sided baking dish over medium-high heat, melt the ghee. When the ghee has melted and is hot, add the chicken thighs, skin-side down, and leave them for about 8 minutes, or until the skin is brown and crispy.
4. Flip the chicken and cook for 2 minutes on the second side. Around the chicken thighs, pour in the chicken broth, and add the lemon slices, lemon juice, and olives.
5. Bake in the oven for about 30 minutes, until the chicken is cooked through.
6. Add the butter to the broth mixture.
7. Divide the chicken and olives between two plates and serve.

Nutrition for Total Servings:

- Calories: 567
- Fat: 47g
- Carbs: 4g
- Protein: 33g

Buttery Garlic Chicken

Preparation time: 5 minutes   **Cooking time:** 40 minutes   **Servings: 2**

Ingredients:

- 2 tbsps. ghee, melted
- Boneless skinless chicken breasts
- Pink Himalayan salt
- Freshly ground black pepper
- 1 tbsp. dried Italian seasoning
- 4 tbsps. butter
- 2 garlic cloves, minced

Directions:

1. Now, preheat the oven to 375°F. Choose a baking dish that is large enough to hold both chicken breasts and coat it with ghee.
2. Pat dry the chicken breasts and season with pink Himalayan salt, pepper, and Italian seasoning. Place the chicken in the baking dish.
3. In a medium skillet over medium heat, melt the butter. Add the minced garlic, and cook for about 5 minutes. You want the garlic very lightly browned but not burned.
4. Remove the butter-garlic mixture from the heat, and pour it over the chicken breasts.
5. Roast the chicken in the oven for 30 to 35 minutes, until cooked through. . Let the chicken rest in the baking dish for 5 minutes.
6. Divide the chicken between two plates, spoon the butter sauce over the chicken, and serve.

Nutrition for Total Servings:

- Calories: 642
- Fat: 45g
- Carbs: 2g
- Protein: 57g

Parmesan Baked Chicken

Preparation time: 5 minutes **Cooking time:** 20 minutes **Servings:** 2

Ingredients:

- 2 tbsps. ghee
- 2 boneless skinless chicken breasts
- Pink Himalayan salt
- Freshly ground black pepper
- 1/2 cup mayonnaise
- 1 tbsp. dried Italian seasoning
- 1/4 cup crushed pork rinds

Directions:

1. Now, preheat the oven to 425°F. Choose a baking dish that is large enough to hold both chicken breasts and coat it with ghee.
2. Pat dry the chicken breasts with a paper towel, season with pink Himalayan salt and pepper, and place in the prepared baking dish.
3. In a small bowl, mix to combine the mayonnaise, and Italian seasoning.
4. Slather the mayonnaise mixture evenly over the chicken breasts, and sprinkle the crushed pork rinds on top of the mayonnaise mixture.
5. Bake until the topping is browned, about 20 minutes, and serve.

Nutrition for Total Servings:

- Calories: 850
- Fat: 67g
- Carbs: 2g
- Protein: 60g

Crunchy Chicken Milanese

Preparation time: 10 minutes **Cooking time:** 10 minutes **Servings:** 2

Ingredients:

- 2 boneless skinless chicken breasts
- 1/2 cup coconut flour
- 1 tsp. ground cayenne pepper
- Pink Himalayan salt
- Freshly ground black pepper
- 1 egg, lightly beaten
- 1/2 cup crushed pork rinds
- 2 tbsps. olive oil

Directions:

1. Pound the chicken breasts with a heavy mallet until they are about 1/2 inch thick. (If you don't have a kitchen mallet, you can use the thick rim of a heavy plate.)
2. Prepare two separate prep plates and one small, shallow bowl
3. On plate 1, put the coconut flour, cayenne pepper, pink Himalayan salt, and pepper. Mix together.
4. Crack the egg into the small bowl, and lightly beat it with a fork or whisk.
5. On plate 2, put the crushed pork rinds.
6. In a large skillet over medium-high heat, heat the olive oil.
7. Dredge 1 chicken breast on both sides in the coconut-flour mixture. Dip the chicken into the egg, & coat both sides. Dredge the chicken in a pork-rind mixture, pressing the pork rinds into the chicken so they stick. Place the coated chicken in a hot skillet & repeat with the other chicken breast.
8. Cook the chicken for 3 to 5 minutes on each side, until brown, crispy, and cooked through, and serve.

Nutrition for Total Servings:

- Calories: 604
- Fat: 29g
- Carbs: 17g
- Protein: 65g

Egg Butter

Preparation time: 5 minutes **Cooking time:** 0 minutes **Servings:** 2

Ingredients:

- 2 large eggs, hard-boiled
- 3-ounce unsalted butter
- 1/2 tsp. dried oregano
- 1/2 tsp. dried basil
- 2 leaves of iceberg lettuce

Seasoning:

- 1/2 tsp. of sea salt
- 1/4 tsp. ground black pepper

Directions:

1. Peel the eggs, then chop them finely and place in a medium bowl.
2. Add remaining ingredients and stir well.
3. Serve egg butter wrapped in a lettuce leaf.

Nutrition for Total Servings:

- Calories: 159
- Fats 16.5 g
- Protein: 3 g
- Carbs: 0.2 g

Cider Chicken

Preparation time: 10 minutes **Cooking time:** 18 minutes **Servings:** 2

Ingredients:
- 2 chicken thighs
- 1/4 cup apple cider vinegar
- 1 tsp. liquid stevia

Seasoning:
- 1/2 tbsp. coconut oil
- 1/3 tsp. salt
- 1/4 tsp. ground black pepper

Directions:
1. Turn on the oven, then set it to 450°F and let it preheat.
2. Meanwhile, place chicken in a bowl, drizzle with oil and then season with salt and black pepper
3. Take a baking sheet, place prepared chicken thighs on it, and bake for 10 to 15 minutes or until its internal temperature reaches 165°F.
4. In the meantime, take a small saucepan, place it over medium heat, pour in vinegar, stir in stevia and bring the mixture to boil.
5. Then switch heat to the low level and simmer sauce for 3 to 5 minutes until reduced by half, set aside until required.
6. When the chicken has roasted, brush it generously with prepared cider sauce, then Turn on the broiler and bake the chicken for 3 minutes until golden brown. Then serve.

Nutrition for Total Servings:
- Calories: 182.5
- Fat: 107.5 g
- Protein: 15.5 g
- Carb: 2.5 g

Bacon-Wrapped Chicken Bites

Preparation time: 10 minutes **Cooking time:** 20 minutes **Servings:** 2

Ingredients:
- 1 chicken thigh, debone, cut into small pieces
- 4 slices of bacon, cut into thirds
- 2 tbsp. garlic powder

Seasoning:
- 1/4 tsp. salt
- 1/8 tsp. ground black pepper

Directions:
1. Turn on the oven, then set it to 400°F and let it preheat.
2. Cut chicken into small pieces, then place them in a bowl, add salt, garlic powder, and black pepper and toss until well coated.
3. Wrap each chicken piece with a bacon strip, place in a baking dish and bake for 15 to 20 minutes until crispy, turning carefully every 5 minutes. Then Serve.

Nutrition for Total Servings:
- Calories: 153
- Fat: 8.7 g
- Protein: 15 g
- Carbs: 2.7 g

Beans and Sausage

Preparation time: 5 minutes **Cooking time:** 6 minutes **Servings:** 2

Ingredients:
- 4 oz. green beans
- 4 oz. chicken sausage, sliced
- 1/2 tsp. dried basil
- 1/2 tsp. dried oregano
- 1/3 cup chicken broth, from chicken sausage

Seasoning:
- 1 tbsp. avocado oil
- 1/4 tsp. salt
- 1/8 tsp. ground black pepper

Directions:
1. Turn on the instant pot, place all the ingredients in its inner pot and shut with lid, in the sealed position.
2. Press the "manual" button, cook for 6 minutes at high-pressure settings and, when done, do a quick pressure release. Serve immediately.

Nutrition for Total Servings:
- Calories: 151
- Fats 9.4 g
- Protein: 11.7 g
- Carbs: 3.4 g

Paprika Rubbed Chicken

Preparation time: 5 minutes   **Cooking time:** 25 minutes   **Servings:** 2

Ingredients:

- 2 chicken thighs, boneless
- 1/4 tbsp. fennel seeds, ground
- 1/2 tsp. hot paprika
- 1/4 tsp. smoked paprika
- 1/2 tsp. minced garlic

Seasoning:

- 1/4 tsp. salt
- 2 tbsp. avocado oil

Directions:

1. Turn on the oven, then set it to 325°F and let it preheat.
2. Prepare the spice mix and for this, take a small bowl, add all the ingredients in it, except for chicken, and stir until well mixed.
3. Brush the mixture on all sides of the chicken, rub it well into the meat, then place chicken onto a baking sheet and roast for 15 to 25 minutes until thoroughly cooked, basting every 10 minutes with the drippings. Then serve.

Nutrition for Total Servings:

- Calories: 102.3
- Fat: 8 g
- Protein: 7.2 g
- Carbs: 0.3 g

Teriyaki Chicken

Preparation time: 5 minutes   **Cooking time:** 18 minutes   **Servings:** 2

Ingredients:

- 2 chicken thighs, boneless
- 2 tbsp. soy sauce
- 1 tbsp. swerve sweetener
- 1 tbsp. avocado oil

Directions:

1. Take a skillet pan, place it over medium heat, add oil and when hot, add chicken thighs and cook for 5 minutes per side until seared.
2. Then sprinkle sugar over chicken thighs, drizzle with soy sauce and bring the sauce to boil.
3. Switch heat to medium-low level, continue cooking for 3 minutes until chicken is evenly glazed, and then transfer to a plate.
4. Serve chicken with cauliflower rice.

Nutrition for Total Servings:

- Calories: 150
- Fat: 9 g
- Protein: 17.3 g
- Carbs: 0 g

Chili Lime Chicken with Coleslaw

Preparation time: 35 minutes   **Cooking time:** 8 minutes   **Servings:** 2

Ingredients:

- 1 chicken thigh, boneless
- 2 oz. coleslaw
- 1/4 tsp. minced garlic
- 3/4 tbsp. apple cider vinegar
- 1/2 of a lime, juiced, zested

Seasoning:

- 1/4 tsp. paprika
- 1/4 tsp. salt
- 2 tbsp. avocado oil
- 1 tbsp. unsalted butter

Directions:

1. Prepare the marinade and for this, take a medium bowl, add vinegar, oil, garlic, paprika, salt, lime juice, and zest and stir until well mixed.
2. Cut chicken thighs into bite-size pieces, toss until well mixed, and marinate it in the refrigerator for 30 minutes.
3. Then take a skillet pan, place it over medium-high heat, add butter and marinated chicken pieces and cook for 8 minutes until golden brown and thoroughly cooked.
4. Serve chicken with coleslaw.

Nutrition for Total Servings:

- Calories: 157.3
- Fat: 12.8 g
- Protein: 9 g
- Carbs: 1 g

Lime Garlic Chicken Thighs

Preparation time: 35 minutes   **Cooking time:** 15 minutes   **Servings:** 2

Ingredients:

- 2 boneless chicken thighs, skinless
- 3/4 tsp. garlic powder
- 1 1/2 tsp. all-purpose seasoning
- 1/2 of lime, juiced, zested
- 1 1/2 tbsp. avocado oil

Directions:

1. Take a medium bowl, place chicken in it, and sprinkle with garlic powder, all-purpose seasoning, and lime zest.
2. Drizzle with lime juice, toss until well coated and let chicken thighs marinate for 30 minutes.
3. Then take a medium skillet pan, place it over medium heat, add oil and when hot, place marinated chicken thighs in it and cook for 5 to 7 minutes per side until thoroughly cooked. Then serve.

Nutrition for Total Servings:

- Calories: 260
- Fat: 15.6 g
- Protein: 26.8 g
- Carbs: 1.3 g

Chicken and Peanut Stir-Fry

Preparation time: 5 minutes   **Cooking time:** 5 minutes   **Servings:** 2

Ingredients:

- 2 chicken thighs, cubed
- 1/2 cup broccoli florets
- 1/4 cup peanuts
- 1 tbsp. sesame oil
- 1 1/2 tbsp. soy sauce

Seasoning:

- 1/2 tsp. garlic powder

Directions:

1. Take a skillet pan, place it over medium heat, add 1/2 tbsp. oil and when hot, add chicken cubes and cook for 4 minutes until browned on all sides.
2. Then add broccoli florets and continue cooking for 2 minutes until tender-crisp.
3. Add remaining ingredients, stir well and cook for another 2 minutes. Then serve.

Nutrition for Total Servings:

- Calories: 266
- Fat: 19 g
- Protein: 18.5 g
- Carbs: 4 g

Garlic Cheddar Chicken Thighs

Preparation time: 5 minutes   **Cooking time:** 25 minutes   **Servings:** 2

Ingredients:

- 2 chicken thighs
- 1/3 tsp. garlic powder
- 1/3 tbsp. dried basil
- 1/2 tsp. coconut oil

Seasoning:

- 1/8 tsp. salt
- 1/3 tsp. ground black pepper

Directions:

1. Turn on the oven, then set it to 450°F, and let preheat.
2. Meanwhile, prepare the herb mix and for this, stir together 1/4 tsp. oil, salt, garlic, black pepper, and basil until combined.
3. Create a pocket into each chicken thigh and then stuff it with half of the prepared herb mix and spread the remaining herb mix evenly on chicken thighs.
4. Take a skillet pan, place it over medium-high heat, add remaining oil and when hot, place stuffed chicken thighs in it and cook for 4 minutes.
5. Then flip the chicken thighs, cook for 5 to 7 minutes until the chicken is no longer pink and then roast the chicken thighs for 10 to 12 minutes until a meat thermometer inserted into the thickest part of the thighs read 160°F.
6. Let chicken thighs rest for 5 minutes and then serve.

Nutrition for Total Servings:

- Calories: 128.5
- Fat: 9.5 g
- Protein: 9 g
- Carbs: 0.2 g

Garlic Chicken Low-Carb

Preparation time: 15 Minutes   **Cooking time: 45 minutes**   **Servings: 4**

Ingredients:

- 2 ounces (57 g) butter
- 2 pounds (907 g) chicken drumsticks
- Salt & freshly ground black pepper, to taste
- 2 tbsps. olive oil
- 1 lemon, the juice
- 7 garlic cloves, sliced
- 1/2 cup fresh parsley, finely chopped

Directions:

1. Start by preheating the oven to 450°F (235°C).
2. Grease the baking pan with butter and put the chicken drumsticks, season with salt and pepper generously.
3. Drizzle the olive oil and lemon juice over the chicken pieces. Sprinkle the garlic and parsley on top.
4. Bake the chicken for 30 to 40 minutes or until the garlic slices become golden and chicken pieces turn brown and roasted, the baking time may be longer if your drumsticks are a large size. Lower the temperature considerably towards the end.

Nutrition for Total Servings:

- Calories: 542
- Fat: 40.0g
- Carbs: 4.0g
- Protein: 42.0g

Chicken and Herb Butter with Keto Zucchini Roll-Ups

Preparation time: 15 minutes   **Cooking time: 40 minutes**   **Servings: 4**

Ingredients:

Zucchini roll-ups:

- 1 1/2 pounds (680 g) zucchini
- 1/2 tsp. salt
- 3 ounces (85 g) butter
- 6 ounces (170 g) mushrooms, finely chopped
- 1/2 green bell pepper, chopped
- 2 ounces (57 g) air-dried chorizo, chopped
- 1 egg
- 1 tsp. onion powder
- 2 tbsps. fresh parsley, chopped
- 1/2 tsp. salt
- 1/4 tsp. pepper

Chicken:

- 4 (6-ounce/170-g) chicken breasts
- Salt & freshly ground pepper, to taste
- 1 ounce (28 g) butter, for frying

Herb butter:

- 4 ounces (113 g) butter, at room temperature
- 1 garlic clove
- 1/2 tsp. garlic powder
- 1 tbsp. fresh parsley, finely chopped
- 1 tsp. lemon juice
- 1/2 tsp. salt

Directions:

1. Now, preheat the oven to 350°F (180°C). Cut the zucchini lengthwise into equal slices, half an inch, Pat dry with paper towels or a clean kitchen towel and place it on a baking tray lined with parchment paper. Sprinkle salt on the zucchini and let stand for 10 minutes.
2. Bake for 20 minutes in the oven, or until the zucchini is tender. Transfer to a cooling rack from the oven, Dry more if needed.
3. Put the butter in the saucepan over medium heat, cut the mushrooms and put it in and stir fry well, let cool.
4. Add the remaining ingredients for the zucchini roll-ups to a bowl. Add the mushrooms and blend well.
5. Roll up and put it inside the baking dish with seams down Raise the temperature to 400°F (205°C). Bake for 20 minutes In the meantime, season your chicken and fry it over medium heat in butter until it is crispy on the outside and cooked through.

Herb butter:

1. To prepare Herb butter mix the butter, garlic, garlic powder, fresh parsley, lemon juice, and salt. Thoroughly in a small bowl. Let sit for 30 minutes and serve on top of the chicken and zucchini roll-ups.

Nutrition for Total Servings:

- Calories: 913
- Fat: 84.0g
- Carbs: 10.0g
- Protein: 30.0g

Keto Buffalo Drumsticks with Chili Aioli and Garlic

Preparation time: 10 minutes   **Cooking time: 40 minutes**   **Servings: 4**

Ingredients:

- 2 pounds (907g) chicken drumsticks or chicken wings
- 1/3 cup mayonnaise, keto-friendly
- 1 tbsp. smoked paprika powder or smoked chili powder
- 1 garlic clove, minced
- 2 tbsps. olive oil, and more for greasing the baking dish
- 2 tbsps. white wine vinegar
- 1 tsp. salt
- 1 tsp. paprika powder
- 1 tbsp. tabasco

Directions:

1. Now, preheat the oven to 450°F (235°C).
2. Make the chili aioli: Combine the mayonnaise, smoked paprika powder, garlic clove, olive oil white wine vinegar, salt, paprika powder and tabasco for the marinade in a small bowl,
3. Put the drumsticks in a plastic bag, and pour the chili aioli into the plastic bag. Shake the bag thoroughly and let marinate for 10 minutes at room temperature.
4. Coat a baking dish with olive oil. Place the drumsticks in the baking dish and let bake in the preheated oven for 30 to 40 minutes or until they are done and have turned a nice color.
5. Remove the chicken wings from the oven and serve warm.

Nutrition for Total Servings:

- Calories: 570
- Fat: 43.0g
- Carbs: 3.0g
- Protein: 43.0g

Coleslaw with Crunchy Keto Chicken Thighs

Preparation time: 15 minutes   **Cooking time: 40 minutes**   **Servings: 8**

Ingredients:

- 1 tsp. salt
- 1/2 cup sour cream
- 2 tbsps. jerk seasoning (cinnamon, paprika, turmeric, ginger, saffron and cumin)
- 2 pounds (907 g) chicken thighs
- 5 ounces (142 g) pork rinds
- 3 ounces (85 g) unsweetened shredded coconut
- 3 tbsps. olive oil
- 1 pound (454 g) green cabbage
- 1 cup mayonnaise, keto-friendly
- Salt & freshly ground black pepper, to taste
- 2 big plastic bags

Directions:

1. Now, preheat the oven to 350°F (180°C).
2. Mix together a marinade of jerk seasoning, salt and sour cream. And pour in a big plastic bag with the drumsticks, please keep the skin on the drumsticks.
3. Thoroughly shake and allow to marinate for 15 minutes.
4. Take the drumsticks out, and into a new, clean bag.
5. Put the pork rinds into a food processor and blend into fine crumbs, add in coconut flakes and blend a few more seconds.
6. Pour the pork mixture into the bag with the marinated chicken and shake.
7. Grease a baking dish, and put the chicken into it, drizzle with olive oil and bake for 40 to 50 minutes, or until the chicken is cooked through. Turn the drumsticks halfway through, if the breading has already turned a desirable golden brown color, lower the heat.
8. In the meantime, cut the cabbage finely with a sharp knife or with a mandolin or even a food processor. Put the coleslaw into a bowl, season with salt and pepper, and add mayonnaise, mix well and let sit for 10 minutes.

Nutrition for Total Servings:

- Calories: 586
- Fat: 51.2g
- Carbs: 6.4g
- Protein: 27.2g

CHAPTER 10:

Beef Lamb Pork

Jerk Pork

Preparation time: 15 minutes **Cooking time:** 20 minutes **Servings:** 6

Ingredients:

- 1/8 tsp cayenne pepper
- 1/4 tsp. salt
- 1/4 tsp. freshly ground black pepper
- 1/2 tbsp. dried thyme
- 1/2 tbsp. garlic powder
- 1/2 tbsp. ground allspice
- 1 tsp. ground cinnamon
- 1 tbsp. granulated erythritol
- 1 (1-pound/454-g) pork tenderloin, cut into 1-inch rounds
- 1/4 cup extra-virgin olive oil
- 2 tbsps. chopped fresh cilantro, for garnish
- 1/2 cup sour cream

Directions:

1. Combine the ingredients for the seasoning in a bowl. Stir to mix well.
2. Put the pork rounds in the bowl of seasoning mixture. Toss to coat well.
3. Pour the olive oil into a nonstick skillet, and heat over medium-high heat.
4. Arrange the pork in the singer layer in the skillet and fry for 20 minutes or until an instant-read thermometer inserted in the center of the pork registers at least 145°F (63°C). Flip the pork rounds halfway through the cooking time. You may need to work in batches to avoid overcrowding.
5. Transfer the pork rounds onto a large platter, and top with cilantro and sour cream, then serve warm.

Nutrition for Total Servings:

- Calories: 289
- Fat: 23.2g
- Carbs: 2.8g
- Protein: 17.2g

Hot Pork and Bell Pepper in Lettuce

Preparation time: 15 minutes **Cooking time:** 20 minutes **Servings:** 4

Ingredients:

Sauce:

- 1 tbsp. fish sauce
- 1 tbsp. rice vinegar
- 1 tbsp. almond flour

Pork filling:

- 2 tbsps. sesame oil, divided
- 1 pound (454 g) ground pork
- 1 tsp. fresh ginger, peeled and grated
- 1 tsp. garlic, minced
- 1 tsp. coconut aminos
- 1 tbsp. granulated erythritol
- 2 tbsps. coconut oil

- 1 red bell pepper, deseeded and thinly sliced
- 1 scallion, white and green parts, thinly sliced
- 8 large romaine or Boston lettuce leaves

Directions:

1. Make the sauce: Combine the ingredients for the sauce in a bowl. Set aside until ready to use.
2. Make the pork filling: In a nonstick skillet, warm a tbsp. sesame oil over medium-high heat.
3. Add the sauté the ground pork for 8 minutes or until lightly browned, then pour the sauce over and keep cooking for 4 minutes more or until the sauce has lightly thickened.
4. Transfer the pork onto a platter and set aside until ready to use.
5. Clean the skillet with paper towels, then warm the remaining sesame oil over medium-high heat.
6. Add and sauté the ginger and garlic for 3 minutes or until fragrant.
7. Add and sauté the sliced bell pepper and scallion for an additional 5 minutes or until fork-tender.
8. Lower the heat, and move the pork back to the skillet. Stir to combine well.
9. Divide and arrange the pork filling over four lettuce leaves and serve hot.

Nutrition for Total Servings:

- Calories: 385
- Fat: 31.1g
- Carbs: 5.8g
- Protein: 20.1g

Italian Sausage, Zucchini, Eggplant, and Tomato Ratatouille

Preparation time: 15 minutes   **Cooking time:** 45 minutes   **Servings:** 4

Ingredients:

- 3 tbsps. extra-virgin olive oil
- 1 pound (454 g) Italian sausage meat (sweet or hot)
- 2 zucchini, diced
- 1 red bell pepper, diced
- 1/2 eggplant, cut into 1/2-inch cubes
- 1 tbsp. garlic, minced
- 1/2 red onion, chopped
- 1 tbsp. balsamic vinegar
- 1 (15-ounce/425-g) can low-sodium tomatoes, diced
- 1 tbsp. fresh basil, chopped
- Red pepper flakes, to taste
- 2 teaspoons chopped fresh oregano, for garnish
- Salt & freshly ground black pepper, to taste

Directions:

1. Add the olive oil in a stock pot, and warm over medium-high heat, then add and sauté the Italian sausage meat for 7 minutes or until lightly browned.
2. Add the zucchini, bell pepper, eggplant, garlic, and onion to the pot and sauté for 10 minutes or until tender.
3. Fold in the balsamic vinegar, tomatoes, basil, and red pepper flakes. Stir to combine well, then bring to a boil.
4. Turn down the heat to low. Simmer the mixture for 25 minutes or until the vegetables are entirely softened.
5. Sprinkle with oregano, salt, and black pepper. Stir to mix well, then serve warm.

Nutrition for Total Servings:

- Calories: 431
- Fat: 33.2g
- Carbs: 11.8g
- Protein: 21.2g

Bacon, Beef, and Pecan Patties

Preparation time: 10 minutes   **Cooking time:** 15 minutes   **Servings:** 8

Ingredients:

- 1/4 cup chopped onion
- 1/4 cup ground pecans
- 1 large egg
- 8 ounces (227 g) bacon, chopped
- 1 pound (454 g) grass-fed ground beef
- Salt & freshly ground black pepper, to taste
- 1 tbsp. extra-virgin olive oil

Directions:

1. Now, preheat the oven to 450°F (235°C). Line a baking sheet with parchment paper.
2. Whisk the ingredients, except for the olive oil, in a bowl.
3. Grease your hands with olive oil, and shape the mixture into 8 patties with your hands.
4. Arrange patties on a baking sheet and bake in the preheated oven for 20 min or until a meat thermometer inserted in the center of the patties reads at least 165°F (74°C). Flip patties halfway through cooking time.
5. Remove the cooked patties from the oven and serve warm.

TIP: You can serve the patties with homemade sauces or store-bought burger toppings for more and different flavors.

Nutrition for Total Servings:

- Calories: 318
- Fat: 27.2g
- Carbs: 1.1g
- Protein: 18.1g

Lemony Anchovy Butter with Steaks

Preparation time: 15 minutes   **Cooking time:** 10 minutes   **Servings:** 4

Ingredients:

Anchovy butter:

- 4 anchovies packed in oil, drained and minced
- 1/2 tsp. freshly squeezed lemon juice
- 1/4 cup unsalted butter, at room temperature
- 1 tsp. minced garlic
- 4 (4-ounce/113-g) rib-eye steaks
- Salt & freshly ground black pepper, to taste

Directions:

1. Make the anchovy butter: Combine the anchovies, lemon juice, butter, and garlic in a bowl. Stir to mix well, then arrange the bowl into the refrigerator to chill until ready to use.
2. Preheat the grill to medium-high heat.
3. Rub the steaks with salt and black pepper on a clean work surface.
4. Arrange the seasoned steaks on the grill grates and grill for 10 minutes or until medium-rare. Flip steaks halfway through cooking time.
5. Allow the steaks to cool for 10 minutes. Transfer the steaks onto four plates, and spread the anchovy butter on top, then serve warm.

TIP: To make this a complete meal, you can serve it with spicy asparagus. They also taste great paired with fresh cucumber salad.

Nutrition for Total Servings:

- Calories: 447
- Fat: 38.1g
- Carbs: 0g
- Protein: 26.1g

Zucchini Carbonara

Preparation time: 10 minutes   **Cooking time:** 15 minutes   **Servings:** 6

Ingredients:

- 8 chopped bacon slices
- 2 large eggs
- 4 large egg yolks
- 1/2 cup heavy whipping cream
- 2 tbsps. chopped fresh basil
- 2 tbsps. chopped fresh parsley
- Salt & freshly ground black pepper, to taste
- 1 tbsp. minced garlic
- 1/2 cup dry white wine
- 4 medium zucchini, spiralized

Directions:

1. In a nonstick skillet, cook the bacon for 6 minutes or until it curls and buckle. Flip bacon halfway through cooking time.
2. Meanwhile, whisk together the eggs, egg yolks, cream, basil, parsley, salt, & black pepper in a large bowl. Set aside.
3. Add the garlic to the skillet and sauté for 3 minutes until fragrant, then pour the dry white wine over and cook for an additional 2 minutes for deglazing.
4. Turn down the heat to low, add and sauté the spiralized zucchini for 2 minutes.
5. Pour egg mixture into skillet and toss for 4 minutes or until the mixture is thickened and coat the spiralized zucchini.
6. Transfer to a platter

TIP: To make this a complete meal, you can serve it with lemony radicchio salad. They also taste great paired with braised fennel and shallots.

Nutrition for Total Servings:

- Calories: 332
- Fat: 26.2g
- Carbs: 6.9g
- Protein: 19.1g

Mushroom, Spinach, and Onion Stuffed Meatloaf

Preparation time: 20 minutes

Cooking time: 1 hour

Servings: 8

Ingredients:

- 3 tbsps. extra-virgin olive oil
- 17 ounces (482 g) ground beef
- 2 teaspoons ground cumin
- 2 garlic cloves, granulated
- Salt & freshly ground black pepper, to taste
- 1/4 cup mushrooms, diced
- 1/2 cup spinach
- 1/4 cup onions, diced
- 1/4 cup green onions, diced

Directions:

1. Now, preheat your oven 350°F (180°C). Coat a meatloaf pan with olive oil.
2. Combine 1 pound (454 g) ground beef, cumin, garlic, salt, and black pepper in a large bowl. Pour the mixture into the meatloaf pan.
3. Make a well in the center of the beef mixture. Put the mushrooms, spinach, and onions in the well, then cover them with the remaining 1 ounce (28 g) ground beef.
4. Place the meatloaf pan into the preheated oven and bake for 1 hour until cooked through.
5. Remove meatloaf from oven and slice to serve.

TIP: To gift this dish with more flavor. You can serve it with homemade spicy or sour sauces, or store-bought toppings.

Nutrition for Total Servings:

- Calories: 254
- Fat: 20.2g
- Carbs: 1.4g
- Protein: 15.3g

Italian Flavor Herbed Pork Chops

Preparation time: 10 minutes   **Cooking time:** 20 minutes   **Servings:** 4

Ingredients:

- 2 tbsps. melted butter, plus for coating
- 2 tbsps. Italian seasoning
- 2 tbsps. olive oil
- Salt & freshly ground black pepper, to taste (if no salt or pepper in the Italian seasoning)
- 4 pork chops, boneless
- 2 tbsps. fresh Italian leaf parsley, chopped

Directions:

1. Now, preheat the oven to 350°F (180°C). Grease a baking dish with melted butter.
2. Combine the Italian seasoning, butter, olive oil, salt, and black pepper in a large bowl. Dredge each pork chop into the bowl to coat well.
3. Arrange the pork chops onto the baking dish, and spread the fresh parsley on top of each chop.
4. Bake in preheated oven for 20 mins. Or until cooked through. An instant-read thermometer inserted in the middle of the pork chops should register at least 145°F (63°C).
5. Transfer the pork chops from the oven and serve warm.

TIP: To make this a complete meal, you can serve it with roasted broccoli. They also taste great paired with creamy spinach and dill.

Nutrition for Total Servings:

- Calories: 335
- Fat: 23.4g
- Carbs: 0g
- Protein: 30.9g

Braised Beef Shanks and Dry Red Wine

Preparation time: 10 minutes   **Servings:** 6
Cooking time: 8 hours
Ingredients:

- 2 tbsps. olive oil
- 2 pounds (907 g) beef shanks
- 2 cups dry red wine
- 3 cups beef stock
- 1 sprig of fresh rosemary
- 5 garlic cloves, finely chopped
- 1 onion, finely chopped
- Salt & freshly ground black pepper, to taste

Directions:

1. In a nonstick skillet, warm olive oil over medium-high heat.
2. Put the beef shanks into the skillet and fry for 5 to 10 minutes until well browned. Flip the beef shanks halfway through. Set aside.
3. Pour the dry red wine into the skillet & bring it to a simmer.
4. Coat the insert of the slow cooker with olive oil.
5. Add the cooked beef shanks, dry red wine, beef stock, rosemary, garlic, onion, salt, and black pepper to the slow cooker. Stir to mix well.
6. Put slow cooker lid on & cook on LOW for 8 hours until the beef shanks are fork-tender.
7. Remove from the slow cooker & serve hot.

TIP: To make this a complete meal, you can serve it with roasted cauliflower. They also taste great paired with tomato and herb salad.

Nutrition for Total Servings:

- Calories: 315
- Fat: 11g
- Carbs: 4g
- Protein: 50g

Beef, Eggplant, Zucchini, and Baby Spinach Lasagna

Preparation time: 10 minutes   **Cooking time:** 4 hours   **Servings:** 8
Ingredients:

- 3 tbsps. olive oil, plus for greasing the slow cooker
- 5 garlic cloves, finely chopped
- 1 onion, finely chopped
- 2 pounds (907 g) beef, minced
- 2 teaspoons dried mixed herbs (oregano, rosemary, thyme)
- 4 tomatoes, chopped
- Salt & freshly ground black pepper, to taste
- 1 large eggplant, cut into round slices crosswise
- 2 large zucchinis, cut into slices lengthwise
- 2 cups baby spinach leaves

Directions:

1. Warm the olive oil in a nonstick skillet over medium-high heat.
2. Add and sauté the garlic and onions for 3 minutes or until the onions are translucent.
3. Add and sauté the beef for 3 more minutes until lightly browned.
4. Add the dried mixed herbs and tomatoes over the beef, and season with salt and black pepper. Sauté for 5 minutes to combine well.
5. Grease the slow cooker with olive oil.
6. Make the lasagna: Spread a layer of beef mixture on the bottom of the slow cooker, and top the beef mixture with a layer of eggplant slices, then spread another layer of beef mixture, and then put on a layer of zucchini slices, after that, top the zucchini slices with a layer of beef mixture, and on the beef mixture, spread a layer of baby spinach leaves, and finally, a layer of beef mixture.
7. Combine the salt and black pepper in a large bowl. Put the slow cooker lid on and bake on HIGH for 4 hours.
8. Remove the hot lasagna from the slow cooker and slice to serve.

N You can use different vegetable slices to replace the eggplant, zucchinis, or baby spinach leaves, such as tomato slices and broccoli slices.

Nutrition for Total Servings:

- Calories: 397
- Total fat: 22.0g
- Carbs: 10.5g
- Protein: 40.8g

Lamb and Tomato Curry

Preparation time: 10 minutes   **Cooking time:** 8 hours   **Servings:** 8

Ingredients:

- 3 tbsps. olive oil, plus for greasing the slow cooker
- 2 1/2 lb. (1.1 kg) boneless lamb shoulder, cubed
- 4 tbsps. curry paste
- 5 garlic cloves, finely chopped
- 2 onions, roughly chopped
- Salt & freshly ground black pepper, to taste
- 1 lamb stock cube
- 2 tomatoes, chopped
- 2 1/2 cups unsweetened oat milk
- 1 cup of water
- Fresh coriander, roughly chopped, for garnish
- Full-fat Greek yogurt, to serve

Directions:

1. Warm the olive oil in a nonstick skillet over medium-high heat.
2. Add and sear the lamb shoulder for 3 minutes until browned on both sides.
3. Grease the slow cooker with olive oil.
4. Place the cooked lamb into the slow cooker, and add the curry paste, garlic, onions, salt, and black pepper. Toss to coat the lamb well.
5. Add the stock cube, tomatoes, oat milk, and water to the slow cooker. Stir to mix well.
6. Put the slow cooker lid on & cook on LOW for 8 hours.
7. Transfer the lamb curry to a large plate, and spread the coriander and yogurt on top to serve.

TIP: To make this a complete meal, you can serve it with Indian raita, cucumber salad, and naan.

Nutrition for Total Servings:

- Calories: 406
- Fat: 28.2g
- Carbs: 10.5g
- Protein: 31.6g

Garlicky Lamb Leg with Rosemary

Preparation time: 15 minutes

Cooking time: 30 minutes

Servings: 8

Ingredients:

- 3 tbsps. extra-virgin olive oil
- 4 pounds (1.8 kg) boneless leg of lamb
- Salt & freshly ground black pepper, to taste
- 2 tbsps. chopped rosemary
- 1 tbsp. garlic
- 2 cups of water

Directions:

1. Warm the olive oil in a nonstick skillet over medium-high heat.
2. Add lamb leg to the skillet, and sprinkle with salt and black pepper. Sear for 3 minutes until browned on both sides.
3. Remove the lamb leg from the skillet to a platter. Allow to cool few minutes, then rub with rosemary and garlic.
4. Pour the water into a pressure cooker with a steamer, then arrange the lamb leg on the steamer.
5. Put the pressure cooker lid on and cook for 30 minutes.
6. Release the pressure, and remove the lamb leg from the pressure cooker. Allow to cool 10 minutes & slice to serve.

TIP: If you think the taste of this recipe is a little plain, you can try to top the lamb leg with your secret glaze or homemade sauce to gift more flavor to the lamb leg.

Nutrition for Total Servings:

- Calories: 366
- Fat: 16.2g
- Carbs: 1.2g
- Protein: 51.1g

Lamb Chops with Dry Red Wine

Preparation time: 10 minutes   **Servings:** 4
Cooking time: 40 minutes
Ingredients:

- 1 tbsp. olive oil
- 1 garlic clove, minced
- 1/2 onion, sliced
- 1 pound (454 g) lamb chops
- 1/2 tsp. mint
- 1/2 tbsp. sage
- Salt & freshly ground black pepper, to taste
- 1/4 cup dry red wine
- 1 cup of water

Directions:

1. Warm the olive oil in a nonstick skillet over medium-high heat.
2. Sauté the garlic and onion in the skillet for 3 minutes or until the onion is translucent.
3. Arrange the lamb chops on a clean work surface and rub with mint, sage, salt, and black pepper on both sides.
4. Add the lamb chops in the skillet and cook for 6 minutes until lightly browned. Flip the chops halfway through. Set aside.
5. Pour the dry red wine and water into the skillet. Bring to a boil, then cook until it reduces to half.
6. Add the cooked lamb chops back to the skillet. Lower the heat, & simmer for 30 minutes.
7. Remove them from the skillet and serve hot.

TIP: If you think the taste of this recipe is a little plain, you can try to top the lamb chops with your secret glaze or homemade sauce to gift more flavor to the lamb chops.

Nutrition for Total Servings:

- Calories: 341
- Fat: 29.8g
- Carbs: 3.6g
- Protein: 14.6g

Pork with Veggies

Preparation time: 15 minutes   **Cooking time:** 15 minutes   **Servings:** 5
Ingredients:

- 1 quid pork loin, cut into thin strips
- 2 tbsps. olive oil, divided
- 1 tsp. garlic, minced
- 1 tsp. fresh ginger, minced
- 2 tbsps. low-sodium soy sauce
- 1 tbsp. fresh lemon juice
- 1 tsp. sesame oil
- 1 tbsp. granulated erythritol
- 1 tsp. arrowroot star
- 10 ounces' broccoli florets
- 1 carrot, peeled and sliced
- 1 big red bell pepper, seeded and cut into strips
- 2 scallions, cut into 2-inch pieces

Directions:

1. In a bowl, mix well pork strips, 1/2 tbsp. of olive oil, garlic, and ginger.

For the sauce:

1. Add the soy sauce, lemon juice, sesame oil, Swerve, and arrowroot starch in a small bowl and mix well.
2. Preheat the oven remaining olive oil in a big nonstick wok over high heat and sear the pork strips for about 3–4 minutes or until cooked through.
3. With a slotted spoon, transfer the pork into a bowl.
4. In the same wok, add the carrot and cook for about 2–3 minutes.
5. Add the broccoli, bell pepper, and scallion, and cook, covered for about 1–2 minutes.
6. Stir the cooked pork, sauce, and stir fry, and cook for about 3–5 minutes or until the desired doneness, stirring occasionally.
7. Remove from the heat and serve.

Nutrition for Total Servings:

- Calories: 268
- Fat: 18 g
- Carbs: 7 g
- Protein: 8 g

Pork Taco Bake

Preparation time: 15 minutes   **Cooking time:** 60 minutes   **Servings:** 6

Ingredients:

Crust:

- 3 organic eggs
- 1/2 tsp. taco seasoning
- 1/3 cup heavy cream

Topping:

- 1 pound lean ground pork
- 4 ounces canned chopped green chilies
- 1/4 cup sugar-free tomato sauce
- 3 teaspoons taco seasoning
- 1/4 cup fresh basil leaves

Directions:

1. Now, preheat the oven to 375°F.
2. Lightly grease a 13x9-inch baking dish.
3. For the crust: In a bowl, add the eggs, and beat until well combined and smooth.
4. Add the taco seasoning and heavy cream, and mix well.
5. Bake for about 25–30 minutes.
6. Remove baking dish from oven and set aside for about 5 minutes.
7. Meanwhile, for the topping: Heat a large nonstick wok over medium-high heat and cook the pork for about 8–10 minutes.
8. Drain the excess grease from the wok.
9. Stir in the green chilies, tomato sauce, and taco seasoning, and remove from the heat.
10. Place the pork mixture evenly over the crust.
11. Bake for about 18–20 minutes or until bubbly.
12. Remove from the oven and set aside for about 5 minutes.
13. Cut into desired size slices and serve with the garnishing of basil leaves.

Nutrition for Total Servings:

- Calories: 198 Cal
- Fat: 12 g
- Carbs: 8 g
- Protein: 19 g

Creamy Pork Stew

Preparation time: 15 minutes   **Cooking time:** 95 minutes   **Servings:** 8

Ingredients:

- 3 tbsps. unsalted butter
- 2 1/2 pounds boneless pork ribs, cut into 3/4-inch cubes
- 1 large yellow onion, chopped
- 4 garlic cloves, crushed
- 1 1/2 cups homemade chicken broth
- 2 (10-ounce) cans of sugar-free diced tomatoes
- 2 teaspoons dried oregano
- 1 tsp. ground cumin
- Salt, to taste
- 2 tbsps. fresh lime juice
- 1/2 cup sour cream

Directions:

1. In a large heavy-bottomed pan, dissolve the butter over medium-high heat and cook the pork, onions, and garlic for about 4–5 min. Or until browned.
2. Add the broth and with a wooden spoon, scrape up the browned bits.
3. Add the tomatoes, oregano, cumin, and salt, and stir to combine well
4. Adjust the temperature to medium-low and simmer, covered for about 1 1/2 hours.
5. Stir in the sour cream and lime juice and remove from the heat. Then serve hot.

Nutrition for Total Servings:

- Calories: 182
- Fat: 18 g
- Carbs: 9 g
- Protein: 18 g

KETO DIET FOR WOMEN OVER 50

Creamy Basil Baked Sausage

Preparation time: 5 minutes   **Cooking time:** 30 minutes   **Servings:** 2

Ingredients:

- 3 lb. of Italian sausage - pork/turkey or chicken
- ¼ cup of heavy cream
- ¼ cup of basil pesto
- 80 g mozzarella

Directions:

1. Set the oven to 400°F.
2. Lightly spritz a casserole dish with cooking oil spray. Add the sausage to the dish and bake for 30 minutes.
3. Combine the heavy cream, pesto
4. Pour the sauce over the casserole
5. Bake for another 10 minutes. The sausage should reach 160°Fahrenheit in the center when checked with a meat thermometer.
6. You can also broil for 3 minutes to brown the cheesy layer.

Nutrition for Total Servings:

- Calories: 298
- Fat: 17 g
- Carbs: 4 g
- Protein: 9 g

Chicken Pan-Grilled With Chorizo Confetti

Preparation time: 5 minutes   **Cooking time:** 30 minutes   **Servings:** 4

Ingredients:

- 4 (6-ounce) skinless, boneless chicken bosom parts
- 1/2 tsp. genuine salt, isolated
- 1/4 tsp. newly ground dark pepper
- Cooking splash
- 1/4 cup Mexican pork chorizo, housings expelled
- 1/4 cup cut onion
- 2 carrots, diced
- 1/4 cup diced yellow ringer pepper
- 1/4 cup diced red chime pepper
- 2 tbsps. diced green chime pepper
- 1/4 cup unsalted chicken stock
- 1 tbsp. cleaved new cilantro Green Salad with Crostini.

Directions:

1. Warmth a flame broil skillet over medium-high warmth.
2. Sprinkle chicken with 1/4 tsp. salt and pepper.
3. Coat dish with cooking splash.
4. Add chicken to the dish; cook 6 minutes on each side or until done.
5. While chicken cooks heat a huge skillet over medium-high warmth. Include chorizo; cook 1 moment, mixing to disintegrate.
6. Include staying 1/4 tsp. salt, onion, and carrot; cook 2 minutes, blending infrequently.
7. Include chime peppers; cook 1 moment or until fresh delicate. Include stock; cook 2 minutes or until fluid nearly vanishes, scratching container to slacken sautéed bits.
8. Spoon chorizo blend over chicken; top with cilantro.

Nutrition for Total Servings:

- Calories: 190
- Fat: 22 g
- Carbs: 5 g
- Protein: 12 g

Italian Pork Dish

Preparation time: 15 minutes　　　　**Cooking time:** 15 minutes　　　　**Servings:** 6

Ingredients:

- 2 lbs. pork tenderloins, cut into 1 1/2-inch each piece
- 1/4 cup of. almond flour
- 1 tsp. garlic salt
- Freshly ground black pepper, to taste
- 2 tbsps. butter
- 1/2 cup of homemade chicken broth
- 1/3 cup of balsamic vinegar
- 1 tbsp. capers
- 2 tsps. fresh lemon zest, grated finely

Directions:

1. In a large bowl, add pork pieces, flour, garlic salt, and black pepper and toss to coat well.
2. Remove pork pieces from the bowl and shake off excess flour mixture.
3. In a large skillet, melt butter over medium-high heat and cook the pork pieces for about 2-3 minutes per side.
4. Add broth & vinegar and bring to a gentle boil.
5. Reduce the heat to medium and simmer for about 3-4 minutes.
6. With a slotted spoon, transfer the pork pieces onto a plate.
7. In the same skillet, add the capers and lemon zest and simmer for about 3-5 minutes or until the desired thickness of the sauce.
8. Pour sauce over pork pieces and serve.

Nutrition for Total Servings:

- Calories: 484
- Fat: 19 g
- Carbs: 8 g
- Protein: 10 g

Classic Pork Tenderloin

Preparation time: 15 minutes　　　　**Cooking time:** 35 minutes　　　　**Servings:** 4

Ingredients:

- 8 bacon slices
- 2 lb. pork tenderloin
- 1 tsp. dried oregano, crushed
- 1 tsp. dried basil, crushed
- 1 tbsp. garlic powder
- 1 tsp. seasoned salt
- 3 tbsp. butter

Directions:

1. Now, preheat the oven to 400°F.
2. Heat a large ovenproof skillet over medium-high heat and cook the bacon for about 6-7 minutes.
3. Transfer the bacon onto a paper towel-lined plate to drain.
4. Then, wrap the pork tenderloin with bacon slices and secure it with toothpicks.
5. With a sharp knife, slice the tenderloin between each bacon slice to make a medallion.
6. In a bowl, mix together the dried herbs, garlic powder and seasoned salt.
7. Now, coat the medallion with herb mixture.
8. With a paper towel, wipe out the skillet.
9. In the same skillet, melt the butter over medium-high heat and cook the pork medallion for about 4 minutes per side.
10. Now, transfer the skillet into the oven.
11. Roast for about 17-20 minutes.
12. Remove the wok from the oven and let it cool slightly before cutting.
13. Cut the tenderloin into desired size slices and serve.

Nutrition for Total Servings:

- Calories: 471
- Carb: 1g
- Protein: 53.5g
- Fat: 26.6g

The Signature Italian Pork Dish

Preparation time: 15 minutes   **Cooking time:** 15 minutes   **Servings:** 6

Ingredients:

- 2 lb. pork tenderloins, cut into 1 1/2-inch piece
- 1/4 C. almond flour
- 1 tsp. garlic salt
- Freshly ground black pepper, to taste
- 2 tbsp. butter
- 1/2 C. homemade chicken broth
- 1/3 C. balsamic vinegar
- 1 tbsp. capers
- 2 tsp. fresh lemon zest, grated finely

Directions:

1. In a large bowl, add pork pieces, flour, garlic salt and black pepper and toss to coat well.
2. Remove pork pieces from the bowl and shake off excess flour mixture.
3. In a large skillet, melt the butter over medium-high heat and cook the pork pieces for about 2-3 minutes per side.
4. Add broth & vinegar and bring to a gentle boil.
5. Reduce the heat to medium and simmer for about 3-4 minutes.
6. With a slotted spoon, transfer the pork pieces onto a plate.
7. In the same skillet, add the capers and lemon zest and simmer for about 3-5 minutes or until the desired thickness of the sauce.
8. Pour sauce over pork pieces and serve.

Nutrition for Total Servings:

- Calories: 373
- Carbos: 1.8g
- Protein: 46.7g
- Fat: 18.6g

Spiced Pork Tenderloin

Preparation time: 15 minutes   **Cooking time:** 18 minutes   **Servings:** 6

Ingredients:

- 2 tsp. fennel seeds
- 2 tsp. coriander seeds
- 2 tsp. caraway seeds
- 1 tsp. cumin seeds
- 1 bay leaf
- Salt & freshly ground black pepper, to taste
- 2 tbsp. fresh dill, chopped
- 2 (1-lb.) pork tenderloins, trimmed

Directions:

1. For the spice rub: in a spice grinder, add the seeds and bay leaf and grind until finely powdered.
2. Add the salt and black pepper and mix.
3. In a small bowl, reserve 2 tbsp. Of spice rub.
4. In another small bowl, mix the remaining spice rub, and dill.
5. Place 1 tenderloin over a piece of plastic wrap.
6. With a sharp knife, slice through the meat to within 1/2-inch of the opposite side.
7. Now, open the tenderloin like a book.
8. Cover with another plastic wrap and with a meat pounder, gently pound into 1/2-inch thickness.
9. Repeat with the remaining tenderloin.
10. Remove the plastic wrap and spread half of the dill mixture over the center of each tenderloin.
11. Roll each tenderloin like a cylinder.
12. With a kitchen string, tightly tie each roll at several places.
13. Rub each roll with the reserved spice rub generously.
14. With 1 plastic wrap, wrap each roll and refrigerate for at least 4-6 hours.
15. Preheat the grill to medium-high heat. Grease the grill grate.
16. Remove the plastic wrap from tenderloins.
17. Place tenderloins onto the grill and cook for about 14-18 minutes, flipping occasionally.
18. Remove from the grill and place tenderloins onto a cutting board and with a piece of foil, cover each tenderloin for at least 5-10 minutes before slicing.
19. With a sharp knife, cut the tenderloins into desired size slices and serve.

Nutrition for Total Servings:

- Calories: 313
- Carbs: 1.4g
- Protein: 45.7g
- Fat: 12.6g

Sticky Pork Ribs

Preparation time: 15 minutes   **Cooking time:** 2 hours 34 minutes   **Servings:** 9

Ingredients:

- 1/4 cup erythritol
- 1 tbsp. garlic powder
- 1 tbsp. Paprika
- 1/2 tsp. red chili powder
- 4 lb. pork ribs, membrane removed
- Salt & freshly ground black pepper, to taste
- 1 1/2 tsp. liquid smoke
- 1 1/2 C. sugar-free BBQ sauce

Directions:

1. Now, preheat the oven to 300°F. Line a large baking sheet with 2 layers of foil, shiny side out.
2. In a bowl, add the Erythritol, garlic powder, paprika and chili powder and mix well.
3. Season the ribs with salt and black pepper and then, coat with the liquid smoke.
4. Now, rub the ribs with the Erythritol mixture.
5. Arrange the ribs onto the prepared baking sheet, meaty side down.
6. Arrange 2 layers of foil on top of ribs and then, roll and crimp edges tightly.
7. Bake for about 2-2 1/2 hours or until the desired doneness.
8. Remove baking sheet from oven and place the ribs onto a cutting board.
9. Now, set the oven to broiler.
10. With a sharp knife, and then cut the ribs into serving sized portions and evenly coat with the barbecue sauce.
11. Arrange the ribs onto a broiler pan, bony side up.
12. Broil for about 1-2 minutes per side.
13. Remove from the oven and serve hot.

Nutrition for Total Servings:

- Calories: 530
- Carbs: 2.8g
- Protein: 60.4g
- Fat: 40.3g

Valentine's Day Dinner

Preparation time: 15 minutes   **Cooking time:** 35 minutes   **Servings:** 4

Ingredients:

- 1 tbsp. olive oil
- 4 large boneless rib pork chops
- 1 tsp. salt
- 1 cup cremini mushrooms, chopped roughly
- 3 tbsp. yellow onion, chopped finely
- 2 tbsp. fresh rosemary, chopped
- 1/3 cup homemade chicken broth
- 1 tbsp. unsalted butter
- 2/3 cup heavy cream
- 2 tbsp. sour cream

Directions:

1. Now, preheat the oven oil in a large skillet over medium heat and sear the chops with the salt for about 3-4 minutes or until browned completely.
2. With a slotted spoon, transfer the pork chops onto a plate and set aside.
3. In the same skillet, add mushrooms, onion and rosemary and sauté for about 3 minutes.
4. Stir in the cooked chops, broth and bring to a boil.
5. Reduce heat to low & cook, covered for about 20 minutes.
6. With a slotted spoon, transfer the pork chops onto a plate and set aside.
7. In the skillet, stir in the butter until melted.
8. Add the heavy cream and sour cream and stir until smooth.
9. Stir in the cooked pork chops and cook for about 2-3 minutes or until heated completely.
10. Serve hot.

Nutrition for Total Servings:

- Calories: 400
- Carbs: 3.6g
- Protein: 46.3g
- Fat: 21.6g

South East Asian Steak Platter

Preparation time: 15 minutes   **Cooking time:** 20 minutes   **Servings:** 4

Ingredients:

- 14 oz. grass-fed sirloin steak, trimmed and cut into thin strips
- Freshly ground black pepper, to taste
- 2 tbsp. olive oil, divided
- 1 small yellow onion, chopped
- 2 garlic cloves, minced
- 1 Serrano pepper, seeded and chopped finely
- 3 C. broccoli florets
- 3 tbsp. low-sodium soy sauce
- 2 tbsp. fresh lime juice

Directions:

1. Season steak with black pepper.
2. In a large skillet, heat 1 tbsp. Of the oil over medium heat and cook the steak for about 6-8 minutes or until browned from all sides. Then transfer the steak onto a plate.
3. In the same skillet, heat remaining oil and sauté onion for about 3-4 minutes.
4. Add the garlic and Serrano pepper and sauté for about 1 minute.
5. Add broccoli and stir fry for about 2-3 minutes.
6. Stir in cooked beef, soy sauce and lime juice and cook for about 3-4 minutes. Then serve hot.

Nutrition for Total Servings:

- Calories: 282
- Carbs: 7.6g
- Protein: 33.1g
- Fat: 13.5g

Pesto Flavored Steak

Preparation time: 15 minutes   **Cooking time:** 17 minutes   **Servings:** 4

Ingredients:

- 1/4 cup fresh oregano, chopped
- 1 1/2 tbsp. garlic, minced
- 1 tbsp. fresh lemon peel, grated
- 1/2 tsp. red pepper flakes and crushed
- Salt & freshly ground black pepper, to taste
- 1 lb. (1-inch thick) grass-fed boneless beef top sirloin steak
- 1 cup pesto

Directions:

1. Preheat gas grill to medium heat. Lightly, grease the grill grate.
2. In a bowl, add oregano, garlic, lemon peel, red pepper flakes, salt & black pepper & mix well.
3. Rub garlic mixture onto the steak evenly.
4. Place steak onto the grill and cook, covered for about 12-17 minutes, flipping occasionally.
5. Remove from the grill and place the steak onto a cutting board for about 5 minutes.
6. With a sharp knife, cut the steak into desired sized slices.
7. Divide the steak slices and pesto onto serving plates and serve

Nutrition for Total Servings:

- Calories: 226
- Carbos: 6.8g
- Protein: 40.5g
- Fat: 7.6g

Flawless Grilled Steak

Preparation time: 10 minutes   **Cooking time:** 21 minutes   **Servings:** 5

Ingredients:

- 1/2 tsp. dried thyme, crushed
- 1/2 tsp. dried oregano, crushed
- 1 tsp. red chili powder
- 1/2 tsp. ground cumin
- 1/4 tsp. garlic powder
- Salt & freshly ground black pepper, to taste
- 1 1/2 lb. grass-fed flank steak, trimmed

Directions:

1. In a large bowl, add the dried herbs and spices and mix well.
2. Add the steaks and rub with mixture generously. Set aside for about 15-20 minutes.
3. Preheat the grill to medium heat. Grease the grill grate.
4. Place the steak onto the grill over medium coals and cook for about 17-21 minutes, flipping once halfway through.
5. Remove the steak from the grill and place onto a cutting board for about 10 minutes before slicing.
6. With a sharp knife, and then cut the steak into desired sized slices.

Nutrition for Total Servings:

- Calories: 271
- Carbos: 0.7g
- Protein: 38.3g
- Fat: 11.8g

Beef and Pepper Kebabs

Preparation time: 30 minutes   **Cooking time:** 10 minutes   **Servings:** 2

Ingredients:

- 2 tbsps. olive oil
- 1 1/2 tbsp. balsamic vinegar
- 2 teaspoons of Dijon mustard
- Salt & pepper

- 8 ounces of beef sirloin, cut into 2-inch pieces
- 1 small red pepper, and then cut into chunks
- 1 small green pepper, and then cut into chunks

Directions:

1. Whisk the olive oil, balsamic vinegar, & mustard in a shallow dish.
2. Season the steak with salt and pepper, then toss in the marinade.
3. Let marinate for 30 minutes, then slide onto skewers with the peppers.
4. Preheat a grill pan to high heat and grease with cooking spray.
5. Cook the kebabs for 2 to 3 min on each side until the beef is done.

Nutrition for Total Servings:

- Calories: 365
- Fat: 21.5g
- Protein: 35.5g
- Carbs: 6.5g

Chinese Pork Bowl

Preparation time: 5 minutes   **Cooking time:** 15 minutes   **Servings:** 4

Ingredients:

- 1 1/4 pounds pork belly, cut into bite-size pieces
- 2 Tbsp. tamari soy sauce
- 1 Tbsp. rice vinegar
- 2 cloves garlic, smashed
- 3 oz. butter

- 1 pound Brussels sprouts, rinsed, trimmed, halved or quartered
- 1/2 leek, chopped
- Salt and ground black pepper, to taste

Directions:

1. Fry the pork over medium-high heat until it is starting to turn golden brown.
2. Combine the garlic cloves, butter, and Brussels sprouts. Add to the pan, whisk well and cook until the sprouts turn golden brown.
3. Stir the soy sauce & rice vinegar together and pour the sauce into the pan.
4. Sprinkle with salt and pepper. Top with chopped leek.

Nutrition for Total Servings:

- Carbs: 7 g
- Fat: 97 g
- Protein: 19 g
- Calories: 993

Flavor Packed Pork Loin

Preparation time: 15 minutes   **Cooking time:** 60 minutes   **Servings:** 6

Ingredients:

- 1/3 cup of low-sodium soy sauce
- 1/4 cup of fresh lemon juice
- 2 tsps. fresh lemon zest, grated
- 1 tbsp. fresh thyme, finely chopped
- 2 tbsps. fresh ginger, grated

- 2 garlic cloves, chopped finely
- 2 tbsps. Erythritol
- Freshly ground black pepper, to taste
- 1/2 tsp. cayenne pepper
- 2 lbs. boneless pork loin

Directions:

1. For pork marinade: in a large baking dish, add all the ingredients except pork loin and mix until well combined.
2. Add pork loin and coat with the marinade generously.
3. Refrigerate for about 24 hours.
4. Now, preheat the oven to 400°F.
5. Remove pork loin from marinade and arrange it into a baking dish.
6. Cover the baking dish and bake for about 1 hour.
7. Remove from the oven and place the pork loin onto a cutting board.
8. With a piece of foil, cover each loin for at least 10 minutes before slicing.
9. With a sharp knife, cut the pork loin into desired size slices and serve.

Nutrition for Total Servings:

- Calories: 230
- Fat: 29 g
- Carbs: 4 g
- Protein: 10 g

Keto Breakfast Cups

Preparation time: 15 minutes   **Cooking time:** 40 minutes   **Servings:** 12

Ingredients:

- 2 lbs. ground pork
- 1 tbsp. freshly chopped thyme
- 2 cloves garlic, minced
- 1/2 tsp. paprika
- 1/2 tsp. ground cumin
- 1 tsp. kosher salt
- Freshly ground black pepper
- 2 1/2 cups chopped fresh spinach
- 12 eggs
- 1 tbsp. freshly chopped chives

Directions:

1. Preheats the oven to 400°c. Combine the pork, thyme, garlic, paprika, cumin, and salt in a large bowl. Season with peppers.
2. Attach a small handful of pork to each tin of muffin well then press the sides to make a cup. Spinach Season with salt and pepper and crack an egg on top of each cup.
3. Bake for about 25 min, until eggs are set, and the pork is cooked through. Garnish and serve with chives.
4. Serve hot.

Nutrition for Total Servings:

- Calories: 418
- Fat: 30 g
- Carbs: 9 g
- Protein: 19 g

Keto Stuffed Cabbage

Preparation time: 15 minutes   **Cooking time:** 45 minutes   **Servings:** 12

Ingredients:

Sauce:

- 1 (14-oz.) can diced tomatoes
- 1 tbsp. apple cider vinegar
- 1/2 tsp. red pepper flakes
- 1 tsp. onion powder
- 1 tsp. garlic powder
- 1 tsp. dried oregano
- Kosher salt
- Freshly ground black pepper
- 1/4 cup of extra-virgin olive oil

Cabbage Rolls:

- 12 cabbage leaves
- 1 lb. ground beef
- 3/4 lb. ground pork
- 1 cup rice cauliflower
- 3 green onions, thinly sliced
- 1/4 cup of chopped parsley, plus for serving
- Freshly ground black pepper and salt

Directions:

Sauce:

1. Now, preheat the oven to 375°C. Puree tomatoes, in a blender, apple cider vinegar, red pepper flakes, onion powder, garlic powder and oregano; salt and pepper seasoning.
2. Heat oil in large, deep pan (or big pot) over medium heat. Add the pureed tomato sauce, bring to a simmer then lower to medium-low, and cook for 20 minutes until thickened slightly.

Cabbage Rolls:

1. Flinch the cabbage leaves in a large pot of boiling water until tender and flexible, around 1 minute set aside
2. For the filling: mix 1/2 c in a large bowl. Tomato sauce, meat from the farm, cauliflower rice, scallions, and parsley. Top with pepper and salt.
3. Put a thin layer of sauce on a large baking dish underneath. Slice the hard-triangular rib out of each cabbage leaf using a paring knife. Place approximately 1/3 cup filling in one end of each leaf, then roll up and tuck into the sides as you move. Layer rolls in a baking dish to seam-side-down on top of the sauce. Remaining spoon sauce over the cabbage rolls. Bake until the meat is properly cooked through and the internal temperature hits 150°F for 45 minutes to 55 minutes. Apply more parsley to garnish before serving.

Nutrition for Total Servings:

- Calories: 229
- Fat: 20 g
- Carbs: 3 g
- Protein: 19 g

Garlic Rosemary Pork Chops

Preparation time: 10 minutes   **Cooking time:** 30 minutes   **Servings:** 4

Ingredients:

- 4 pork loin chops
- Kosher salt
- Freshly ground black pepper
- 1 tbsp. freshly minced rosemary
- 2 cloves garlic, minced
- 1/2 cup (1 stick) butter, melted
- 1 tbsp. extra-virgin olive oil

Directions:

1. Now, preheat the oven to 375°F. Spice the pork with salt and pepper generously.
2. Mix the butter, rosemary, and garlic together in a small bowl. Set aside.
3. Heat olive oil over medium-high flame, then places pork chops in an oven-safe skillet. Sear for 4 minutes until crispy, flip over and cook for 4 minutes. Clean the pork with garlic butter, generously.
4. Place the bucket in the oven and cook for 10-12 minutes until cooked (145°F for medium). Serve with more butter over garlic.

Nutrition for Total Servings:

- Calories: 390
- Fat: 30 g
- Carbs: 6 g
- Protein: 19g

Chicken Parmesan

Preparation time: 20 minutes

Cooking time: 15 minutes

Servings: 4

Ingredients:

- 1/4 cup of avocado oil
- 1/4 cup of almond flour
- 3/4 cup of marinara sauce, sugar-free
- 2 eggs, beaten
- 2 tsps. Italian seasoning
- 3 oz. pork rinds, pulverized
- 4 lbs. chicken breasts, boneless & skinless
- Sea salt & pepper, to taste
- 1/3 cup parmesan cheese

Directions:

1. Now, preheat the oven to 450°Fahrenheit and grease a baking dish.
2. Place the beaten egg into one shallow dish. Place the almond flour in another. In a third dish, combine the pork rinds, parmesan, pepper, salt and Italian seasoning and mix well.
3. Pat the chicken breasts dry and pound them down to about 1/2" thick.
4. Dredge the chicken in the almond flour, then coat in egg, then coat in the crumb.
5. Heat a large sauté pan over medium-high heat and warm oil until shimmering.
6. Once the oil is hot, lay the breasts into the pan and do not move them until they've had a chance to cook. Cook for about two minutes, then flip as gently as possible (a fish spatula is perfect) then cook for two more. Remove the pan from the heat.
7. Place the breasts in the greased baking dish and top with marinara sauce Bake for about 10 minutes and then serve.

Nutrition for Total Servings:

- Calories: 621
- Fat: 24 g
- Carbs: 6 g
- Protein: 14 g

Potluck Lamb Salad

Preparation time: 20 minutes   **Cooking time:** 10 minutes   **Servings:** 4

Ingredients:

- 2 tbsp. olive oil, divided
- 12 oz. grass-fed lamb leg steaks, trimmed
- 200 g halloumi
- Salt & freshly ground black pepper, to taste
- 2 jarred roasted red bell peppers, sliced thinly
- 2 cucumbers, cut into thin ribbons
- 3 C. fresh baby spinach
- 2 tbsp. balsamic vinegar

Directions:

1. In a skillet, heat 1 tbsp. Of the oil over medium-high heat and cook the lamb steaks for about 4-5 minutes per side or until desired doneness.
2. Transfer the lamb steaks onto a cutting board for about 5 minutes.
3. Then cut the lamb steaks into thin slices.
4. In the same skillet, add haloumi and cook for about 1-2 minutes per side or until golden.
5. In a salad bowl, add the lamb, haloumi, bell pepper, cucumber, salad leaves, vinegar, and remaining oil and toss to combine.
6. Serve immediately.

Nutrition for Total Servings:

- Calories: 420
- Carbs: 8g
- Protein: 35.4g
- Fat: 27.2g

Balsamic-Glazed Lamb Chops

Preparation time: 10 minutes   **Cooking time:** 15 minutes   **Servings:** 4

Ingredients:

Lamb chops:

- 3/4 tsp. dried rosemary
- 1/4 tsp. dried basil
- Salt and black pepper, to taste to taste
- 1/2 tsp. dried thyme
- 4 lamb chops, 3/4-inch (1.9 cm) thick
- 1 tbsp. olive oil

Balsamic reduction:

- 1/4 cup minced shallots
- 1/3 Cup aged balsamic vinegar
- 3/4 cup chicken broth
- 1 tbsp. butter

Directions:

1. Take a small-sized bowl and add the rosemary, basil, salt, black pepper, and thyme. Mix the ingredients well.
2. Place the cleaned lamb chops in a baking tray and liberally rub them with rosemary mixture. Cover the chops with aluminum foil and leave them for 15 minutes at room temperature.
3. Meanwhile, take a large-sized nonstick skillet over medium-high heat. Add olive oil to the skillet & let it heat for 1 minute.
4. Add lamb chops to the skillet and cook for 3 1/2 to 4 minutes per side until the chops are well done.
5. Once cooked, remove the chops from the skillet and keep them on a serving platter. Cover them with a plastic sheet until ready to serve.
6. Make the balsamic reduction: Add shallots to the same skillet and sauté until brown and caramelized. Add vinegar to deglaze the pan then pour in chicken broth.
7. Cook this mixture for 5 minutes on medium-high heat until the broth is reduced to half. Stir in butter and mix well.
8. Pour this balsamic reduction over the seared chops and serve warm.
9. Storage: Store in airtight container in the fridge for up to 4 days or in the freezer for up to one month.
10. Reheat in microwave, covered, until the desired temperature is reached or reheat in a frying pan or air fryer/instant pot, covered, on medium.
11. Serve: To make this a complete meal, serve the lamb chops with cauliflower mash. They also taste great paired with kale cucumber cream salad.

Nutrition for Total Servings:

- Calories: 256
- Fat: 19.4g
- Protein: 14.6g
- Carbs: 5.1g

Beef and Egg Bake

Preparation time: 5 minutes   **Cooking time:** 10 minutes   **Servings:** 1

Ingredients:

- 1 tsp. extra-virgin olive oil
- 3 ounces (85 g) ground beef, lamb or pork, cooked
- 2 eggs

Directions:

1. Begin by preheating the oven and set its temperature to 400°F (205°C).
2. Meanwhile, take a small baking pan and grease it with olive oil. Spread the cooked ground meat in the prepared pan.
3. Use a medium-sized spoon and make two holes in the beef mixture. Crack one egg into each hole.
4. Transfer the baking pan to the oven and bake it for 10 to 15 minutes.
5. Once baked, remove pan from the oven and leave it for 5 minutes at room temperature.
6. Slice and serve warm.
7. Storage: Store in airtight container in the fridge for up to 4 days or in the freezer for up to one month.
8. Reheat: Microwave, covered, until the desired temperature is reached or reheat in a frying pan or air fryer/instant pot, covered, on medium.
9. Serve: To make this complete meal, serve the egg bake with green salad or avocado. They also taste great paired with homemade keto-friendly mayonnaise.

Nutrition for Total Servings:

- Calories: 498
- Fat: 35.2g
- Protein: 41.1g
- Carbs: 2.3g

Butter Dipped Lamb Chops

Preparation time: 5 minutes   **Cooking time:** 10 minutes   **Servings:** 4

Ingredients:

Lamb chops:

- 8 lamb chops
- 1 tbsp. butter
- 1 tbsp. olive oil
- Salt and black pepper, to taste

For serving:

- 4 ounces (113 g) herb butter
- 1 lemon, in wedges

Directions:

1. Remove the lamb chops from refrigerator and leave them at room temperature for 15 minutes.
2. Use a sharp knife and make few cuts into the fat portion of the chops. Liberally, season these chops with salt and black pepper.
3. Take a large-sized frying pan and place it over medium-high heat. Add butter and olive oil to the hot pan and heat for 2 minutes.
4. Add the seasoned chops to the pan and sear them for 4 minutes per side until thoroughly cooked from inside out.
5. Transfer the lamb chops to the serving plates and garnish them with herb butter and lemon wedges. Devour!
6. Storage: Store in airtight container in the fridge for up to 4 days or in the freezer for up to one month.
7. Reheat: Microwave, covered, until the desired temperature is reached or reheat in a frying pan or air fryer/instant pot, covered, on medium.
8. Serve: To make this a complete meal, serve the lamb chops with tomato relish. They also taste great paired with crispy kale Salad.

Nutrition for Total Servings:

- Calories: 723
- Fat: 62g
- Protein: 43.3g
- Carbs: 0.3g

Steaks with Béarnaise Sauce

Preparation time: 10 minutes   **Cooking time:** 15 minutes   **Servings:** 4

Ingredients:

Béarnaise sauce:
- 4 egg yolks, at room temperature
- 2 teaspoons white wine vinegar
- 1/2 tsp. onion powder
- 2 tbsps. fresh tarragon, finely chopped
- 10 ounces (284 g) butter
- Salt and black pepper, to taste

Rib eye steaks:
- 4 (2 pounds/907 g) rib eye steaks, at room temperature
- 2 tbsps. butter
- Salt and black pepper, to taste

Salad:
- 2 ounces (57 g) arugula lettuce, chopped
- 2 ounces (57 g) lettuce, chopped
- 8 ounces (227 g) cherry tomatoes, quartered

Directions:

1. Make the béarnaise sauce: separate egg yolks from their whites and transfer the yolks to a small heat-proof bowl. Keep the egg whites for other recipes.
2. Take another small bowl and add the onion powder, tarragon, and vinegar. Mix them well and keep the mixture aside.
3. Beat the egg yolks with a hand mixer until pale in color and smooth in texture.
4. Place butter in a microwave-safe bowl and heat it for 30 seconds until completely melted. Pour the melted butter into the beaten egg yolks.
5. Rub all the rib eye steaks with butter, salt, and black pepper liberally. Then grill these steaks in the preheated charcoal grill or a pan grill until their internal temperature reaches to 145°F (63°C).
6. To serve, divide the lettuce, arugula lettuce, and cherry tomatoes into the four serving plates. Place one grilled steak on each plate and pour the warm béarnaise sauce over the steaks. Serve warm and fresh.
7. Storage: Store béarnaise sauce in an airtight container in the fridge for up to 1 day and store the grilled steaks in a sealed container for 3 to 5 days in the refrigerator.
8. Reheat: To reheat, béarnaise sauce, microwave, covered, on low heat, until the desired temperature is reached and reheat the steaks in a well-greased frying pan, on medium heat.
9. Serve: To make this a complete meal, serve the steaks on a bed of baby spinach. They also taste great paired with freshly prepared cucumber dill salad.

Nutrition for Total Servings:
- Calories: 1124
- Fat: 103.1g
- Protein: 49g
- Carbs: 3.4g

Grilled Garlic Lamb Chops

Preparation time: 10 minutes   **Servings:** 6
Cooking time: 6 minutes

Ingredients:
- 1/2 tsp. black pepper
- 2 teaspoons salt
- 1/4 cup distilled white vinegar
- 1 onion, thinly sliced
- 1 tbsp. minced garlic
- 2 tbsps. and 1 tsp. olive oil
- 2 pounds (907 g) lamb chops

Directions:

1. Add the black pepper, salt, vinegar, onion, garlic, and 2 tbsps. Olive oil to a large-sized Ziploc
2. Bag. Shake the Ziploc bag well to mix all the ingredients inside.
3. Place lamb chops in this bag and seal it again. Shake well to coat the chops and refrigerate it for 2 hours for marinating.
4. Meanwhile, prepare an outdoor grill and preheat it at medium-high heat. And grease its grilling grates with 1 tsp. olive oil.
5. Remove the lamb chops from the Ziploc bag and discard the marinade.
6. Wrap the exposed bones at one end of the chops with aluminum foil and place them in the preheated grill. Cook the marinated lamb chops for 3 minutes per side. Serve warm and fresh.

Nutrition for Total Servings:
- Calories: 519
- Fat: 44.8g
- Protein: 25.2g
- Carbs: 2.4g

CHAPTER 11:

Meatless Meal

Spicy Steak Curry

Preparation time: 15 minutes   **Cooking time:** 40 minutes   **Servings:** 6

Ingredients:

- 1 cup plain yogurt
- 1/2 tsp. garlic paste
- 1/2 tsp. ginger paste
- 1/2 tsp. ground cloves
- 1/2 tsp. ground cumin
- 2 teaspoons red pepper flakes
- 1/4 tsp. ground turmeric
- Salt
- 2 pounds grass-fed round steak
- 1/4 cup olive oil
- 1 medium yellow onion
- 1 1/2 tbsps. lemon juice
- 1/4 cup cilantro

Directions:

1. Mix yogurt, garlic paste, ginger paste and spices. Add the steak pieces. Set aside.
2. Sauté the onion within 4-5 minutes. Add the steak pieces with marinade and mix.
3. Simmer within 25 minutes. Stir in the lemon juice and simmer 10 minutes.
4. Garnish with cilantro and serve.

Nutrition for Total Servings:

- Calories: 440
- Carbs: 5.5g
- Fiber: 0.7g
- Fat: 14.5 g

Beef Stew

Preparation time: 15 minutes   **Cooking time:** 1 hour 40 minutes   **Servings:** 4

Ingredients:

- 1 1/3 pounds grass-fed chuck roast
- Salt
- Ground black pepper
- 1 yellow onion
- 2 garlic cloves
- 1 cup beef broth
- 1 bay leaf
- 1/2 tsp. dried thyme
- 1/2 tsp. dried rosemary
- 1 carrot
- 4 ounces celery stalks
- 1 tbsp. lemon juice

Directions:

1. Put salt and black pepper in beef cubes.
2. Sear the beef cubes within 4-5 minutes. Add the onion and garlic, then adjust the heat to medium and cook within 4-5 minutes. Add the broth, bay leaf and dried herbs and boil.
3. Simmer within 45 minutes. Stir in the carrot and celery and simmer within 30-45 minutes.
4. Stir in lemon juice, salt, and black pepper. Serve.

Nutrition for Total Servings:

- Calories: 413
- Carbs: 5.9g
- Fat: 7.53 g
- Protein: 52g

Beef & Cabbage Stew

Preparation time: 15 minutes   **Cooking time:** 2 hours 10 minutes   **Servings:** 8

Ingredients:

- 2 pounds grass-fed beef stew meat
- 1 1/3 cups hot chicken broth
- 2 yellow onions
- 2 bay leaves
- 1 tsp. Greek seasoning
- Salt
- ground black pepper
- 3 celery stalks
- 1 package cabbage
- 1 can sugar-free tomato sauce
- 1 can sugar-free whole plum tomatoes

Directions:

1. Sear the beef within 4-5 minutes. Stir in the broth, onion, bay leaves, Greek seasoning, salt, and black pepper, and boil. Adjust the heat to low and cook within 1 1/4 hours.
2. Stir in the celery and cabbage and cook within 30 minutes. Stir in the tomato sauce and chopped plum tomatoes and cook, uncovered within 15-20 minutes. Stir in the salt, discard bay leaves and serve.

Nutrition for Total Servings:

- Calories: 247
- Carbs: 7g
- Protein: 36.5g
- Fat: 14.54 g

Beef & Mushroom Chili

Preparation time: 15 minutes   **Cooking time:** 3 hours 10 minutes   **Servings:** 8

Ingredients:

- 2 pounds grass-fed ground beef
- 1 yellow onion
- 1/2 cup green bell pepper
- 1/2 cup carrot
- 4 ounces mushrooms
- 2 garlic cloves
- 1 can sugar-free tomato paste
- 2 tbsps. red chili powder
- 1 tbsp. ground cumin
- 1 tsp. ground cinnamon
- 1 tsp. red pepper flakes
- 1/2 tsp. ground allspice
- Salt
- ground black pepper
- 4 cups of water
- 1/2 cup sour cream

Directions:

1. Cook the beef within 8-10 minutes. Stir in the remaining fixing except for sour cream and boil. Cook on low, covered, within 3 hours.
2. Top with sour cream and serve.

Nutrition for Total Servings:

- Calories: 246
- Carbs: 8.2g
- Fat: 22.44 g
- Protein: 25.1g

Steak

Preparation time: 15 minutes   **Cooking time:** 17 minutes   **Servings:** 4

Ingredients:

- 18 ounces grass-fed filet mignon
- Salt
- Ground black pepper
- 1/2 cup yellow onion
- 1 cup heavy cream
- 1 garlic clove
- Ground nutmeg

Directions:

1. Cook onion within 5-8 minutes. Add the heavy cream, garlic, nutmeg, salt, and black pepper and stir.
2. Cook for about 3-5 minutes.
3. Put salt and black pepper in filet mignon steaks. Cook the steaks within 4 minutes per side.
4. Transfer and set aside.

Nutrition for Total Servings:

- Calories: 521
- Carbs: 3.3g
- Fat: 28.54 g
- Protein: 44.7g

Steak with Blueberry Sauce

Preparation time: 15 minutes **Cooking time:** 20 minutes **Servings:** 4

Ingredients:

For Sauce:
- 2 tbsps. butter
- 2 tbsps. yellow onion
- 2 garlic cloves
- 1 tsp. thyme
- 1 1/3 cups beef broth
- 2 tbsps. lemon juice
- 3/4 cup blueberries

For Steak:
- 4 grass-fed flank steaks
- Salt
- ground black pepper

Directions:
1. For the sauce: sauté the onion within 2-3 minutes.
2. Add the garlic and thyme and sauté within 1 minute. Stir in the broth and simmer within 10 minutes.
3. For the steak: put salt and black pepper. Cook steaks within 3-4 minutes per side.
4. Transfer and put aside. Add sauce to the skillet and stir. Stir in the lemon juice, blueberries, salt, and black pepper, and cook within 1-2 minutes. Put blueberry sauce over the steaks. Serve.

Nutrition for Total Servings:
- Calories: 467
- Carbs: 4.6g
- Fat: 6.22 g
- Protein: 49.5g

Grilled Steak

Preparation time: 15 minutes
Cooking time: 12 minutes
Servings: 6
Ingredients:
- 1 tsp. lemon zest
- 1 garlic clove
- 1 tbsp. red chili powder
- 1 tbsp. paprika
- 1 tbsp. ground coffee
- Salt
- Ground black pepper
- 2 grass-fed skirt steaks

Directions:
1. Mix all the ingredients except steaks. Marinate the steaks and keep them aside within 30-40 minutes.
2. Grill the steaks within 5-6 minutes per side.
3. Remove then cool before slicing. Serve.

Nutrition for Total Servings:
- Calories: 473
- Carbos: 1.6g
- Fat: 2.27 g
- Protein: 60.8g

Roasted Tenderloin

Preparation time: 10 minutes **Cooking time:** 50 minutes **Servings:** 10

Ingredients:
- 1 grass-fed beef tenderloin roast
- 4 garlic cloves
- 1 tbsp. rosemary
- Salt
- ground black pepper
- 1 tbsp. olive oil

Directions:
1. Warm-up oven to 425°F.
2. Place beef meat into the prepared roasting pan. Massage with garlic, rosemary, salt, and black pepper, and oil. Roast the beef within 45-50 minutes.
3. Remove, cool, slice, and serve.

Nutrition for Total Servings:
- Calories: 295
- Carbs: 0.4g
- Protein: 39.5g
- Fat: 13.9g

Chocolate Chili

Preparation time: 15 minutes   **Cooking time:** 2 1/4 hours   **Servings:** 8

Ingredients:

- 2 tbsps. olive oil
- 1 small onion
- 1 green bell pepper
- 4 garlic cloves
- 1 jalapeño pepper
- 1 tsp. dried thyme
- 2 tbsps. red chili powder
- 1 tbsp. ground cumin
- 2 pounds lean ground pork
- 2 cups fresh tomatoes
- 4 ounces sugar-free tomato paste
- 1 1/2 tbsps. cacao powder
- 2 cups chicken broth
- 1 cup of water
- Salt
- Ground black pepper

Directions:

1. Sauté the onion and bell pepper within 5-7 minutes.
2. Add the garlic, jalapeño pepper, thyme, and spices and sauté within 1 minute.
3. Add the pork and cook within 4-5 minutes. Stir in the tomatoes, tomato paste, and cacao powder and cook within 2 minutes.
4. Add the broth and water, boil. Simmer, covered within 2 hours. Stir in the salt and black pepper.

Nutrition for Total Servings:

- Calories: 326
- Carbs: 9.1g
- Protein: 23.3g
- Fat: 22.9g

Pork & Chiles Stew

Preparation time: 15 minutes   **Cooking time:** 2 hours & 10 minutes   **Servings:** 8

Ingredients:

- 2 1/2 pounds boneless pork ribs
- 1 large yellow onion
- 4 garlic cloves
- 1 1/2 cups chicken broth
- 2 cans sugar-free tomatoes
- 1 cup canned roasted poblano chilies
- 2 teaspoons dried oregano
- 1 tsp. ground cumin
- Sal
- 1/4 cup cilantro
- 2 tbsps. lime juice

Directions:

1. Cook the pork, onions, and garlic within 5 minutes.
2. Add the broth, tomatoes, poblano chilies, oregano, cumin, and salt and boil.
3. Simmer, covered within 2 hours. Mix with fresh cilantro and lime juice and remove it. Serve.

Nutrition for Total Servings:

- Calories: 288
- Carbs: 8.8g
- Fat: 13.88 g
- Protein: 39.6g

Keto Rib Eye Steak

Preparation time: 5 minutes
Cooking time: 20 minutes
Servings: 2
Ingredients:

- 1/2 pound grass-fed rib eye steak, preferably 1" thick
- 1 tsp. adobo seasoning
- 1 tbsp. extra-virgin olive oil

Directions:

1. Add steak in a large-sized mixing bowl and drizzle both sides with a small amount of olive oil. Dust the seasonings on both sides, rubbing the seasonings into the meat.
2. Let sit for a couple of minutes and heat up your grill in advance. Once hot; place the steaks over the grill, and cook until both sides are cooked through, for 15 to 20 minutes, flipping occasionally.

Nutrition for Total Servings:

- Calories: 257
- Fat: 19g
- Carbs: 0.3g
- Protein: 24g

Bacon Bleu Zoodle Salad

Preparation time: 5 minutes   **Cooking time:** 0 minutes   **Servings:** 2

Ingredients:

- 4 cups zucchini noodles
- 1/2 cup bacon, cooked and crumbled
- 1 cup fresh spinach, chopped
- Fresh cracked pepper, to taste

Directions:

1. Toss the entire ingredients together in a large-sized mixing bowl.
2. Serve immediately, and enjoy.

Nutrition for Total Servings:

- Calories: 214
- Fat: 17g
- Carbs: 6g
- Protein: 33g

Garlic Baked Butter Chicken

Preparation time: 10 minutes   **Cooking time:** 40 minutes   **Servings:** 4

Ingredients:

- 1 tbsp. rosemary leaves, fresh
- 3 chicken breasts, boneless, skinless (approximately 12 oz.); washed and cleaned
- 1 stick butter (1/2 cup)
- 6 garlic cloves, minced
- Fresh ground pepper and salt to taste

Directions:

1. Grease a large-sized baking dish lightly with a pat of butter, and preheat your oven to 375°F.
2. Season chicken breasts with pepper and salt to taste; arrange them in the prepared baking dish, preferably in a single layer; set aside.
3. Now, over medium heat in large skillet, heat the butter until melted, and then cook the garlic until lightly browned, for 4 to 5 minutes, stirring every now and then. Keep an eye on the garlic; don't burn it.
4. Add the rosemary; give everything a good stir; remove the skillet from heat.
5. Transfer the already prepared garlic butter over the meat.
6. Bake in preheated oven for 30 min.
7. Remove from oven & let stand for a couple of minutes. Transfer the cooked meat to large serving plates. Serve and enjoy.

Nutrition for Total Servings:

- Calories: 375
- Fat: 27g
- Carbs: 2.3g
- Protein: 30g

Lemon Rosemary Chicken Thighs

Preparation time: 10 minutes   **Cooking time:** 45 minutes   **Servings:** 4

Ingredients:

- 4 chicken thighs
- 2 garlic cloves, roughly chopped
- 4 sprigs of Rosemary, fresh
- 1 lemon, medium
- 2 tbsps. butter
- Pepper, and salt to taste

Directions:

1. Now, preheat the oven to 400°F in advance and heat up a cast-iron skillet over high heat as well.
2. Season both sides of chicken with pepper, and salt. When the skillet is hot; carefully place the coated thighs, preferably skin side down into the hot skillet and sear them for 4 to 5 minutes, until nicely brown.
3. Carefully flip and flavor the thighs with the lemon juice (only use 1/2 of the lemon). Quarter the leftover lemon halves and throw the pieces into the pan with the chicken.
4. Add the chopped garlic cloves together with some rosemary into the skillet.
5. Place the skillet inside the oven and bake for 30 minutes.
6. Remove the skillet from the oven. To add flavor, moisture, and more crispiness; add a portion of butter over the chicken thighs. Bake for 10 more minutes.
7. Serve hot and enjoy.

Nutrition for Total Servings:

- Calories: 159
- Fat: 8.8g
- Carbs: 6.9g
- Protein: 13.9g

Coffee Butter Rubbed Tri-Tip Steak

Preparation time: 20 minutes   **Cooking time:** 15 minutes   **Servings:** 2

Ingredients:

- 2 Tri-tip steaks, preferably 1/2 pound
- 1 package of coffee blocks
- 1/2 tbsp. garlic powder
- 1 tsp. black pepper,
- 2 tbsps. olive oil
- 1/2 tbsp. sea salt

Directions:

1. Pound the meat using a mallet until tenderize; let the meat to sit for 20 minutes at room temperature.
2. Combine everything together (except the steaks) in a large-sized mixing bowl.
3. Rub the sides, top and bottom of the meat steaks entirely with the mixture.
4. Over medium-high heat in a large skillet; heat the olive oil until hot.
5. Carefully add the coated steaks into the hot oil and cook for 5 min.
6. Flip & cook the other side until cooked through, for 5 more minutes.
7. Remove the meat from pan and let sit for a minute in its own juices.
8. Cut into slices against the grain. Serve warm and enjoy.

Nutrition for Total Servings:

- Calories: 371
- Fat: 35g
- Carbs: 0.5g
- Protein: 22g

Garlicky Prime Rib Roast

Preparation time: 15 minutes   **Cooking time:** 1 hour 35 minutes   **Servings:** 15

Ingredients:

- 10 garlic cloves
- 2 teaspoons dried thyme
- 2 tbsps. olive oil
- Salt
- Ground black pepper
- 1 grass-fed prime rib roast

Directions:

1. Mix the garlic, thyme, oil, salt, and black pepper. Marinate the rib roast with garlic mixture within 1 hour.
2. Warm-up oven to 500°F.
3. Roast within 20 minutes. Lower to 325°F and roast within 65-75 minutes.
4. Remove then cool down within 10-15 minutes, slice and serve.

Nutrition for Total Servings:

- Calories: 499
- Carbs: 0.7g
- Protein: 61.5g
- Fat: 25.9g

Meatballs

Preparation time: 20 minutes   **Cooking time:** 25 minutes   **Servings:** 5

Ingredients:

For Meatballs:

- 1-pound ground pork
- 1 organic egg
- 1/2 tbsp. dried basil
- 1 tsp. garlic powder
- 1/2 tsp. onion powder
- Salt
- Ground black pepper
- 3 tbsps. olive oil

For Sauce:

- 1 can sugar-free tomatoes
- 2 tbsps. butter
- 7 ounces spinach
- 2 tbsps. parsley
- Salt
- Ground black pepper

Directions:

For meatballs:

1. Mix all the fixing except oil in a large bowl. Make small-sized balls from the mixture.
2. Cook the meatballs within 3-5 minutes. Add the tomatoes. Simmer within 15 minutes.
3. Stir fry the spinach within 1-2 minutes in butter. Put salt and black pepper.
4. Remove then put the cooked spinach, parsley and stir.
5. Cook within 1-2 minutes. Remove and serve.

Nutrition for Total Servings:

- Calories: 398
- Carbs: 6.6g
- Protein: 38.6g
- Fat: 24.8g

Pork Stew

Preparation time: 15 minutes   **Cooking time:** 45 minutes   **Servings:** 6

Ingredients:

- 2 tbsps. olive oil
- 2 pounds pork tenderloin
- 1 tbsp. garlic
- 2 teaspoons paprika
- 3/4 cup chicken broth
- 1 cup sugar-free tomato sauce
- 1/2 tbsp. Erythritol
- 1 tsp. dried oregano
- 2 dried bay leaves
- 2 tbsps. lemon juice
- Salt
- Ground black pepper

Directions:

1. Cook the pork within 3-4 minutes. Add the garlic and cook within 1 minute.
2. Stir in the remaining fixing and boil. Simmer, covered within 30-40 minutes
3. Remove then discard the bay leaves. Serve.

Nutrition for Total Servings:

- Calories: 277
- Carbs: 3.6g
- Protein: 41g
- Fat: 10.4g

Meatballs Curry

Preparation time: 15 minutes
Cooking time: 25 minutes
Servings: 6
Ingredients:
For Meatballs:

- 1-pound lean ground pork
- 2 organic eggs
- 3 tbsps. yellow onion
- 1/4 cup fresh parsley leaves
- 1/4 tsp. fresh ginger
- 2 garlic cloves
- 1 jalapeño pepper
- 1 tsp. Erythritol
- 1 tbsp. red curry paste
- 3 tbsps. olive oil

For Curry:

- 1 yellow onion
- Salt
- 2 garlic cloves
- 1/4 tsp. ginger
- 2 tbsps. red curry paste
- 1 can unsweetened soy milk
- Ground black pepper
- 1/4 cup fresh parsley

Directions:

For meatballs:

1. Mix all the ingredients except oil. Make small-sized balls from the mixture.
2. Cook meatballs within 3-5 minutes. Transfer and put aside.

For curry:

1. Sauté onion, and salt within 4-5 minutes. Add the garlic and ginger. Add the curry paste, and sauté within 1-2 minutes. Add soy milk, and meatballs then simmer.
2. Simmer again within 10-12 minutes. Put salt and black pepper. Remove then serve with parsley.

Nutrition for Total Servings:

- Calories: 444
- Fat: 6.59 g
- Carbs: 8.6g
- Protein: 17g

Beef Taco Bake

Preparation time: 15 minutes
Cooking time: 1 hour
Servings: 6
Ingredients:
For Crust:

- 3 organic eggs
- 1/2 tsp. taco seasoning
- 1/3 cup heavy cream

For Topping:

- 1-pound grass-fed ground beef
- 4 ounces green chilies
- 1/4 cup sugar-free tomato sauce
- 3 teaspoons taco seasoning

Directions:

1. Warm-up oven to 375°F.
2. For the crust: beat the eggs, taco seasoning, and heavy cream.
3. Bake within 25-30 minutes. Remove then set aside within 5 minutes.

For topping:

1. Cook the beef within 8-10 minutes.
2. Stir in the green chilies, tomato sauce, and taco seasoning and transfer.
3. Place the beef mixture over the crust. Bake within 18-20 minutes.
4. Remove then slice and serve.

Nutrition for Total Servings:

- Calories: 569
- Carbs: 4g
- Fat: 21.04 g
- Protein: 38.7g

CHAPTER 12:

Seafood and Fish

Keto Fish

Preparation time: 40 minutes   **Cooking time:** 30 minutes   **Servings:** 4

Ingredients:

For the Tartar Sauce:
- 4 tbsps. dill pickle relish
- 1 cup mayonnaise
- 1/2 tbsp. curry powder

For the Fish:
- 1 1/2 pounds white fish
- 1 cup almond flour
- 2 eggs
- 2 cups coconut oil, for frying

- 1 tbsp. olive oil
- 1 1/2 pounds rutabaga (peeled and cleaned)
- Salt and pepper, to taste

- 1 tsp. paprika powder
- 1/4 tsp. pepper
- 1/2 tsp. onion powder
- 1 tsp. salt

Directions:
1. Take a small bowl and mix mayonnaise, curry powder, and pickle relish thoroughly. Refrigerate the tartar sauce until you finish the remaining dish.
2. Now, preheat the oven to 400°F.
3. Slice the peeled rutabaga into thin rods and brush them with oil.
4. Line baking tray with parchment paper and spread the oil-coated rutabaga rods.
5. Sprinkle the pepper and salt over the spread rutabaga.
6. Bake for 30 minutes until the rods become golden brown.
7. As the rutabaga gets cooked, prepare the fish.
8. Crack eggs into small bowl and beat it well with a fork.
9. Mix the almond flour, paprika powder, pepper, onion powder, and salt on a plate. Set aside.
10. Dip the flour-coated fix into the beaten eggs and coat it again with the flour mix.
11. Pour the oil in a shallow skillet and heat over high heat.
12. If the rutabaga chips are ready by now, turn off the oven and let it sit for a while.
13. Fry the flour-egg coated fish in the hot oil until the fish is completely cooked and turns golden brown.
14. Repeat steps 11 and 14 with the remaining fish.
15. Transfer the fried fish, baked rutabaga fries, and tartar into a serving bowl. Serve hot and enjoy!

Nutrition for Total Servings:
- Calories: 463
- Fat: 26.2 g
- Protein: 49.2 g
- Carbs: 4 g

Zingy Lemon Fish

Preparation time: 50 minutes   **Cooking time:** 40 minutes   **Servings:** 4

Ingredients:

- 14 ounces fresh Gurnard fish fillets
- 2 tbsps. lemon juice
- 6 tbsps. butter
- 1/2 cup fine almond flour
- 2 teaspoons dried chives
- 1 tsp. garlic powder
- 2 teaspoons dried dill
- 2 teaspoons onion powder
- Salt and pepper to taste

Directions:

1. Add almond flour, dried herbs, salt, and spices on a large plate and stir until well combined. Spread it all over the plate evenly.
2. Place a large pan over medium-high heat. Add half the butter and half the lemon juice. When butter just melts, place fillets on the pan and cook for 3 minutes. Move the fillets around the pan so that it absorbs the butter and lemon juice.
3. Add remaining half butter and lemon juice. When butter melts, flip sides and cook the other side for 3 minutes.
4. Serve fillets with any butter remaining in the pan.

Nutrition for Total Servings:

- Calories: 406
- Fat: 30.33 g
- Protein: 29 g
- Carb: 3.55 g

Creamy Keto Fish Casserole

Preparation time: 1 hour   **Cooking time:** 50 minutes   **Servings:** 4

Ingredients:

- 25 ounces of white fish (slice into bite-sized pieces)
- 15 ounces broccoli (small florets, include the step too)
- 3 ounces butter + extra
- 6 scallions (finely chopped)
- 1 1/4 cups heavy whipping cream
- 2 tbsps. small capers
- 1 tbsp. dried parsley
- 1 tbsp. Dijon mustard
- 1/4 tsp. black pepper (ground)
- 1 tsp. salt
- 2 tbsps. olive oil
- 5 ounces leafy greens (finely chopped), for garnishing

Directions:

1. Now, preheat the oven to 400°F
2. Now, preheat the oven oil in a saucepan over medium-high heat.
3. Fry the broccoli florets in the hot oil for 5 minutes until tender and golden.
4. Transfer the fried florets to a small bowl and season it with salt and pepper. Toss the contents to ensure all the florets get an equal amount of seasoning.
5. Add the chopped scallions and capers to the same saucepan and fry for 2 minutes. Return the florets to the pan and mix well.
6. Grease a baking tray with a little amount of butter and spread the fried veggies (broccoli, scallions, and capers) in the baking tray.
7. Add the sliced fish to the tray and nestle it among the veggies.
8. Mix the heavy cream, mustard, and parsley in a small bowl and pour this mixture over the fish-veggie mixture
9. Top this with the remaining butter and spread gently over the contents using a spatula
10. Transfer to a plate and garnish with chopped greens. Serve warm and enjoy!

Nutrition for Total Servings:

- Calories: 822
- Fat: 69 g
- Protein: 41 g
- Carb: 8 g

Keto Fish Casserole with Mushrooms and French Mustard

Preparation time: 1 hour   **Cooking time:** 50 minutes   **Servings:** 6

Ingredients:

- 25 ounces of white fish
- 15 ounces mushrooms (cut into wedges)
- 20 ounces cauliflower (cut into florets)
- 2 cups heavy whipping cream
- 2 tbsps. Dijon mustard
- 3 ounces olive oil
- 2 tbsps. fresh parsley
- Salt & pepper, to taste

Directions:

1. Now, preheat the oven to 350°F
2. Fry the mushroom for 5 minutes until tender and soft.
3. Add the parsley, salt, and pepper to the mushrooms as you continue to mix well.
4. Reduce the heat and add the mustard and heavy whipping cream to the mushroom.
5. Allow it simmer for 10 minutes until the sauce thickens and reduces a bit.
6. Season the fish slices with pepper and salt. Set aside.
7. Spread the creamy mushroom over the top.
8. Boil cauliflower florets in lightly salted water for 5 minutes and strain the water.
9. Place the strained florets in a bowl and add the olive oil. Mash thoroughly with a fork until you get a coarse texture—season with salt and pepper. Mix well.

Nutrition for Total Servings:

- Calories: 828
- Fat: 71 g
- Protein: 39 g
- Carb: 8 g

Keto Thai Fish with Curry and Coconut

Preparation time: 50 minutes   **Cooking time:** 40 minutes   **Servings:** 4

Ingredients:

- 25 ounces salmon (slice into bite-sized pieces)
- 15 ounces cauliflower (bite-sized florets)
- 14 ounces coconut cream
- 1-ounce olive oil
- 4 tbsps. butter
- Salt and pepper, to taste

Directions:

1. Now, preheat the oven to 400°F
2. Sprinkle salt and pepper over the salmon generously. Toss it once, if possible.
3. Place the butter generously over all the salmon pieces and set aside.
4. Pour this cream mixture over the fish in the baking tray.
5. Meanwhile, boil the cauliflower florets in salted water for 5 minutes, strain and mash the florets coarsely. Set aside.
6. Transfer the creamy fish to a plate and serve with mashed cauliflower. Enjoy!

Nutrition for Total Servings:

- Calories: 880
- Fat: 75 g
- Protein: 42 g
- Carb: 6 g

Keto Salmon Tandoori with Cucumber Sauce

Preparation time: 15 minutes   **Cooking time:** 20 minutes   **Servings:** 4

Ingredients:

- 25 ounces salmon (bite-sized pieces)
- 2 tbsps. coconut oil
- 1 tbsp. tandoori seasoning

For the cucumber sauce:

- 1/2 shredded cucumber (squeeze out the water completely)
- Juice of 1/2 lime
- 2 minced garlic cloves
- 1 1/4 cups sour cream or mayonnaise
- 1/2 tsp. salt (optional)

For the crispy salad:

- 3 1/2 ounces lettuce (torn)
- 3 scallions (finely chopped)
- 2 avocados (cubed)
- 1 yellow bell pepper (diced)
- Juice of 1 lime

Directions:

1. Now, preheat the oven to 350°F.
2. Mix the tandoori seasoning with oil in a small bowl and coat the salmon pieces with this mixture.
3. Bake for 20 minutes until soft and the salmon flakes with a fork.
4. Take another bowl and place the shredded cucumber in it. Add the mayonnaise, minced garlic, and salt (if the mayonnaise doesn't have salt) to the shredded cucumber.
5. Mix the lettuce, scallions, avocados, and bell pepper in another bowl. Drizzle the contents with the lime juice.
6. Transfer the veggie salad to a plate and place the baked salmon over it. Top the veggies and salmon with cucumber sauce. Serve immediately and enjoy!

Nutrition for Total Servings:

- Calories: 847
- Fat: 73 g
- Protein: 35 g
- Carb: 6 g

Creamy Mackerel

Preparation time: 10 minutes   **Cooking time:** 20 minutes   **Servings:** 4

Ingredients:

- 2 shallots, minced
- 2 spring onions, chopped
- 2 tbsps. olive oil
- 4 mackerel fillets, skinless and cut into medium cubes
- 1 cup heavy cream
- 1 tsp. cumin, ground
- 1/2 tsp. oregano, dried
- A pinch of salt and black pepper
- 2 tbsps. chives, chopped

Directions:

1. Heat a pan with the oil over medium heat, add the spring onions and the shallots, stir and sauté for 5 minutes.
2. Add the fish and cook it for 4 minutes.
3. Add the rest of the ingredients, bring to a simmer, cook everything for 10 minutes more, divide between plates, and serve.

Nutrition for Total Servings:

- Calories: 403
- Fat: 33.9g
- Carbs: 2.7g
- Protein: 22g

Lime Mackerel

Preparation time: 10 minutes   **Cooking time:** 30 minutes   **Servings:** 4

Ingredients:

- 4 mackerel fillets, boneless
- 2 tbsps. lime juice
- 2 tbsps. olive oil
- A pinch of salt and black pepper
- 1/2 tsp. sweet paprika

Directions:

1. Arrange the mackerel on a baking sheet lined with parchment paper, add the oil and the other ingredients, rub gently, introduce in the oven at 360°F and bake for 30 minutes.
2. Divide the fish between plates and serve.

Nutrition for Total Servings:

- Calories: 297
- Fat: 22.7g
- Carbs: 2g
- Protein: 21.1g

Turmeric Tilapia

Preparation time: 10 minutes **Cooking time:** 12 minutes **Servings:** 4

Ingredients:
- 4 tilapia fillets, boneless
- 2 tbsps. olive oil
- 1 tsp. turmeric powder
- A pinch of salt and black pepper
- 2 spring onions, chopped
- 1/4 tsp. basil, dried
- 1/4 tsp. garlic powder
- 1 tbsp. parsley, chopped

Directions:
1. First, Heat pan with the oil over medium heat, add the spring onions and cook them for 2 minutes.
2. Add the fish, turmeric, and the other ingredients, cook for 5 minutes on each side, divide between plates and serve.

Nutrition for Total Servings:
- Calories: 205
- Fat: 8.6g
- Carbs: 1.1g
- Protein: 31.8g

Walnut Salmon Mix

Preparation time: 10 minutes **Cooking time:** 14 minutes **Servings:** 4

Ingredients:
- 4 salmon fillets, boneless
- 2 tbsps. avocado oil
- A pinch of salt and black pepper
- 1 tbsp. lime juice
- 2 shallots, chopped
- 2 tbsps. walnuts, chopped
- 2 tbsps. parsley, chopped

Directions:
1. Heat a pan with the oil over medium-high heat, add the shallots, stir and sauté for 2 minutes.
2. Add the fish and the other ingredients, cook for 6 minutes on each side, divide between plates and serve.

Nutrition for Total Servings:
- Calories: 276
- Fat: 14.2g
- Carbs: 2.7g
- Protein: 35.8g

Chives Trout

Preparation time: 10 minutes **Cooking time:** 12 minutes **Servings:** 4

Ingredients:
- 4 trout fillets, boneless
- 2 shallots, chopped
- A pinch of salt and black pepper
- 3 tbsps. chives, chopped
- 2 tbsps. avocado oil
- 2 teaspoons lime juice

Directions:
1. First, heat a pan with the oil over medium heat, add the shallots and sauté them for 2 minutes.
2. Add the fish and the rest of the ingredients, cook for 5 minutes on each side, divide between plate sand serve.

Nutrition for Total Servings:
- Calories: 320
- Fat: 12g
- Carbs: 2g
- Protein: 24g

Salmon and Tomatoes

Preparation time: 10 minutes **Cooking time:** 25 minutes **Servings:** 4

Ingredients:
- 2 tbsps. avocado oil
- 4 salmon fillets, boneless
- 1 cup cherry tomatoes, halved
- 2 spring onions, chopped
- 1/2 cup chicken stock
- A pinch of salt and black pepper
- 1/2 tsp. rosemary, dried

Directions:
1. In a roasting pan, combine the fish with the oil and the other ingredients, introduce in the oven at 400°F & bake for 25 minutes.
2. Divide between plates and serve.

Nutrition for Total Servings:
- Calories: 200
- Fat: 12g
- Carbs: 3g
- Protein: 21g

Herbed Salmon

Preparation time: 10 minutes
Cooking time: 8 minutes
Servings: 4

Ingredients:
- 2 garlic cloves, minced
- 1 tsp. dried oregano, crushed
- 1 tsp. dried basil, crushed
- Salt and ground black pepper, to taste
- 1/4 cup olive oil
- 2 tbsps. fresh lemon juice
- 4 (4-ounce) salmon fillets

Directions:
1. For salmon: In large bowl, add all ingredients (except salmon) and mix well.
2. Add salmon and coat with marinade generously.
3. Cover & refrigerate to marinate for at least 1 hour.
4. Preheat the grill to medium-high heat. Grease the grill grate.
5. Place the salmon in the grill and cook for about 4 minutes per side.
6. Serve hot.

Nutrition for Total Servings:
- Calories: 263
- Fat: 19.7 g
- Carbs: 0.9 g
- Protein: 22.2 g

Buttered Salmon

Preparation time: 10 minutes
Cooking time: 10 minutes
Servings: 4

Ingredients:
- 4 (5-ounce) skin-on, boneless salmon fillets
- Salt and ground black pepper, to taste
- 1 tbsp. olive oil
- 3 tbsps. butter
- 2 tbsps. lemon juice
- 2 tbsps. fresh rosemary, minced
- 1 tsp. lemon zest, grated

Directions:
1. Season the salmon fillets with salt & black pepper evenly.
2. In non-stick wok, heat oil over medium heat.
3. Place salmon fillets, skin side down and cook for about 3–5 minutes, without stirring.
4. Flip the salmon fillets and cook for about 2 minutes.
5. Add the butter, lemon juice, rosemary, and lemon zest, and cook for about 2 minutes, spooning the butter sauce over the salmon fillets occasionally.
6. Serve hot.

Nutrition for Total Servings:
- Calories: 301
- Fat: 21.2 g
- Carbs: 1.3 g
- Protein: 27.7 g

Lemony Salmon

Preparation time: 10 minutes
Cooking time: 10 minutes
Servings: 4
Ingredients:

- 1 tbsp. butter, melted
- 1 tbsp. fresh lemon juice
- 1 tsp. Worcestershire sauce
- 1 tsp. lemon zest, grated finely.
- 4 (6-ounce) salmon fillets
- Salt and ground black pepper, to taste

Directions:

1. In a baking dish, place butter, lemon juice, Worcestershire sauce, and lemon zest, and mix well.
2. Coat the fillets with mixture and then arrange skin side-up in the baking dish.
3. Set aside for about 15 minutes.
4. Preheat the broiler of oven.
5. Arrange the oven rack about 6-inch from heating element.
6. Line a broiler pan with a piece of foil.
7. Remove the salmon fillets from baking dish and season with salt and black pepper.
8. Arrange the salmon fillets onto the prepared broiler pan, skin side down.
9. Broil for about 8–10 minutes.
10. Serve hot.

Nutrition for Total Servings:

- Calories: 253
- Fat: 13.4 g
- Carbs: 0.4 g
- Protein: 33.1 g

Cheesy Tilapia

Preparation time: 10 minutes
Cooking time: 15 minutes
Servings: 8
Ingredients:

- 2 pounds tilapia fillets
- 3 tbsps. mayonnaise
- 1/4 cup unsalted butter, softened
- 2 tbsps. fresh lemon juice
- 1/4 tsp. dried thyme, crushed
- Salt and ground black pepper, to taste

Directions:

1. Preheat the broiler of oven.
2. Grease a broiler pan.
3. In a large bowl, mix the ingredients except tilapia fillets. Set aside.
4. Place the fillets onto prepared broiler pan in a single layer.
5. Broil the fillets for about 2–3 minutes.
6. Remove the broiler pan from oven and top the fillets.
7. Broil for about 2 minutes further.
8. Serve hot.

Nutrition for Total Servings:

- Calories: 185
- Fat: 9.8 g
- Carbs: 1.4 g
- Protein: 23.2 g

Roasted Mackerel

Preparation time: 10 minutes   **Cooking time:** 20 minutes   **Servings:** 2

Ingredients:

- 2 (7-ounce) mackerel fillets
- 1 tbsp. butter, melted
- Salt and ground black pepper, to taste

Directions:

1. Now, preheat the oven to 350°F.
2. Arrange a rack, in the middle of oven.
3. Lightly, grease a baking dish.
4. Brush the fish fillets with melted butter and then season with salt and black pepper.
5. Arrange the fish fillets into the prepared baking dish in a single layer.
6. Bake for about 20 minutes.
7. Serve hot.

Nutrition for Total Servings:

- Calories: 571
- Fat: 41.1 g
- Carbs: 0 g
- Protein: 47.4 g

Herbed Sea Bass

Preparation time: 15 minutes
Cooking time: 20 minutes
Servings: 2
Ingredients:

- 2 (1 1/4-pound) whole sea bass; gutted, gilled, scaled, and fins removed
- Salt and ground black pepper, to taste
- 6 fresh bay leaves
- 2 fresh thyme sprigs
- 2 fresh parsley sprigs
- 2 fresh rosemary sprigs
- 2 tbsps. butter, melted
- 2 tbsps. fresh lemon juice

Directions:

1. Season the cavity and outer side of each fish with salt and black pepper evenly.
2. With a plastic wrap, cover each fish and refrigerate for 1 hour.
3. Now, preheat the oven to 450°F.
4. Lightly, grease a baking dish.
5. Arrange 2 bay leaves in the bottom of prepared baking dish.
6. Divide herb sprigs and remaining bay leaves inside the cavity of each fish.
7. Arrange the both fish over bay leave in baking dish and drizzle with butter.
8. Roast for about 15-20 minutes or until fish is cooked through.
9. Remove the baking dish from oven and place the fish onto a platter.
10. Drizzle the fish with lemon juice and serve.

Nutrition for Total Servings:

- Calories: 811
- Fat: 26.2 g
- Carbs: 0.8 g
- Protein: 134.5 g

Shrimp Stew

Preparation time: 15 minutes   **Cooking time:** 20 minutes   **Servings:** 6

Ingredients:

- 1/4 cup olive oil
- 1/4 cup onion, chopped
- 1/4 cup roasted red pepper, chopped
- 1 garlic clove, minced
- 1 1/2 pounds raw shrimp, peeled and deveined
- 1 (14-ounce) can sugar-free diced tomatoes with chilies
- 1 cup unsweetened soy milk
- 2 tbsps. Sriracha
- 2 tbsps. fresh lime juice
- Salt and ground black pepper, to taste
- 1/4 cup fresh cilantro, chopped

Directions:

1. In a wok, heat the oil over medium heat and sauté the onion for about 4-5 minutes.
2. Add the red pepper and garlic and sauté for about 4-5 minutes.
3. Add the shrimp and tomatoes and cook for about 3-4 minutes.
4. Stir in the soy milk and Sriracha and cook for about 4-5 minutes.
5. Stir in the lime juice, salt, & black pepper, and remove from the heat.
6. Garnish with cilantro and serve hot.

Nutrition for Total Servings:

- Calories: 289
- Fat: 16 g
- Carbs: 7 g
- Protein: 27.1 g

Shrimp Casserole

Preparation time: 15 minutes   **Cooking time:** 30 minutes   **Servings:** 6

Ingredients:

- 1/4 cup unsalted butter
- 1 tbsp. garlic, minced
- 1 1/2 pounds large shrimp, peeled & deveined
- 3/4 tsp. dried oregano, crushed
- 1/4 tsp. red pepper flakes, crushed
- 1/4 cup fresh parsley, chopped
- 1/2 cup homemade chicken broth
- 1 tbsp. fresh lemon juice
- 1 (14 1/2-ounce) can sugar-free diced tomatoes, drained

Directions:

1. Now, preheat the oven to 3500F.
2. In a large wok, melt butter over medium-high heat and sauté the garlic for about 1 minute.
3. Add the shrimp, oregano and red pepper flakes and cook for about 4-5 minutes.
4. Stir in the parsley and salt and immediately transfer into a casserole dish evenly.
5. In the same wok, add broth and lemon juice over medium heat and simmer for about 2-3 minutes or until liquid reduces to half.
6. Stir in tomatoes and cook for about 2-3 minutes.
7. Pour the tomato mixture over shrimp mixture evenly.
8. Bake for approximately 15-20 minutes or until top becomes golden-brown.
9. Remove from the oven and serve hot.

Nutrition for Total Servings:

- Calories: 272
- Fat: 13.9 g
- Carbs: 6 g
- Protein: 29.8 g

Super Salmon Parcel

Preparation time: 15 minutes

Cooking time: 20 minutes

Servings: 6

Ingredients:

- 6 (3-oz.) salmon fillets
- Salt & freshly ground black pepper, to taste
- 1 yellow bell pepper, seeded and cubed
- 1 red bell pepper, seeded and cubed
- 4 plum tomatoes, cubed
- 1 small yellow onion, sliced thinly
- 1/2 C. fresh parsley, chopped
- 1/4 C. olive oil
- 2 tbsp. fresh lemon juice

Directions:

1. Now, preheat the oven to 400°F.
2. Arrange 6 pieces of foil onto a smooth surface. Place 1 salmon fillet onto each foil piece and sprinkle with salt and black pepper. In a bowl, add the bell peppers, tomato and onion and mix. Place veggie mixture over each fillet evenly and top with parsley. Drizzle with oil and lemon juice. Fold the foil around salmon mixture to seal it. Arrange the foil packets onto a large baking sheet in a single layer. Bake for about 20 minutes.
3. Serve hot.

Nutrition for Total Servings:

- Calories: 224
- Carbs: 8.2g
- Protein: 18.2g
- Fat: 14g

New England Salmon Pie

Preparation time: 20 minutes   **Cooking time:** 50 minutes   **Servings:** 5

Ingredients:

For Crust:

- 3/4 C. almond flour
- 4 tbsp. coconut flour
- 4 tbsp. sesame seeds
- 1 tbsp. psyllium husk powder
- 1 tsp. organic baking powder

- Pinch of salt
- 1 organic egg
- 3 tbsp. olive oil
- 4 tbsp. water

For Filling:

- 8 oz. smoked salmon
- 1 C. mayonnaise
- 3 organic eggs

- 2 tbsp. fresh dill, finely chopped
- 1/2 tsp. onion powder
- 1/4 tsp. ground black pepper

Directions:

1. Now, preheat the oven to 350°F. Line a 10-inch spring form pan with parchment paper.
2. For crust: place all the ingredients in a food processor, fitted with a plastic pastry blade and pulse till a dough ball is formed.
3. Place dough into prepared spring form pan and with your fingers, gently press in the bottom.
4. Bake for about 12-15 min or until lightly browned.
5. Remove the pie crust from oven and let it cool slightly.
6. Meanwhile, for filling: in a bowl add all the ingredients and mix well.
7. Bake for 35 min or until the pie is golden brown.
8. Remove the pie from oven & let it cool slightly.
9. Cut into 5 equal-sized slices and serve warm.

Nutrition for Total Servings:

- Calories: 762
- Carbs: 10.8g
- Protein: 24.8g
- Fat: 70g

Juicy Garlic Butter Shrimp

Preparation time: 10 minutes   **Cooking time:** 5 minutes   **Servings:** 4

Ingredients:

- 2 lbs. shrimp, peeled and deveined
- 2 tbsps. fresh herbs, chopped
- 2 tbsps. fresh lemon juice
- 1 tsp. paprika
- 1 tbsp. garlic, minced
- 1/4 cup butter
- Pepper
- Salt

Directions:

1. Melt your butter in pan over medium heat.
2. Add garlic and sauté for 30 seconds.
3. Add shrimp, paprika, pepper, and salt. Cook shrimp for about 2 min, on each side.
4. Add remaining ingredients and stir well and cook for 1 minute.
5. Serve and enjoy.

Nutrition for Total Servings:

- Calories: 379
- Fat: 15.5 g
- Carbs: 5 g
- Protein: 52.1 g

Simple Lemon Garlic Shrimp

Preparation time: 5 minutes   **Cooking time:** 15 minutes   **Servings:** 4

Ingredients:

- 1 1/2 lbs. shrimp, peeled and deveined
- 1/4 cup fresh parsley, chopped
- 1/4 cup fresh lemon juice
- 1 tbsp. garlic, minced
- 1/4 cup butter
- Pepper
- Salt

Directions:

1. Melt butter in pan over medium heat. Add garlic and sauté for 30 seconds.
2. Add shrimp and season with pepper and salt and cook for 4-5 minutes or until it turns to pink.
3. Add lemon juice & parsley and stir well and cook for 2 minutes.
4. Serve and enjoy.

Nutrition for Total Servings:

- Calories: 312
- Fat: 14.6 g
- Carbs: 3.9 g
- Protein: 39.2 g

Flavourful Shrimp Creole

Preparation time: 10 minutes   **Cooking time:** 1 hour 30 minutes   **Servings:** 8

Ingredients:

- 2 lbs. shrimp, peeled
- 3/4 cup green onions, chopped
- 1 tsp. garlic, minced
- 2 1/2 cups water
- 1 tbsp. hot sauce
- 8 oz. can tomato sauce, sugar-free
- 8 oz. can tomato paste
- 1/2 cup bell pepper, chopped
- 3/4 cup celery, chopped
- 1 cup onion, chopped
- 2 tbsps. olive oil
- Pepper
- Salt

Directions:

1. Now, preheat the oven oil in a saucepan over medium heat.
2. Add celery, onion, bell pepper, pepper, and salt and sauté until onion is softened.
3. Add tomato paste & cook for 5 minutes.
4. Add hot sauce, tomato sauce, and water and cook for 1 hour.
5. Add garlic and shrimp and cook for 15 minutes.
6. Add green onions & cook for 2 minutes more.
7. Serve and enjoy.

Nutrition for Total Servings:

- Calories: 208
- Fat: 5.7 g
- Carbs: 11.6 g
- Protein: 27.9 g

Perfect Pan-Seared Scallops

Preparation time: 10 minutes   **Cooking time:** 4 minutes   **Servings:** 4

Ingredients:

- 1 lb. scallops, rinse and pat dry
- 1 tbsp. olive oil
- 2 tbsps. butter
- Pepper
- Salt

Directions:

1. Season scallops with pepper and salt.
2. Heat butter & oil in pan over medium heat.
3. Add scallops and sear for 2 minutes then turn to other side and cook for 2 minutes more.
4. Serve and enjoy.

Nutrition for Total Servings:

- Calories: 181
- Fat: 10.1 g
- Carbs: 2.7 g
- Protein: 19.1 g

Easy Baked Shrimp Scampi

Preparation time: 10 minutes   **Cooking time:** 10 minutes   **Servings:** 4

Ingredients:

- 2 lbs. shrimp, peeled
- 3/4 cup olive oil
- 2 tsp. dried oregano
- 1 tbsp. garlic, minced
- 1/2 cup fresh lemon juice
- 1/4 cup butter, sliced Pepper
- Salt

Directions:

1. Now, preheat the oven to 350 F. Add shrimp in a baking dish. In a bowl, whisk together lemon juice, oregano, garlic, oil, pepper, and salt and pour over shrimp. Add butter on top of shrimp.
2. Bake in preheated oven for 10 min or until shrimp cooked. Serve and enjoy.

Nutrition for Total Servings:

- Calories: 708
- Fat: 53.5 g
- Carbs: 5.3 g
- Protein: 52.2 g

Delicious Blackened Shrimp

Preparation time: 10 minutes

Cooking time: 5 minutes

Servings: 4

Ingredients:

- 1 1/2 lbs. shrimp, peeled
- 1 tbsp. garlic, minced
- 1 tbsp. olive oil
- 1 tsp. garlic powder
- 1 tsp. dried oregano
- 1 tsp. cumin
- 1 tbsp. paprika
- 1 tbsp. chili powder
- Pepper
- Salt

Directions:

1. In a mixing bowl, mix together garlic powder, oregano, cumin, paprika, chili powder, pepper, and salt.
2. Add shrimp and mix until well coated. Set aside for 30 minutes.
3. Heat an oil in a pan over medium-high heat.
4. Add shrimp and cook for 2 minutes. Turn shrimp and cook for 2 minutes more.
5. Add garlic and cook for 30 seconds.
6. Serve and enjoy.

Nutrition for Total Servings:

- Calories: 252
- Fat: 7.1 g
- Carbs: 6.3 g
- Protein: 39.6 g

Creamy Parmesan Shrimp

Preparation time: 10 minutes   **Cooking time:** 20 minutes   **Servings:** 4

Ingredients:

- 1 1/2 lbs. shrimp
- 1/2 cup chicken stock
- 1/4 tsp. red pepper flakes
- 1 cup fresh basil leaves
- 1 1/2 cups heavy cream
- 1/4 tsp. paprika
- 3 oz. roasted red peppers, sliced
- 1/2 onion, minced
- 1 tbsp. garlic, minced
- 3 tbsps. butter
- Pepper
- Salt

Directions:

1. Melt 2 tbsps. Butter in a pan over medium heat.
2. Season shrimp with pepper and salt and sear in a pan for 1-2 minutes. Transfer shrimp on a plate.
3. Add remaining butter in a pan.
4. Add red chili flakes, paprika, roasted peppers, garlic, onion, pepper, and salt and cook for 5 minutes.
5. Add stock and stir well and cook until liquid is reduced by half.
6. Turn heat to low and add cream and stir for 1-2 minutes.
7. Add basil and stir for 1-2 minutes.
8. Return shrimp to pan and cook for 1-2 minutes.
9. Serve and enjoy.

Nutrition for Total Servings:

- Calories: 524
- Fat: 33.2 g
- Carbs: 8.3 g
- Protein: 47.8 g

Pan Fry Shrimp & Zucchini

Preparation time: 10 minutes   **Cooking time:** 20 minutes   **Servings:** 4

Ingredients:

- 1 lb. shrimp, peeled and deveined
- 1/2 small onion, chopped
- 1 summer squash, chopped
- 1 zucchini, chopped
- 2 tbsps. olive oil
- 1/2 tsp. paprika
- 1/2 tsp. garlic powder
- 1/2 tsp. onion powder
- Pepper
- Salt

Directions:

1. In a large bowl, mix together paprika, garlic powder, onion powder, pepper, and salt. Add shrimp and toss well.
2. Heat 1 tbsp. oil in a pan over medium heat,
3. Add shrimp & cook for 2 min on each side or until shrimp turns to pink. Transfer shrimp on a plate.
4. Add remaining oil in a pan.
5. Add onion, summer squash, and zucchini and cook for 6-8 minutes or until vegetables are softened.
6. Return shrimp to the pan & cook for 1 minute.
7. Serve and enjoy.

Nutrition for Total Servings:

- Calories: 215
- Fat: 9.1 g
- Carbs: 6.1 g
- Protein: 27 g

CHAPTER 13:

Soup and Stew Recipes

Hearty Fall Stew

Preparation time: 15 minutes **Cooking time:** 8 hrs. **Servings:** 6

Ingredients:
- 3 tbsps. extra-virgin olive oil, divided
- 1 (2-pound/907-g) beef chuck roast, cut into 1-inch chunks
- 1/2 tsp. salt
- 1/4 tsp. freshly ground black pepper
- 1/4 cup apple cider vinegar
- 1/2 sweet onion, chopped
- 1 cup diced tomatoes
- 1 tsp. dried thyme
- 1 1/2 cups pumpkin, cut into 1-inch chunks
- 2 cups beef broth
- 2 teaspoons minced garlic
- 1 tbsp. chopped fresh parsley, for garnish

Directions:
1. Add beef to the skillet, and sprinkle salt and pepper to season.
2. Cook the beef for 7 minutes or until well browned.
3. Put the cooked beef into the slow cooker and add the remaining ingredients, except for the parsley, to the slow cooker. Stir to mix well.
4. Slow cook for 8 hrs. And top with parsley before serving.

Nutrition for Total Servings:
- Calories: 462
- Fat: 19.1g
- Carbs: 10.7 g
- Protein: 18.6 g

Chicken Mushroom Soup

Preparation time: 15 minutes **Cooking time:** 10-15 minutes **Servings:** 4

Ingredients:
- 6 cups of chicken stock
- 5 slices of chopped bacon
- 4 cups cooked chicken breast, chopped
- 3 cups of water
- 2 cups of chopped celery root
- 2 cups of sliced yellow squash
- 2 tbsps. of olive oil
- 1/2 tsp. of avocado oil
- 1/4 cup of chopped basil
- 1/4 cup of chopped onion
- 1/4 cup of chopped tomatoes
- 1 tbsp. of ground garlic
- 1 cup of sliced white mushrooms
- 1 cup green beans
- Salt
- Black pepper

Directions:
1. Heat oil in a skillet, add in half of the onions, sauté until soft.
2. Put in bacon and fry for a minute and a half.
3. Then, add in onions, garlic, tomatoes, and mushrooms, stir fry for three minutes.
4. Put in stock and fat water with the rest of the ingredients. Let it simmer for 10-15 minutes. Serve hot.

Nutrition for Total Servings:
- Calories: 268
- Fat: 10.5g
- Carbs: 3.1 g
- Protein: 12.9g

Cold Green Beans and Avocado Soup

Preparation time: 15 minutes **Cooking time:** 15 minutes **Servings:** 4

Ingredients:

- 1 tbsp. butter
- 2 tbsp. almond oil
- 1 garlic clove, minced
- 1 cup (227 g) green beans (fresh or frozen)
- 1/4 avocado
- 1 cup heavy cream
- 1/2 tsp. coconut aminos
- Salt to taste

Directions:

1. Now, preheat the oven butter and almond oil in a large skillet and sauté the garlic for 30 seconds.
2. Add the green beans and stir-fry for 10 minutes or until tender.
3. Add the mixture to a food processor and top with the avocado, heavy cream, coconut aminos, and salt.
4. Blend the ingredients until smooth.
5. Pour the soup into serving bowls, cover with plastic wraps and chill in the fridge for at least 2 hours.

Nutrition for Total Servings:

- Calories: 301
- Fat: 3.1g
- Carb: 2.8 g
- Protein: 3.1g

Creamy Mixed Seafood Soup

Preparation time: 15 minutes **Cooking time:** 15 minutes **Servings:** 4

Ingredients:

- 1 tbsp. avocado oil
- 2 garlic cloves, minced
- 3/4 tbsp. almond flour
- 1 cup vegetable broth
- 1 tsp. dried dill
- 1 lb. frozen mixed seafood
- Salt and black pepper to taste
- 1 tbsp. plain vinegar
- 2 cups cooking cream
- Fresh dill leaves to garnish

Directions:

1. Heat oil sauté the garlic for 30 seconds or until fragrant.
2. Stir in the almond flour until brown.
3. Mix in the vegetable broth until smooth and stir in the dill, seafood mix, salt, and black pepper.
4. Bring soup to a boil and then simmer for 3 to 4 minutes or until the seafood cooks.
5. Add the vinegar, cooking cream, and stir well. Garnish with dill, serve.

Nutrition for Total Servings:

- Calories: 361
- Fat: 12.4g
- Carbs: 3.9 g
- Protein: 11.7g

Roasted Tomato and Cheddar Soup

Preparation time: 10 minutes **Cooking time:** 15-20 minutes **Servings:** 4

Ingredients:

- 2 tbsp. butter
- 2 medium yellow onions, sliced
- 4 garlic cloves, minced
- 5 thyme sprigs
- 8 basil leaves + extra for garnish
- 8 tomatoes
- 1/2 tsp. red chili flakes
- 2 cups vegetable broth
- Salt and black pepper to taste

Directions:

1. Melt the butter in a pot and sauté the onions and garlic for 3 minutes or until softened.
2. Stir in the thyme, basil, tomatoes, red chili flakes, and vegetable broth.
3. Season with salt and black pepper.
4. Boil it then simmer for 10 minutes or until the tomatoes soften.
5. Puree all ingredients until smooth. Season.
6. Garnish with the basil. Serve warm.

Nutrition for Total Servings:

- Calories: 341
- Fat: 12.9g
- Carbs: 4.8 g
- Protein: 4.1g

Cauliflower Kale Soup

Preparation time: 10 minutes   **Cooking time:** 50 minutes   **Servings:** 4

Ingredients:

- 4 cups cauliflower florets
- 6 cups vegetable stock
- 1 tbsp. garlic, minced
- 1/4 cup onion, chopped
- 6 oz. kale, chopped
- 6 tbsp. olive oil
- Pepper
- Salt

Directions:

1. Now, preheat the oven to 425 F.
2. Spread cauliflower onto the baking tray and drizzle with two tbsps. Of oil and season with pepper and salt.
3. Roast cauliflower in a preheated oven for 25 minutes. Remove from the oven and set aside.
4. In a bowl, toss kale with two tbsps. Of oil and season with salt. Arrange kale onto the baking tray and bake at 300 F for 30 minutes. Toss halfway through.
5. Heat oil.
6. Add onion and sauté for 3-4 minutes. Add garlic and sauté for a minute.
7. Add stock and roasted cauliflower and bring to boil.
8. Simmer it for 10 minutes.
9. Add kale and cook for 10 minutes more.
10. Puree the soup until smooth. Serve and enjoy.

Nutrition for Total Servings:

- Calories: 287
- Fat: 15.1g
- Carbs: 3.1 g
- Protein: 5.8g

Healthy Celery Soup

Preparation time: 10 minutes   **Cooking time:** 20 minutes   **Servings:** 4

Ingredients:

- 3 cups celery, chopped
- 1 cup vegetable broth
- 1 1/2 tbsp. fresh basil, chopped
- 1/4 cup onion, chopped
- 1 tbsp. garlic, chopped
- 1 tbsp. olive oil
- 1/4 tsp. pepper
- 1/2 tsp. salt

Directions:

1. Heat some oil.
2. Add celery, onion & garlic to the saucepan and sauté for 4-5 minutes or until softened.
3. Add broth and bring to boil. Turn heat to low and simmer.
4. Add basil.
5. Season soup with pepper and salt.
6. Puree the soup until smooth, serve and enjoy.

Nutrition for Total Servings:

- Calories: 201
- Fat: 5.4g
- Carbs: 3.9 g
- Protein: 5.1g

Creamy Asparagus Soup

Preparation time: 10 minutes   **Cooking time:** 15 minutes   **Servings:** 4

Ingredients:

- 2 lbs. asparagus, cut the ends and chop into 1/2-inch pieces
- 2 tbsp. olive oil
- 3 garlic cloves, minced
- 1/2 cup heavy cream
- 1/4 cup onion, chopped
- 4 cups vegetable stock
- Pepper and salt

Directions:

1. Heat olive oil in large pot over medium heat.
2. Add onion to the pot and sauté until onion is softened.
3. Add asparagus and sauté for 2-3 minutes.
4. Add garlic and sauté for a minute. Season with pepper and salt.
5. Add stock and bring to boil. Turn heat to low and simmer until asparagus is tender.
6. Remove pot from heat and puree the soup using an immersion blender until creamy.
7. Return pot on heat. Add cream and stir well and cook over medium heat until just soup is hot. Do not boil the soup.
8. Remove from heat, serve and enjoy.

Nutrition for Total Servings:

- Calories: 202
- Fat: 8.4g
- Carb: 3.1g
- Protein: 5.3g

Coconut Curry Cauliflower Soup

Preparation time: 15 minutes   **Cooking time:** 30 minutes   **Servings:** 4

Ingredients:

- 1 tbsp. olive oil
- 2-3 tsp. curry powder
- 1 medium onion
- 2 tsp. ground cumin
- 3 garlic cloves
- 1/2 tsp. turmeric powder
- 1 tsp. ginger
- 14 oz. oat milk
- 14 oz. tomatoes
- 1 cup vegetable broth
- 1 cauliflower
- Salt and pepper

Directions:

1. Take a pot, adds olive oil and onion, and set it on a medium flame for sautéing.
2. After 3 minutes, add garlic, ginger, curry powder, cumin, and turmeric powder and sauté for more than 5 minutes.
3. Now add oat milk, tomatoes, vegetable broth, and cauliflower and mix it well.
4. Let the mixture heat and bring to boil.
5. Now on low flame, cook it for at least 20 minutes until cauliflower turns into soft, blend the mixture well through a blender and heat the soup for more 5 minutes and add salt & pepper as per taste, serve the hot seasonal soup.

Nutrition for Total Servings:

- Calories: 281
- Fat: 8.1g
- Carbs: 3.2g
- Protein: 4.8g

Gazpacho Soup

Preparation time: 25 minutes　　　**Cooking time:** 0 minutes　　　**Servings:** 3

Ingredients:

- 1 large cucumber (to be sliced into chunks)
- 4 big ripe tomatoes (coarsely chopped)
- 1/2 bell pepper (any color)
- 2 cloves of garlic (minced)
- 1 celery rib (chopped)
- 1 tbsp. of lemon juice
- 1/4 tbsp. of celery pepper
- 1 tbsp. of fresh basil (chopped)
- 1 tbsp. of fresh parsley (chopped)
- Dash black pepper
- 1/2 tbsp. salt
- 3 tbsps. of red wine (vinegar/balsamic vinegar)
- 1/2 sweet onions (quartered)

Directions:

1. To make the gazpacho, place the cucumber chunks, chopped tomatoes, bell pepper, garlic, celery, lemon juice, and onion in food processor or blender.
2. You may choose to blend or process in batches if needed
3. Add the vinegar (red/balsamic), salt, pepper to the blender or food processor and blend or process together until it is smooth or nearly smooth (the texture depends on you)
4. The next step is to pour soup into a serving bowl and stir in the fresh chopped parsley and basil
5. Cover the serving bowl with plastic wrap or foil or cover it with a plastic wrap and put the bowl inside the refrigerator for about 30 minutes or until when you are set to serve the gazpacho soup.
6. You can decide to add some extra fresh herbs to the soup for presentation as well as some avocado slices or crusty croutons
7. Serve gazpacho soup with a green salad, some artisanal or homemade bread as a substitute, balsamic vinegar, and olive oil for dipping for a light but a complete meal.
8. Serve and enjoy!

Nutrition for Total Servings:

- Calories: 131
- Fat: 9.4g
- Carbs: 2.4 g
- Protein: 4.1g

Nutmeg Pumpkin Soup

Preparation time: 15 minutes　　　**Cooking time:** 20 minutes　　　**Servings:** 4

Ingredients:

- 1 tbsp. of butter
- 1 onion (diced)
- 1 16-ounce can of pumpkin puree
- 1 1/3 cups of vegetable broth
- 1/2 tbsp. of nutmeg
- 1/2 tbsp. of sugar
- Salt (to taste)
- Pepper (to taste)
- 3 cups of soymilk or any milk as a substitute

Directions:

1. Using a large saucepan, add onion to margarine and cook it between 3 and 5 minutes until the onion is clear.
2. Add pumpkin puree, vegetable broth, sugar, pepper, and other ingredients and stir to combine.
3. Cook in medium heat for between 10 and fifteen minutes
4. Before serving the soup, taste and add more spices, pepper, and salt if necessary
5. Serve soup and enjoy it!

Nutrition for Total Servings:

- Calories: 165
- Fat: 4.9g
- Carbs: 3.5 g
- Protein: 4.2g

Thai Coconut Vegetable Soup

Preparation time: 15 minutes   **Cooking time:** 20 minutes   **Servings:** 4

Ingredients:

- 1 onion (diced)
- 2 bell peppers (red, diced)
- 1/4 tsp. of cayenne
- 1/2 tbsp. of coriander
- 1/2 tbsp. of cumin
- 4 tbsps. of olive oil
- 1 can of chickpeas
- 1 carrot (sliced)
- 3 cloves of garlic
- 1/2 cup of basil or cilantro (fresh chopped)
- 1 tsp. of salt
- 3 limes (freshly squeezed juice)
- 1/2 cup of vegetable broth
- 1 cup of soy milk
- 1 cup of peanut butter
- 2 1/2 cups of tomatoes (finely diced)

Directions:

1. Sauté garlic and onions. Make ingredients to be soft for at least 3 to 5 minutes
2. Leaving out basil, add the rest of the ingredients and allow it to simmer. Cook over low heat for an hour.
3. Put the half amount to the food processor, allow it to be very smooth, and return to the pot.
4. Add either basil or cilantro, and your coconut food is ready. Before serving the soup, taste and add more seasoning if necessary. Serve, and enjoy!

Nutrition for Total Servings:

- Calories: 151
- Fat: 6.9g
- Carbs: 3.1 g
- Protein: 4.9g

Keto Cabbage Soup

Preparation time: 10 minutes   **Cooking time:** 30 minutes   **Servings:** 6

Ingredients:

- 1/4 cup onion, diced
- 1 clove garlic, minced
- 1 tsp. cumin
- 1 head cabbage, chopped
- 1 1/4 cup canned diced tomatoes
- 5 oz. canned green chilies
- 4 cups vegetable stock
- Salt and pepper to taste

Directions:

1. Heat a heavy stockpot over medium-high heat. Add the onions and sauté for 5- 7 minutes more. Add the garlic and sauté for one more minute.
2. Bring to a low simmer & cook until the vegetables are tender about 30 minutes. Add water, if necessary, during cooking.
3. Transfer to serving bowls and serve hot.

Nutrition for Total Servings:

- Calories: 131
- Fat: 4.3g
- Carbs: 1.2 g
- Protein: 5.1g

Mixed Vegetable Stew

Preparation time: 15 minutes   **Cooking time:** 30 minutes   **Servings:** 6

Ingredients:

- 1 turnip, cut into bite-size pieces
- 1 onion, chopped
- 6 stalks celery, diced
- 1 carrot, sliced
- 15 oz. pumpkin puree
- 1 lb. green beans frozen or fresh
- 8 cups chicken stock
- 2 cups of water
- 1 Tbsp. fresh basil, chopped
- 1/4 tsp. thyme leaves
- 1/8 tsp. rubbed sage
- Salt to taste
- 1 lb. fresh spinach, chopped

Directions:

1. Put all the ingredients, excluding the spinach, into a heavy stockpot.
2. Bring to a low simmer & cook until the vegetables are tender about 30 minutes. Add water, if necessary.
3. Add the spinach & stir until it's wilted about 5 minutes.
4. Transfer to serving bowls and serve hot.

Nutrition for Total Servings:

- Calories: 198
- Fat: 6.4g
- Carb: 2.5 g
- Protein: 8.2g

Vegetarian Green Chili

Preparation time: 15 minutes **Cooking time:** 20 minutes **Servings:** 6

Ingredients:
- 3 tomatillos, sliced
- 3 jalapeno peppers, seeded and chopped
- 2 New Mexico green chili peppers, seeded and chopped
- 6 cloves garlic, minced
- 1 tomato, chopped
- 3 cups vegetable stock
- 2 tsp. cumin
- Salt and pepper to taste

Directions:
1. Put the tomatillos, jalapenos, New Mexico chilies, garlic, chicken stock, and tomato into a heavy stockpot.
2. Add the cumin, salt, and pepper on top of the meat.
3. Simmer and cook until fragrant, about 20 minutes. Add water, if necessary, during cooking.
4. Puree the soup until smooth.
5. Transfer the chili to serving bowls and serve hot,
6. Garnished with chopped fresh cilantro.

Nutrition for Total Servings:
- Calories: 201
- Fat: 6.1g
- Carbs: 2.1 g
- Protein: 5.1g

Chinese Tofu Soup

Preparation time: 5 minutes **Cooking time:** 5 minutes **Servings:** 2

Ingredients:
- 2 cups chicken stock
- 1 tbsp. soy sauce, sugar-free
- 2 spring onions, sliced
- 1 tsp. sesame oil, softened
- 2 eggs, beaten
- 1-inch piece ginger, grated
- Salt and black ground, to taste
- 1/2 pound extra-firm tofu, cubed
- A handful of fresh cilantros, chopped

Directions:
1. Boil in a pan over medium heat, soy sauce, chicken stock, and sesame oil.
2. Place in eggs as you whisk to incorporate thoroughly.
3. Change heat to low and add salt, spring onions, black pepper, ginger; cook for 5 minutes.
4. Place in tofu and simmer for 1 to 2 minutes.
5. Divide into soup bowls and serve sprinkled with fresh cilantro.

Nutrition for Total Servings:
- Calories: 178
- Fat: 4.1g
- Carbs: 0.4g
- Protein: 5.5g

Sausage & Beer Soup

Preparation time: 15 minutes **Cooking time:** 8 hrs. **Servings:** 4

Ingredients:
- 2 tbsp. butter
- 1/2 cup celery, chopped
- 1/2 cup heavy cream
- 5 oz. turkey sausage, sliced
- 1 small carrot, chopped
- 2 garlic cloves, minced
- 1/2 tsp. red pepper flakes
- 1 cup beer of choice
- 3 cups beef stock
- 1 yellow onion, diced
- Kosher salt and black pepper, to taste

Directions:
1. To the crockpot, add butter, beef stock, beer, turkey sausage, carrot, onion, garlic, celery, salt, red pepper flakes, & black pepper, and stir to combine.
2. Cook for 6 hrs. On low.
3. Then add in the cream, and cook for two more hours.

Nutrition for Total Servings:
- Calories: 345
- Fat: 10.4g
- Carbs: 4.1 g
- Protein: 11.2g

Egg Drop Soup

Preparation time: 5 minutes   **Cooking time:** 10 minutes   **Servings:** 2

Ingredients:

- 4 cups chicken broth
- 1 tsp. pink Himalayan sea salt
- 1/2 tsp. ground ginger
- 1/2 tsp. toasted sesame oil
- Pinch of ground white pepper
- 2 large eggs
- 1 scallion

Directions:

1. In a medium saucepan, combine the broth, salt, ginger, sesame oil, and white pepper.
2. Cook over medium-high heat until the soup is boiling.
3. In small bowl, lightly beat the eggs.
4. Stirring the soup in a circular motion, slowly drizzle the beaten egg into the center of the vortex.
5. When all the egg is mixed in, stop stirring.
6. Cook for an additional 2 minutes, until the egg is cooked through, then pour into 2 bowls, sprinkle with the scallions, and serve.

Nutrition for Total Servings:

- Calories: 121
- Fat: 5.1g
- Carbs: 1.2 g
- Protein: 10g

New England Clam Chowder

Preparation time: 15 minutes   **Cooking time:** 25 minutes   **Servings:** 2

Ingredients:

- 2 bacon slices, chopped
- 1 celery stalk, chopped
- 1/4 medium onion, chopped
- 1 garlic clove, minced
- 1 cup chicken broth
- 2 (6.5-ounce) cans chopped clams, drained, juices reserved
- 1 medium kohlrabi, peeled and cubed
- 1 bay leaf
- 1/2 tsp. pink Himalayan sea salt
- 1/4 tsp. freshly ground black pepper
- 1/4 tsp. dried thyme
- Pinch of ground white pepper
- 1 1/2 cups heavy (whipping) cream

Directions:

1. Cook bacon
2. The pot with the bacon grease, sauté the celery and onion for 8 to 10 minutes until the onion is translucent. Add the garlic.
3. Add the broth, reserved clam juice (not the clams yet), the kohlrabi, bay leaf, salt, black pepper, thyme, and white pepper.
4. Simmer for 10 to 15 min, until the kohlrabi is tender.
5. Add the cream and clams. Stir to combine.
6. Simmer the soup for roughly 20 minutes, or until it reduces to your desired consistency.
7. Remove and discard the bay leaf.
8. Stir in the bacon crumbles and serve.

Nutrition for Total Servings:

- Calories: 376
- Fat: 15.9g
- Carbs: 4.1g
- Protein: 13.1g

Chicken Noodle Soup

Preparation time: 15 minutes

Cooking time: 25 minutes

Servings: 2

Ingredients:

- 1 tbsp. extra-virgin olive oil
- 8 ounces boneless, skinless chicken thighs, cubed
- 1/4 medium onion, chopped
- 1/2 celery stalk, thinly sliced
- 1 tsp. minced garlic
- 2 cups chicken broth
- 1 tsp. pink Himalayan sea salt
- 1/2 tsp. freshly ground black pepper
- 1 tsp. dried thyme
- 1 (7-ounce) package shirataki noodles, drained

Directions:

1. Heat oil.
2. Cook the chicken (10 minutes), until almost cooked through.
3. Put in celery, onion, and garlic. Cook for 7 to 10 minutes until the onion is translucent.
4. Pour the chicken broth into the pot. Add the salt, pepper, and thyme. Simmer for about 10 minutes.
5. Rinse the shirataki noodles, then add them to the pot right before serving.

Nutrition for Total Servings:

- Calories: 368
- Fat: 12.1g
- Carbs: 3.1 g
- Protein: 9.4g

CHAPTER 14:

Side Dishes and Salads

Bacon Avocado Salad

Preparation time: 20 minutes   **Cooking time:** 0 minutes   **Servings:** 4

Ingredients:

- 2 hard-boiled eggs, chopped
- 2 cups spinach
- 2 large avocados, 1 chopped and 1 sliced
- 2 small lettuce heads, chopped
- 1 spring onion, sliced
- 4 cooked bacon slices, crumbled
- 2 tbsp. olive oil
- 1 tsp. mustard
- 1/4 cup apple cider vinegar

Directions:

1. In a large bowl, mix the eggs, spinach, avocados, lettuce, and onion. Set aside.
2. Make the vinaigrette: In a separate bowl, add the olive oil, mustard, and apple cider vinegar. Mix well.
3. Pour vinaigrette in the large bowl and toss well.
4. Serve topped with bacon slices and sliced avocado.

Nutrition for Total Servings:

- Calories: 268
- Fat: 16.9 g
- Carbs: 8 g
- Protein: 5 g

Cauliflower, Shrimp, and Cucumber Salad

Preparation time: 10 minutes   **Cooking time:** 15 minutes   **Servings:** 6

Ingredients:

- 1/4 cup olive oil
- 1 pound (454 g) medium shrimp
- 1 cauliflower head, florets only
- 2 cucumbers, peeled and chopped
- 1/3 tsp. salt
- 1/4 tsp. ground black pepper
- 2 tbsp. fresh dill, chopped
- 1/4 cup of fresh lemon juice
- 2 tsps. fresh lemon zest, grated

Directions:

1. In skillet over medium heat, heat the olive oil until sizzling hot. Add the shrimp and cook for 8 minutes, stirring occasionally, or until the flesh is pink and opaque.
2. Meanwhile, in a microwave-safe bowl, add the cauliflower florets and microwave for about 5 minutes until tender.
3. Remove the shrimp from the heat to a large bowl. Add the cauliflower and cucumber to the shrimp in the bowl. Set aside.
4. Make dressing: Mix olive oil, lemon juice, lemon zest, dill, salt, and pepper in a third bowl. Pour the dressing into the bowl of shrimp mixture. Toss well until the shrimp and vegetables are coated thoroughly.
5. Serve immediately or refrigerate for 1 hr. before serving.

Nutrition for Total Servings:

- Calories: 308
- Fat: 19 g
- Carbs: 4 g
- Protein: 5 g

Cauliflower and Cashew Nut Salad

Preparation time: 10 minutes   **Cooking time:** 5 minutes   **Servings:** 4

Ingredients:

- 1 head cauliflower, cut into florets
- 1/2 cup of black olives, pitted and chopped
- 1 cup roasted bell peppers, chopped
- 1 red onion, sliced
- 1/2 cup cashew nuts
- Chopped celery leaves, for garnish
- 1/4 cup olive oil
- 1/3 tsp. salt
- 1/4 tsp. ground black pepper
- 1/4 tsp. mustard
- 2 tbsp. balsamic vinegar

Directions:

1. Add the cauliflower into a pot of boiling salted water. Allow to boil for 4 to 5 minutes until fork-tender but still crisp.
2. Remove from the heat & drain on paper towels, then transfer the cauliflower to a bowl.
3. Add the olives, bell pepper, and red onion. Stir well.
4. Make the dressing: In a separate bowl, mix the olive oil, mustard, vinegar, salt, and pepper. Pour the dressing over the veggies & toss to combine.
5. Serve topped with cashew nuts and celery leaves.

Nutrition for Total Servings:

- Calories: 298
- Fat: 20 g
- Carbs: 4 g
- Protein: 8 g

Salmon and Lettuce Salad

Preparation time: 10 minutes   **Cooking time:** 0 minutes   **Servings:** 4

Ingredients:

- 1 tbsp. extra-virgin olive oil
- 2 slices smoked salmon, chopped
- 3 tbsps. mayonnaise
- 1 tbsp. lime juice
- Sea salt, to taste
- 1 cup romaine lettuce, shredded
- 1 tsp. onion flakes
- 1/2 avocado, sliced

Directions:

1. In a bowl, stir the olive oil, salmon, mayo, lime juice, and salt. Stir well until the salmon is coated fully.
2. Divide evenly the romaine lettuce and onion flakes among four serving plates. Spread the salmon mixture over the lettuce, then serve topped with avocado slices.

Nutrition for Total Servings:

- Calories: 271
- Fat: 18 g
- Carbs: 4 g
- Protein: 6 g

Prawns Salad with Mixed Lettuce Greens

Preparation time: 10 minutes   **Cooking time:** 3 minutes   **Servings:** 4

Ingredients:

- 1/2 pound (227 g) prawns, peeled and deveined
- Salt and chili pepper, to taste
- 1 tbsp. olive oil
- 2 cups mixed lettuce greens
- 1 tbsp. mustard
- 1 tbsp. lemon juice

Directions:

1. In a bowl, add the prawns, salt, and chili pepper. Toss well.
2. Warm the olive oil over medium heat. Add the seasoned prawns and fry for about 6 to 8 minutes, stirring occasionally, or until the prawns are opaque.
3. Remove from the heat and set the prawns aside on a platter.
4. Make the dressing: In a small bowl, mix the mustard, and lemon juice until creamy and smooth.
5. Make the salad: In a separate bowl, add the mixed lettuce greens. Pour the dressing over the greens and toss to combine.
6. Divide salad among 4 serving plates and serve it alongside the prawns.

Nutrition for Total Servings:

- Calories: 228
- Fat: 17 g
- Carbs: 3 g
- Protein: 5 g

Beef Salad with Vegetables

Preparation time: 10 minutes   **Cooking time:** 10 minutes   **Servings:** 4

Ingredients:

- 1-pound (454 g) ground beef
- 1/4 cup pork rinds, crushed
- 1 egg, whisked
- 1 onion, grated
- 1 tbsp. fresh parsley, chopped

- 1/2 tsp. dried oregano
- 1 garlic clove, minced
- Salt and black pepper, to taste
- 2 tbsps. olive oil, divided

Salad:

- 1 cup chopped arugula
- 1 cucumber, sliced
- 1 cup cherry tomatoes, halved

- 1 1/2 tbsps. lemon juice
- Salt and pepper, to taste

Directions:

1. Stir together the beef, pork rinds, whisked egg, onion, parsley, oregano, garlic, salt, and pepper in a large bowl until completely mixed.
2. Make the meatballs: On a lightly floured surface, using a cookie scoop to scoop out equal-sized amounts of the beef mixture and form into meatballs with your palm.
3. Heat 1 tbsp. olive oil in a large skillet over medium heat, fry the meatballs for about 4 minutes on each side until cooked through.
4. Remove from the heat & set aside on a plate to cool.
5. In a salad bowl, mix the arugula, cucumber, cherry tomatoes, 1 tbsp. olive oil, and lemon juice. Season with salt and pepper.
6. Make the dressing: In a third bowl, whisk the soy milk, yogurt, and mint until well blended. Pour the mixture over the salad. Serve topped with the meatballs.

Nutrition for Total Servings:

- Calories: 302
- Fat: 13 g
- Carbs: 6 g
- Protein: 7 g

Niçoise Salad

Preparation time: 5 minutes   **Cooking time:** 30 minutes   **Servings:** 6

Ingredients:

- 2 tbsps. butter
- 3 cups oil-packed tuna
- 2 ounces lettuce
- 1 cup green beans

- 3 anchovies packed in oil
- 2 avocado
- 1 cup diced tomatoes
- 1/2 cup of black olives

For the dressing:

- 3/4 cup MCT oil
- 1/2 cup lemon juice
- 1 tsp. Dijon mustard
- 1 tbsp. fresh thyme leaves, minced
- 1 medium shallot, minced

- 2 teaspoons fresh oregano leaves, minced
- 2 tbsps. fresh basil leaves, minced
- Celtic sea salt & freshly ground black pepper, to taste

Directions:

1. Melt the butter and heat the olive oil in a nonstick skillet over medium-high heat. Place tuna steaks in the skillet, and sear for 3 minutes or until opaque, flipping once. Set aside.
2. Make the dressing: Combine all the ingredients for the dressing in a bowl.
3. Make six niçoise salads: Dunk the lettuce and tuna steaks in the dressing bowl to coat well, then arrange the tuna in the middle of the lettuce. Set aside.
4. Blanch green beans in a pot of boiling salted water for 3 to 5 minutes or until soft but still crisp. Drain and dry with paper towels.
5. Dunk the green beans in the dressing bowl to coat well. Arrange them around the tuna steaks on the lettuce.
6. Top the tuna and green beans with hard-boiled eggs, anchovies, avocado chunks, tomatoes, and olives. Sprinkle 2 tbsps. Dressing over each egg, then serve.

Nutrition for Total Servings:

- Calories: 197
- Fat: 16 g
- Carbs: 8 g
- Protein: 6 g

Baked Carrot with Bacon

Preparation time: 10 minutes   **Cooking time:** 35 minutes   **Servings:** 4

Ingredients:

- 1 1/2 lb. carrots, peeled
- 12 slices bacon
- 1 tbsp. black pepper
- 1/3 cup maple syrup
- 1 pinch parsley

Directions:

1. Now, preheat the oven to 400°F.
2. Wrap the bacon slices around your carrots from top to bottom. Add black pepper, sprinkle with maple syrup, and bake for about 20-25 minutes. Top with parsley and serve.

Nutrition for Total Servings:

- Carbs: 16 g
- Fat: 26 g
- Protein: 10 g
- Calories: 421

Standard Greek Salad

Preparation time: 15 minutes   **Cooking time:** 0 minutes   **Servings:** 4

Ingredients:

- 1 large tomato, cut into cubes
- 1 cucumber, sliced into half-moons
- 1/3 cup kalamata olives, halved
- 1/2 white onion, sliced
- 3/4 cup feta, crumbled
- 2 tbsp. red wine vinegar
- 2 tbsp. lemon juice
- 1 tsp. oregano, dried
- Salt and pepper to taste
- 1/4 cup extra-virgin olive oil

Directions:

1. In separate bowl, combine the tomatoes, cucumbers, olives, and onion. Stir and top the mix with feta.
2. Another bowl, stir together the lemon juice, vinegar, oregano, salt, pepper, and olive oil. Gently whisk.
3. Sprinkle the salad with the dressing.

Nutrition for Total Servings:

- Carbs: 7 g
- Fat: 20 g
- Protein: 5 g
- Calories: 230

Creamy Mushrooms with Garlic and Thyme

Preparation time: 5 minutes   **Cooking time:** 15 minutes   **Servings:** 4

Ingredients:

- 1 lb. button mushrooms
- 2 tsp. garlic, diced
- 1 tbsp. fresh thyme
- 1 tbsp. parsley, chopped
- 1/2 tsp. salt
- 1/4 tsp. black pepper

Directions:

1. Melt the butter in a pan. Place the mushrooms into the pan. Add salt and pepper. Cook the mushroom mix for about 5 minutes until they're browned on both sides.
2. Add the garlic and thyme. Additionally, sauté the mushrooms for 1-2 minutes. Top them with parsley.

Nutrition for Total Servings:

- Carbs: 45 g
- Fat: 8 g
- Protein: 3 g
- Calories: 99

Easy Roasted Broccoli

Preparation time: 2 minutes   **Cooking time:** 19 minutes   **Servings:** 4

Ingredients:

- 1 lb. frozen broccoli, cut into florets
- 3 tsp. olive oil
- Sea salt to taste

Directions:

1. Place broccoli florets on a baking sheet greased with oil and put it in the oven (preheated to 400°F). Sprinkle the olive oil over the florets.
2. Cook for 12 minutes. Whisk well and bake for an additional 7 minutes.

Nutrition for Total Servings:

- Carbs: 8 g
- Fat: 3 g
- Protein: 3 g
- Calories: 58

Roasted Cabbage with Bacon

Preparation time: 10 minutes **Cooking time:** 40 minutes **Servings:** 4

Ingredients:

- 1/2 head cabbage, quartered
- 8 slices bacon, cut into thick pieces
- 1 tsp. garlic powder
- Salt and pepper to taste
- 1 pinch parsley, chopped

Directions:

1. Lightly sprinkle the cabbage wedges with the garlic powder. Wrap 2 pieces of bacon around each cabbage wedge.
2. Place your wrapped cabbage wedges on the baking sheet and put into the oven preheated to 350°F oven. Bake for 35-40 minutes. Top with parsley.

Nutrition for Total Servings:

- Carbs: 7 g
- Fat: 19 g
- Protein: 9 g
- Calories: 236

Baked Radish Snack

Preparation time: 8 minutes **Cooking time:** 22 minutes **Servings:** 2

Ingredients:

- 8 oz. red radishes, washed and trimmed
- 2 tbsp. olive oil
- 2 tbsp. unsalted butter
- 1 clove garlic, diced
- 1 tsp. lemon juice
- 1/4 tsp. oregano, dried
- Salt and pepper to taste

Directions:

1. Place the halved or quartered radishes into a separate bowl. Drizzle over the olive oil and add oregano. Stir gently.
2. Put the radish on the baking sheet and place it in the oven (preheated to 450°F).
3. Bake for 18-22 minutes. Mix a few times while baking.
4. Melt the butter in a saucepan. Add garlic and cook for about 3-5 minutes.
5. Remove your roasted radishes from the oven, sprinkle them with lemon juice, and top with the butter mix.

Nutrition for Total Servings:

- Carbs: 4 g
- Fat: 17 g
- Protein: 1 g
- Calories: 164

Boiled Asparagus with Sliced Lemon

Preparation time: 5 minutes **Cooking time:** 7 minutes **Servings:** 1

Ingredients:

- 10 large asparagus
- 3 tbsp. avocado oil
- 1/4 tbsp. lemon juice
- 2-3 pieces lemon
- 1/4 cup water
- 1/2 tsp. salt

Directions:

1. Place the asparagus in a pot of water. Boil for about 5-7 minutes.
2. Take the asparagus out of the pot. Sprinkle with lemon juice, avocado oil, and salt. Serve with the pieces of lemon.

Nutrition for Total Servings:

- Carbs: 10.7 g
- Fat: 43 g
- Protein: 4.7 g
- Calories: 447

Stuffed Eggs with Bacon-Avocado Filling

Preparation time: 10 minutes

Cooking time: 10 minutes

Servings: 1

Ingredients:

- 2 eggs, boiled and halved
- 1 tbsp. mayonnaise
- 1/4 tsp. mustard
- 1/8 Lemon, squeezed
- 1/4 tsp. garlic powder
- 1/8 Tsp. salt
- 1/4 avocado
- 16 small pieces of bacon

Directions:

1. Fry the bacon for 3 minutes in a pan. Add the avocado and fry for another 3 minutes (on lower heat).
2. Combine the mayonnaise, mustard, lemon, garlic powder, and salt in a separate bowl. Stir well.
3. Remove the yolk from the halved eggs and fill the egg halves with the mayonnaise mix. Top with the bacon-avocado filling.

Nutrition for Total Servings:

- Carbs: 4 g
- Fat: 30 g
- Protein: 16 g
- Calories: 342

CHAPTER 15:

Desserts Recipes

Mocha Mousse

Preparation time: 2 hours and 35 minutes   **Cooking time:** 0 minutes   **Servings:** 4

Ingredients:
- 3 tbsps. sour cream, full-fat
- 2 tbsps. butter, softened
- 1 1/2 teaspoons vanilla extract, unsweetened

- 1/3 cup erythritol
- 1/4 cup cocoa powder, unsweetened
- 3 teaspoons instant coffee powder

For the Whipped Cream:
- 2/3 cup heavy whipping cream, full-fat
- 1 1/2 tsp. erythritol

- 1/2 tsp. vanilla extract, unsweetened

Directions:
1. Add sour cream and butter then beat until smooth.
2. Now add erythritol, cocoa powder, coffee, and vanilla and blend until incorporated, set aside until required.
3. Prepare whipping cream: For this, place whipping cream in a bowl and beat until soft peaks form.
4. Beat in vanilla and erythritol until stiff peaks form, and fold until just mixed.
5. Then add remaining whipping cream mixture and fold until evenly incorporated.
6. Spoon the mousse into a freezer-proof bowl and place in the refrigerator for 2 1/2 hours until set.
7. Serve straight away.

Nutrition for Total Servings:
- Calories: 421.7
- Fat: 42 g
- Protein: 6 g
- Carbs: 6.5 g

Pumpkin Pie Pudding

Preparation time: 4 hours and 25 minutes   **Cooking time:** 20 minutes   **Servings:** 4

Ingredients:
- 2 eggs
- 1 cup heavy whipping cream, divided
- 3/4 cup erythritol sweetener
- 15 ounces pumpkin puree

- 1 tsp. pumpkin pie spice
- 1 tsp. vanilla extract, unsweetened
- 1 1/2 cup water

Directions:
1. Crack eggs in a bowl, add 1/2 cup cream, sweetener, pumpkin puree, pumpkin pie spice, and vanilla and whisk until blended.
2. Take a 6 by 3-inch baking pan, grease it well with avocado oil, then pour in egg mixture, smooth the top and cover with aluminum foil.
3. Switch on the instant pot, pour in water, insert a trivet stand and place baking pan on it.
4. Shut the instant pot with its lid in the sealed position, then press the 'manual' button, press '+/-' to the set the cooking time to 20 minutes & cook at high-pressure setting; when the pressure builds in the pot, the cooking timer will start.
5. When the instant pot buzzes, press the 'keep warm' button, release pressure naturally for 10 min, and then do quick pressure release and open the lid.
6. Take out the baking pan, uncover it, let cool for 15 minutes at room temperature, then transfer the pan into the refrigerator for 4 hours or until cooled.
7. Top pie with remaining cream, then cut it into slices and serve.

Nutrition for Total Servings:
- Calories: 184
- Fat: 16 g
- Protein: 3 g
- Carbs: 5 g

Avocado & Chocolate Pudding

Preparation time: 20 minutes   **Cooking time:** 10 minutes   **Servings:** 2

Ingredients:

- 1 ripe medium avocado
- 1 tsp. natural sweetener
- 1/4 tsp. vanilla extract
- 4 tbsp. unsweetened cocoa powder
- 1 pinch pink salt

Directions:

1. Combine the avocado, sweetener, vanilla, cocoa powder, and salt into the blender or processor.
2. Pulse until creamy smooth.
3. Measure into fancy dessert dishes and chill for at least 1/2 hour.

Nutrition for Total Servings:

- Calories: 281
- Carbs: 2 g
- Protein: 8 g
- Fat: 27 g

Cake Pudding

Preparation time: 5 min   **Cooking time:** 5 min   **Servings:** 4

Ingredients:

- ½ heavy whipping cream
- 1 tsp. lemon juice
- ½ sour cream
- 20 drops liquid stevia
- 1 tsp. vanilla extract

Directions:

1. Whip the sour cream and whipping cream together with the mixer until soft peaks form. Combine with the rest of the ingredients and whip until fluffy.
2. Portion into four dishes to chill. Place a layer of the wrap over the dish and store in the fridge.
3. When ready to eat, garnish with some berries if you like.
4. Note: If you add berries, be sure to add the carbs.

Nutrition for Total Servings:

- Calories: 356
- Carbs: 5 g
- Protein: 5 g
- Fat: 36 g

Carrot Almond Cake

Preparation time: 45 minutes
Cooking time: 15 minutes
Servings: 8
Ingredients:

- 3 eggs
- 1 ½ tsp. apple pie spice
- 1 cup almond flour
- 2/3 cup swerve
- 1 tsp. baking powder
- 1/4 cup coconut oil
- 1 cup shredded carrots
- 1/2 cup heavy whipping cream
- 1/2 cup chopped walnuts

Directions:

1. Grease cake pan. Combine all of the ingredients with the mixer until well mixed. Pour the mix into the pan and cover with a layer of foil.
2. Pour two cups of water into the Instant Pot bowl along with the steamer rack.
3. Arrange the pan on the trivet and set the pot using the cake button (40 min.).
4. Natural-release the pressure for ten minutes. Then, quick-release the rest of the built-up steam pressure.
5. Cool then start frosting or serve it plain.

Nutrition for Total Servings:

- Calories: 268
- Carbs: 4 g
- Fat: 25 g
- Protein: 6 g

Chocolate Lava Cake

Preparation time: 20 minutes   **Cooking time:** 10 minutes   **Servings:** 4

Ingredients:

- ½ cup unsweetened cocoa powder
- ¼ cup melted butter
- 4 eggs
- ¼ tsp. sugar-free chocolate sauce
- ½ tsp. sea salt
- ½ tsp. ground cinnamon
- Pure vanilla extract
- ¼ cup Stevia
- Also Needed: Ice cube tray & 4 ramekins

Directions:

1. Pour one tbsp. of the chocolate sauce into four of the tray slots and freeze.
2. Warm up the oven to 350°Fahrenheit. Lightly grease the ramekins with butter or a spritz of oil.
3. Mix salt, cinnamon, cocoa powder, & stevia until combined. Whisk in the eggs – one at a time. Stir in the melted vanilla extract and butter.
4. Fill each of the ramekins halfway & add one of the frozen chocolates. Cover the rest of the container with the cake batter.
5. Bake 13-14 min. When they're set, place on a wire rack to cool for about five minutes. Remove and put on a serving dish.
6. Enjoy by slicing its molten center.

Nutrition for Total Servings:

- Calories: 189
- Carbs: 3 g
- Protein: 8 g
- Fat: 17 g

Glazed Pound Cake

Preparation time: 1 hour   **Cooking time:** 1 hours   **Servings:** 16

Ingredients:

- ½ tsp. salt
- 2 ½ cup almond flour
- ½ cup unsalted butter
- 1 ½ cup erythritol

- 8 unchilled eggs
- ½ tsp. lemon extract
- 1 ½ tsp. vanilla extract
- 1 ½ tsp. baking powder

The Glaze:

- ¼ cup powdered erythritol
- 3 tbsp. heavy whipping cream

- ½ tsp. vanilla extract

Directions:

1. Warm the oven to 350°Fahrenheit.
2. Whisk together baking powder, almond flour, and salt
3. Cream the erythritol, butter. Mix until smooth in a large mixing container.
4. Whisk and add the eggs with the lemon and vanilla extract. Blend with the rest of the ingredients using a hand mixer until smooth.
5. Dump the batter into a loaf pan. Bake for one to two hours.
6. Prepare a glaze. Mix in vanilla extract, powdered erythritol, and heavy whipping cream until smooth.
7. You should let the cake cool completely before adding the glaze.

Nutrition for Total Servings:

- Calories: 254
- Carbs: 2.5 g
- Protein: 7.9 g
- Fat: 23.4 g

Lemon Cake

Preparation time: 1.5 hours
Cooking time: 2 hours
Servings: 8
Ingredients:

- ½ cup coconut flour
- 2 tsp. baking powder.
- 1 ½ cups almond flour
- 3 tbsp. Swerve (or) Pyure A-P.
- ½ tsp. Xanthan gum
- ½ cup whipping cream
- ½ cup melted butter
- 2 lemons zested & juiced
- 2 Eggs

Ingredients for the Topping:

- 3 tbsp. Pyure all-purpose/Swerve
- 2 tbsp. lemon juice
- ½ cup boiling water
- 2 tbsp. melted butter
- Suggested: 2-4-quart slow cooker

Directions:
For the Cake:
1. Mix the dry ingredients in a container.
2. Whisk the egg with the lemon juice and zest, butter, and whipping cream.
3. Whisk all of the ingredients and scoop out the dough into the prepared slow cooker.

For the Topping:
1. Mix all of the topping ingredients in a container and empty over the batter in the cooker.
2. Place the lid on the cooker for two to three hours on the high setting.
3. Serve warm with some fresh fruit or whipped cream.

Nutrition for Total Servings:

- Calories: 350
- Net Carbs: 5.2 g
- Protein: 7.6 g
- Fat: 33 g

Spice Cakes

Preparation time: 15 minutes   **Cooking time:** 10 minutes   **Servings:** 12
Ingredients:

- ½ cup salted butter
- ¾ cup erythritol
- 4 eggs
- 1 tsp. vanilla extract
- ¼ tsp. ground cloves
- 2 tsp. baking powder
- ½ tsp. allspice

- ½ tsp. nutmeg
- 2 cups almond flour
- ½ tsp. cinnamon
- ½ tsp. ginger
- 5 tbsp. water
- Also Needed: Cupcake tray

Directions:
1. Warm the oven temperature to 350°Fahrenheit. Prepare the baking tray with liners (12).
2. Mix the butter and erythritol with a hand mixer. Once it's smooth, combine with two eggs and the vanilla. Add the rest of the eggs and mix well.
3. Grind the clove to a fine powder and add with the rest of the spices. Whisk into the mixture. Stir in the baking powder and almond flour. Blend in the water. When the batter is smooth, add to the prepared tin.
4. Bake for 15 minutes. Enjoy any time.

Nutrition for Total Servings:

- Calories: 277
- Carbs: 3 g
- Protein: 6 g
- Fat: 27 g

Vanilla-Sour Cream Cupcakes

Preparation time: 20 minutes **Cooking time:** 25 minutes **Servings:** 12

Ingredients:

- 4 tbsp. butter
- 1 ½ cups Swerve or your favorite sweetener
- ¼ tsp. salt
- 4 eggs
- ¼ cup sour cream
- 1 tsp. vanilla
- 1 cup almond flour
- 1 tsp. baking powder
- ¼ cup coconut flour

Directions:

1. Warm the oven at 350°Fahrenheit.
2. Prepare the butter and sweetener until creamy and fluffy using the mixer.
3. Blend in the vanilla and sour cream. Mix well.
4. 1 at a time, fold in the eggs.
5. Sift and blend in both types of flour, salt, and baking powder.
6. Divide the batter between the cups.
7. Bake for 20 to 25 minutes. Times may vary according to your oven hotness.
8. Cool completely and place in the fridge for fresher results.

Nutrition for Total Servings:

- Calories: 128
- Carbs: 2 g
- Fat: 11 g
- Protein: 4 g

Browned Butter Chocolate Chip Blondies

Preparation time: 20 minutes **Cooking time:** 15 minutes **Servings:** 16

Ingredients:

- ½ cup butter
- 2 cups almond flour
- ¼ cup Swerve sweetener
- 1 tsp. baking powder
- ½ tsp. salt
- ¼ cup Sukrin or more swerve + molasses 2 tsp.
- 1 large egg
- 1/3 cup sugar-free chocolate chips
- ½ tsp. vanilla extract
- Also needed: 9x9-inch baking pan

Directions:

1. Set the oven temperature at 325°F. Lightly grease the pan.
2. Toss the butter into the pan using the medium temperature setting. Cook until the butter is melted and becomes a deep amber (4-5 min.).
3. Remove pan from the burner to cool.
4. Whisk the almond flour with the salt, baking powder, and sweeteners.
5. Whisk the egg & add it to the mixture with the browned butter and vanilla extract until thoroughly combined. Fold in the chocolate chips.
6. Press dough evenly in the prepared pan.
7. Set a timer to bake for 15-20 minutes or until just set and golden brown.
8. Let the blondies cool in the pan. Slice into squares and serve as desired.

Nutrition for Total Servings:

- Calories: 161
- Carbs: 3 g
- Protein: 3.8 g
- Fat: 14.4 g

Key Lime Bars

Preparation time: 30 minutes   **Cooking time:** 20 minutes + chilling time (1 hr.)   **Servings:** 16

Ingredients:

The Crust:

- 1 ¼ cups almond flour
- 1/3 cup Swerve sweetener
- ¼ tsp. salt
- ¼ cup melted butter

The Filling:

- 2 tsp. lime zest
- 1 cup sugar-free oat milk
- 4 egg yolks
- 6 tbsp. key lime juice
- Also suggested: 8x8-inch baking pan

Directions:

The Crust:

1. Warm the oven to 325°F.
2. Whisk the almond flour with the salt and sweetener.
3. Melt the butter and add to the mixture to make the batter.
4. Pour the batter into the pan. Press firmly into the bottom.
5. Bake 'til just golden brown around the edges (for 12-15 min.).
6. Transfer to the countertop to cool.

The Key Lime:

1. Lime zest until creamy smooth.
2. Whisk and fold in the egg yolks until well mixed.
3. Slowly pour in the juice from the lime and oat milk. Stir until the filling is creamy smooth.
4. Add the filling into the crust. Bake it for 15-20 minutes.
5. Remove and cool. Store in the fridge for one hour to set.
6. Top with lightly sweetened whipped cream and lime slices if desired.

Nutrition for Total Servings:

- Calories: 188
- Carbs: 2.4 g
- Protein: 3.4 g
- Fat: 17.5 g

Raspberry Fudge

Preparation time: 1 hour and 15 minutes   **Cooking time:** 1 hour   **Servings:** 12

Ingredients:

- 1 cup butter
- ¼ cup white sugar substitute
- 6 tbsp. unsweetened cocoa powder
- 2 tbsp. heavy cream
- 2 tsp. vanilla extract
- 1 tsp. raspberry extract
- 1/3 cup chopped walnuts

Directions:

1. Put the butter in the mixing bowl with the mixer.
2. When smooth, mix with the rest of the ingredients until well incorporated.
3. Microwave using the high setting for 30 seconds. Blend with the mixer again until smooth.
4. Empty into the prepared pan (1-inch layer). Cover & chill for two hours in the fridge.
5. Slice into 12 portions.
6. Serve and enjoy or store in the fridge for a delicious treat later.

Nutrition for Total Servings:

- Calories: 242
- Carbs: 4.4 g
- Protein: 2.6 g
- Fat: 25.3 g

Sunflower Seed Surprise Cookies

Preparation time: 15 minutes   **Cooking time:** 10 minutes   **Servings:** 12

Ingredients:

- 1 large egg
- ¾ cup sugar-free sunflower seed butter
- 1 rounded tbsp. coconut oil
- Optional: 1 tbsp. Truvia
- ½ tsp. vanilla extract
- 1 tbsp. salt
- 1 tbsp. baking powder & soda

Directions:

1. Warm the oven temperature setting to 350°Fahrenheit. Set the rack in the upper portion of the oven.
2. Prepare a cookie tray using a layer of parchment baking paper.
3. Mix the ingredients in a large container.
4. Roll and flatten the mixture into 12 balls about the width of a quarter.
5. Bake the cookies for seven to nine minutes until they're firm in the center.
6. Cool the cookies for a couple of hours.

Nutrition for Total Servings:

- Calories: 69
- Carbs: 0.64 g
- Protein: 2.3 g
- Fat: 6.3 g

Keto Pie Crust

Preparation time: 10 minutes

Cooking time: 20-30 minutes

Servings: 10

Ingredients:

- Salt ¼ tsp.
- Butter - melted ¼ cup
- Almond flour 1
- Coconut flour 1 ½ tps

Directions:

1. Whisk the salt, sweetener, and flour in a mixing container. Fold in the melted butter to form coarse crumbs.
2. Dump it into a pie plate and press it firmly to the sides and bottom. Prick it using a toothpick or fork.

For unfilled Crust:

1. Bake 325° Fahrenheit for about 20 minutes.

For filled Crust:

1. Pre-bake it for 10-12 minutes before adding the ingredients. Cover the edges to avoid over-browning.

Nutrition for Total Servings:

- Carbs: 1.8 g
- Calories: 187
- Fat: 12.7 g
- Protein: 3.7 g

Delicious Cake

Preparation time: 30 minutes   **Cooking time:** 22 minutes   **Servings:** 12

Ingredients:

- 2 eggs
- 2 tsp. vanilla extract
- 1 ½ cups sour cream
- ½ cup Splenda granules/another keto-friendly sweetener
- 2 tbsp. melted butter
- 2 tsp. raspberry flavoring
- Also Needed: 12 ramekins or 10-inch spring form pan

Directions:

1. Warm the oven temperature at 350°Fahrenheit.
2. Whisk the eggs, vanilla, sour cream, and Splenda in a large mixing container. Work in the butter.
3. Spoon and combine about 1/2 cup of the mixture into another bowl and add the raspberry flavoring.
4. Spoon the rest of the mix into the chosen container.
5. Scoop a spoon of the raspberry batter over the top. Swirl it through the plain mixture.
6. Prepare a crust from 1/4 cup of Splenda, 1/4 cup of butter, and 1 1/2 cups ground almonds. Mix it like a graham cracker crust and add it to the ramekins/pan.
7. Arrange the ramekins in a water bath (a shallow pan with water) in the oven below the ramekins/pan.
8. Bake for 20-25 minutes for ramekins or 35-40 minutes in a spring form pan. The cake will firm up when refrigerated.
9. Top it off using raspberries and whipped cream - but add the carbs. Freeze if desired.

Note: The nutritional calculations do not include crust.

Nutrition for Total Servings:

- Calories: 231.8
- Carbs: 3.4 g
- Protein: 4.9 g
- Fat: 22.3 g

Cocoa Brownies

Preparation time: 20 min   **Cooking time:** 40 min   **Servings:** 9 servings

Ingredients:

- 1/2 cup salted butter, melted
- 1 cup granular Swerve sweetener
- 2 large eggs
- 2 tsp. vanilla extract
- 12 squares unsweetened baking chocolate, melted
- 2 tbsp. coconut flour
- 2 tbsp. cocoa powder
- 1/2 tbsp. baking powder
- 1/2 tsp. salt
- 1/2 cup walnuts, chopped (optional)

Directions:

1. Now, preheat the oven to 350°F.
2. Spray square baking pan with cooking spray or grease pan well with butter.
3. In a large mixing bowl, use an electric mixer or whisk and mix together butter and sweetener.
4. Add the eggs and vanilla extract to bowl and mix with an electric mixer for 1 minute until smooth.
5. Add melted chocolate & stir with a wooden spoon or spatula until the chocolate is incorporated into the butter mixture.
6. In separate bowl, mix the dry ingredients (remaining ingredients besides walnuts) until combined.
7. Add dry ingredients into the bowl with the wet ingredients and stir with a wooden spoon until combined.
8. Add walnuts if desired.
9. Pour batter into prepared pan. Spread to cover an entire bottom of the pan and into corners.
10. Place in a center rack of the oven & bake for 30 minutes.
11. After the brownies are baked, take them out and leave them in the pan to cool.
12. When cool, cut them into 9 servings, and they are ready to eat.

These have to be a once-in-a-while treat because they are sweet, and if you're like me, that sugar will continue to call your name. These are so good you will have to work to eat only one serving.

Nutrition for Total Servings:

- Calories: 201
- Carbs: 5g
- Protein: 3g
- Fat: 19g

Chocolate Chip Cookies

Preparation time: 10 minutes   **Cooking time:** 30 minutes   **Servings:** 24 cookies

Ingredients:

- 1 1/2 c almond flour
- 1 tsp. baking powder
- 1/2 tsp. salt
- 1/2 cup butter, softened
- 1/2 cup stevia
- 1 tsp. vanilla extract
- 1 large egg
- 1 cup sugar-free chocolate chips
- 1/2 cup nuts, chopped

Directions:

1. Now, preheat the oven to 350°F.
2. Grease cookie sheets with butter & set aside.
3. In large bowl, cream butter and stevia.
4. Add the large egg and vanilla extract to the butter and stevia.
5. Mix until the egg is incorporated into the butter.
6. In a second bowl, mix together almond flour, baking powder, and salt until mixed well.
7. Add ingredients to the large bowl & mix until it is combined.
8. Add sugar-free chocolate chips and nuts and stir until they are distributed evenly.
9. Drop by spoonful onto the cookie sheet.
10. Bake until golden brown and the surface of cookies appear dry on the top and are cooked all the way through.
11. Remove the cookies from the sheet to a wire rack to cool.

Note: Make these with or without nuts. Cocoa nibs can be used in place of sugar-free chocolate chips. This is a good recipe to keep on hand so you can have a cookie along with everyone else. Make it a fun project with kids or friends. Baking is always a good way to bring people together, and this a recipe everyone will enjoy.

Nutrition for Total Servings:

- Calories: 120
- Carbs: 3g
- Protein: 2g
- Fat: 11g

Keto Brown Butter Pralines

Preparation time: 10 minutes   **Cooking time:** 16 minutes   **Servings:** 10 servings

Ingredients:

- 2 sticks salted butter
- 2/3 cup heavy cream
- 2/3 cup monk fruit sweetener
- 1/2 tsp. xanthan gum
- 2 cup pecans, chopped
- Sea salt

Directions:

1. Line a cookie sheet with parchment paper or use a silicone baking mat.
2. Prepare a cookie sheet with parchment paper or a silicone baking mat.
3. In a medium-size, medium weight saucepan, brown the butter until it smells nutty. Don't burn the butter. This will take about 5 minutes.
4. Stir in heavy cream, xanthan gum, and sweetener.
5. Take the pan off the heat & stir in the nuts.
6. Place pan in the refrigerator for an hour.
7. Stir the mixture occasionally while it is getting colder.
8. After an hour, scoop the mixture onto the cookie sheets and shape into cookies.
9. Sprinkle with sea salt.
10. Refrigerate on cookies sheet until the pralines are hard.
11. After the cookies are hard, transfer them to an airtight container in the refrigerator.

Nutrition for Total Servings:

- Calories: 338
- Carbs: 1g
- Protein: 2g
- Fat: 36g

Chocolate and Nut Butter Cups

Preparation time: 35 minutes

Cooking time: 2 minutes

Servings: 6

Ingredients:

- 1-ounce chocolate, unsweetened
- 1/3 cup stevia
- 1 stick of unsalted butter
- 4 tbsps. peanut butter
- 2 tbsps. heavy cream

Directions:

1. Take a medium-sized bowl, place unsalted butter in it, and then microwave for 1–2 minutes until butter melts, stirring every 30 seconds.
2. Add stevia, peanut butter, and cream, and then stir until combined.
3. Take a muffin tray, line six cups with a cupcake liner, fill them evenly with chocolate mixture, and freeze for a minimum of 30 minutes until firm.
4. Serve straight away.

Nutrition for Total Servings:

- Calories: 120
- Fat: 17 g
- Carbs: 5 g
- Protein: 9 g

CHAPTER 16:

Drinks Recipes

Bulletproof Coffee

Preparation time: 5 minutes　　　**Cooking time:** 0 minutes　　　**Servings:** 1

Ingredients:

- 1 1/2 cups hot coffee
- 2 tbsps. MCT oil powder or Bulletproof Brain Octane Oil
- 2 tbsps. butter or ghee

Directions:

1. Pour the hot coffee into the blender.
2. Add the oil powder and butter, and blend until thoroughly mixed and frothy.
3. Pour into a large mug and enjoy.

Nutrition for Total Servings:

- Calories: 245
- Fat: 9.4g
- Carbs: 1.2 g
- Protein: 2.3g

Morning Berry-Green Smoothie

Preparation time: 15 minutes　　　**Cooking time:** 0 minutes　　　**Servings:** 4

Ingredients:

- 1 avocado, pitted and sliced
- 3 cups mixed blueberries and strawberries
- 2 cups unsweetened oat milk
- 6 tbsp. heavy cream
- 2 tsp. erythritol
- 1 cup of ice cubes
- 1/3 cup nuts and seeds mix

Directions:

1. Combine the avocado slices, blueberries, strawberries, oat milk, heavy cream, erythritol, ice cubes, nuts, and seeds in a smoothie maker; blend in high-speed until smooth and uniform.
2. Pour the smoothie into drinking glasses, and serve immediately.

Nutrition for Total Servings:

- Calories: 290
- Fat: 5.1g
- Carbs: 1.4 g
- Protein: 2g

Dark Chocolate Smoothie

Preparation time: 10 minutes　　　**Cooking time:** 0 minutes　　　**Servings:** 2

Ingredients:

- 8 pecans
- 3/4 cup of oat milk
- 1/4 cup of water
- 1 1/2 cups watercress
- 2 tsp. vegan protein powder
- 1 tbsp. chia seeds
- 1 tbsp. unsweetened cocoa powder
- 4 fresh dates, pitted

Directions:

1. In a blender, all ingredients must be blended until creamy and uniform.
2. Place into two glasses and chill before serving.

Nutrition for Total Servings:

- Calories: 299
- Fat: 10g
- Carbs: 2.1 g
- Protein: 4.4g

Super Greens Smoothie

Preparation time: 15 minutes   **Cooking time:** 0 minutes   **Servings:** 2

Ingredients:

- 6 kale leaves, chopped
- 3 stalks celery, chopped
- 1 ripe avocado, skinned, pitted, sliced
- 1 cup of ice cubes
- 2 cups spinach, chopped
- 1 large cucumber, peeled and chopped
- Chia seeds to garnish

Directions:

1. In a blender, add the kale, celery, avocado, and ice cubes, and blend for 45 seconds. Add the spinach and cucumber, and process for another 45 seconds until smooth.
2. Pour the smoothie into glasses, garnish it with chia seeds, and serve the drink immediately.

Nutrition for Total Servings:

- Calories: 290
- Fat: 9.4g
- Carbs: 3.1 g
- Protein: 8.5g

Kiwi Coconut Smoothie

Preparation time: 5 minutes   **Cooking time:** 0 minutes   **Servings:** 2

Ingredients:

- 2 kiwis, pulp scooped
- 1 tbsp. xylitol
- 4 ice cubes
- 2 cups unsweetened soy milk
- 1 cup of coconut yogurt
- Mint leaves to garnish

Directions:

1. Process the kiwis, xylitol, soy milk, yogurt, and ice cubes in a blender, until smooth, for about 3 minutes.
2. Transfer to serving glasses, garnish with mint leaves and serve.

Nutrition for Total Servings:

- Calories: 298
- Fat: 1.2g
- Carbs: 1.2 g
- Protein: 3.2g

Avocado-Coconut Shake

Preparation time: 5 minutes   **Cooking time:** 0 minutes   **Servings:** 2

Ingredients:

- 3 cups soy milk, chilled
- 1 avocado, pitted, peeled, sliced
- 2 tbsp. erythritol
- Coconut cream for topping

Directions:

1. Combine soy milk, avocado, and erythritol, into the smoothie maker, and blend for 1 minute to smooth.
2. Pour the drink into serving glasses, add some coconut cream on top of them, and garnish with mint leaves. Serve immediately.

Nutrition for Total Servings:

- Calories: 301
- Fat: 6.4g
- Carbs: 0.4 g
- Protein: 3.1g

Creamy Vanilla Cappuccino

Preparation time: 5 minutes   **Cooking time:** 0 minutes   **Servings:** 2

Ingredients:

- 2cups unsweetened vanilla soy milk, chilled
- 1 tsp. swerve sugar
- 1/2 tbsp. powdered coffee
- 1/2 tsp. vanilla bean paste
- 1/4 tsp. xanthan gum
- Unsweetened chocolate shavings to garnish

Directions:

1. In a blender, combine the soy milk, swerve sugar, coffee, vanilla bean paste, and xanthan gum and process on high speed for 1 minute until smooth.
2. Pour into tall shake glasses, sprinkle with chocolate shavings, and serve immediately.

Nutrition for Total Servings:

- Calories: 190
- Fat: 4.1g
- Carbs: 0.5 g
- Protein: 2g

Golden Turmeric Latte with Nutmeg

Preparation time: 5 minutes   **Cooking time:** 5 minutes   **Servings:** 2

Ingredients:
- 2 cups oat milk
- 1/3 tsp. cinnamon powder
- 1/2 cup brewed coffee
- 1/4 tsp. turmeric powder
- 1 tsp. xylitol
- Nutmeg powder to garnish

Directions:
1. Add the oat milk, cinnamon powder, coffee, turmeric and xylitol to the blender.
2. Blend the ingredients at medium speed for 50 seconds and pour the mixture into a saucepan.
3. Over low heat, set the pan and heat through for 6 minutes, without boiling.
4. Keep swirling the pan to prevent boiling. Turn the heat off, and serve in latte cups, topped with nutmeg powder.

Nutrition for Total Servings:
- Calories: 254
- Fat: 9.1g
- Carbs: 1.2g
- Protein: 1 g

Almond Smoothie

Preparation time: 5 minutes   **Cooking time:** 0 minutes   **Servings:** 2

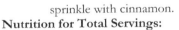

Ingredients:
- 2 cups soy milk
- 2 tbsp. almond butter
- 1/2 cup Greek yogurt
- 1 tsp. almond extract
- 1 tsp. cinnamon
- 4 tbsp. flax meal
- 30 drops of stevia
- A handful of ice cubes

Directions:
1. Put the yogurt, soy milk, almond butter, flax meal, almond extract, and stevia in the bowl of a blender.
2. Blend until uniform and smooth, for about 30 seconds.
3. Pour in smoothie glasses, add the ice cubes and sprinkle with cinnamon.

Nutrition for Total Servings:
- Calories: 288
- Fat: 6.4g
- Carbs: 1 g
- Protein: 1.4g

Raspberry Vanilla Shake

Preparation time: 5 minutes   **Cooking time:** 0 minutes   **Servings:** 2

Ingredients:
- 2 cups raspberries
- 2 tbsp. erythritol
- 6 raspberries to garnish
- 1/2 cup cold unsweetened soy milk
- 2/3 tsp. vanilla extract
- 1/2 cup heavy whipping cream

Directions:
1. In a large blender, process the raspberries, soy milk, vanilla extract, whipping cream, and erythritol for 2 minutes; work in two batches if needed.
2. The shake should be frosty.
3. Pour into glasses, stick in straws, garnish with raspberries, and serve.

Nutrition for Total Servings:
- Calories: 298
- Fat: 5.1g
- Carbs: 1.2g
- Protein: 1.4 g

CHAPTER 17:

Measurement Conversion

But if you must move from stressing about work to stressing about what you'll eat for lunch, then those precious minutes of break time kiss us goodbye! And that's not where the stress ends. Upon the breakdown of carbohydrates into glucose, the glucose is then absorbed into the bloodstream for transportation to different parts of the body. The increasing blood glucose concentrations signal the body to secrete insulin from the beta cells of the pancreas. The role of insulin in this case is to help the cells to take up glucose as the glucose-rich blood flows in different parts of the body. We have gone to great length in order to make sure that the measurements on the following Measurement Chart are accurate.

American and British Variances					
Term	Abbreviation	Nationality	Dry or liquid	Metric equivalent	Equivalent in context
cup	c., C.		usually liquid	237 milliliters	16 tablespoons or 8 ounces
ounce	fl oz, fl. oz.	American	liquid only	29.57 milliliters	
		British	either	28.41 milliliters	
gallon	gal.	American	liquid only	3.785 liters	4 quarts
		British	either	4.546 liters	4 quarts
inch	in, in.			2.54 centimeters	
ounce	oz, oz.	American	dry	28.35 grams	1/16 pound
			liquid	see OUNCE	see OUNCE
pint	p., pt.	American	liquid	0.473 liter	1/8 gallon or 16 ounces
			dry	0.551 liter	1/2 quart
		British	either	0.568 liter	
pound	lb.		dry	453.592 grams	16 ounces
Quart	q., qt, qt.	American	liquid	0.946 liter	1/4 gallon or 32 ounces
			dry	1.101 liters	2 pints
		British	either	1.136 liters	
Teaspoon	t., tsp., tsp		either	about 5 milliliters	1/3 tablespoon
Tablespoon	T., tbs., tbsp.		either	about 15 milliliters	3 teaspoons or 1/2 ounce

Volume (Liquid)

American Standard (Cups & Quarts)	American Standard (Ounces)	Metric (Milliliters & Liters)
2 tbsp.	1 fl. oz.	30 ml
1/4 cup	2 fl. oz.	60 ml
1/2 cup	4 fl. oz.	125 ml
1 cup	8 fl. oz.	250 ml
1 1/2 cups	12 fl. oz.	375 ml
2 cups or 1 pint	16 fl. oz.	500 ml
4 cups or 1 quart	32 fl. oz.	1000 ml or 1 liter
1 gallon	128 fl. oz.	4 liters

Volume (Dry)

American Standard	Metric
1/8 teaspoon	5 ml
1/4 teaspoon	1 ml
1/2 teaspoon	2 ml
3/4 teaspoon	4 ml
1 teaspoon	5 ml
1 tablespoon	15 ml
1/4 cup	59 ml
1/3 cup	79 ml
1/2 cup	118 ml
2/3 cup	158 ml
3/4 cup	177 ml
1 cup	225 ml
2 cups or 1 pint	450 ml
3 cups	675 ml
4 cups or 1 quart	1 liter
1/2 gallon	2 liters
1 gallon	4 liters

Oven Temperatures

American Standard	Metric
250° F	130° C
300° F	150° C
350° F	180° C
400° F	200° C
450° F	230° C

Weight (Mass)

American Standard (Ounces)	Metric (Grams)
1/2 ounce	15 grams
1 ounce	30 grams
3 ounces	85 grams
3.75 ounces	100 grams
4 ounces	115 grams
8 ounces	225 grams
12 ounces	340 grams
16 ounces or 1 pound	450 grams

Dry Measure Equivalents

3 teaspoons	1 tablespoon	1/2 ounce	14.3 grams
2 tablespoons	1/8 cup	1 ounce	28.3 grams
4 tablespoons	1/4 cup	2 ounces	56.7 grams
5 1/3 tablespoons	1/3 cup	2.6 ounces	75.6 grams
8 tablespoons	1/2 cup	4 ounces	113.4 grams
12 tablespoons	3/4 cup	6 ounces	.375 pound
32 tablespoons	2 cups	16 ounces	1 pound

References

- Types of ketogenic diets are retrieved from:
Health.com. (2020). https://www.health.com. [Online] Available at: https://www.health.com/weight-loss/keto-diet-types.

- Healthy habits for women after 50 is retrieved from:
https://chealth.canoe.com/healthfeature/gethealthfeature/your-50s-a-health-guide-for-women

- Precautions before exercise when you are on a keto diet is retrieved from:
https://www.cheatsheet.com/health-fitness/can-you-exercise-on-the-keto-diet-best-workouts-for-weight-loss.html/

- Supplements for improving exercise performance is retrieved from:
https://www.ruled.me/complete-guide-exercise-ketogenic-diet/

- How keto can work for women is retrieved from:
https://opportuniteas.com/blogs/news/is-keto-the-right-diet-for-women-over-50

- Low carb cucumber green tea detox smoothie recipe is retrieved from:
https://www.sugarfreemom.com/recipes/low-carb-cucumber-green-tea-detox-smoothie/

- Keto roasted pumpkin and halloumi salad recipe is retrieved from:
https://www.ruled.me/keto-recipes/lunch/

- Keto peanut butter fat bombs recipe is retrieved from:
https://diabetesstrong.com/keto-peanut-butter-fat-bombs/

Conclusion

Now that you are familiar with the Keto diet on many levels, you should feel confident in your ability to start your own Keto journey. This diet plan isn't going to hinder you or limit you, so do your best to keep this in mind as you begin changing your lifestyle and adjusting your eating habits. Packed with good fats and plenty of protein, your body is going to go through a transformation as it works to see these things as energy. Before you know it, your body will have an automatically accessible reserve that you can utilize at any time. Whether you need a boost of energy first thing in the morning or a second wind to keep you going throughout the day, this will already be inside of you.

As you take care of yourself through the afterward few years, you can feel great knowing that the Keto diet aligns with the anti-aging lifestyle you seek. Not only does it keep you looking great and feeling younger, but it also acts as a preventative barrier from various ailments and conditions. The body tends to weaken as you age, but Keto helps keep a shield up in front of it by giving you plenty of opportunities to burn energy and create muscle mass. Instead of taking the things you need to feel great, Keto only takes what you have in abundance. This is how you will always end up feeling your best each day.

Arguably one of the best diets around, Keto keeps you feeling great because you have many meal options! There is no shortage of delicious and filling meals you can eat while you are on any Keto diet plans. You can even take this diet with you as you eat out at restaurants and friends' houses. As long as you can remember the simple guidelines, you should have no problems staying on track with Keto. Cravings become almost non-existent as your body works to change the way it digests. Instead of relying on glucose in your bloodstream, your body switches focus. It begins using fat as soon as you reach the state of ketosis that you are aiming for. The best part is, you do not have to do anything other than eating within your fat/protein/carb percentages. Your body will do the rest on its own.

Because this is a way that your body can properly function for long periods, Keto is proven to be more than a simple fad diet. Originating with a medical background for helping epilepsy patients, the Keto diet has been tried and tested for decades. Many successful studies align with the knowledge that Keto works. Whether you are trying to be on a diet for a month or a year, both are just as healthy for you. Keto is an adjustment, but it will continue benefiting you for as long as you can keep it up. Good luck on your journey ahead!

Made in the USA
Monee, IL
20 August 2021